St Josemaría Escrivá and the Origins of Opus Dei: The Day the Bells Rang Out

St Josemaría Escrivá and the Origins of Opus Dei: The Day the Bells Rang Out

William Keenan

GRACEWING

First published in 2004

Gracewing
2 Southern Avenue, Leominster
Herefordshire HR6 0QF

All rights reserved. No part of this publication may be reproduced, stored in a retrieval system, or transmitted in any form, or by any means, electronic, mechanical, photocopying, recording or otherwise, without the written permission of the publisher.

© William Keenan 2004

The right of William Keenan to be identified as the author of this work has been asserted in accordance with the Copyright, Designs and Patents Act 1988.

ISBN 0 85244 581 4

Typeset by Action Publishing Technology Ltd,
Gloucester GL1 5SR

Contents

Part I	PRELUDE TO CIVIL WAR	
1	The House Facing the Barracks	3
2	Boyhood Memories	5
3	Cops and Robbers	11
4	Tragedies in the Family	17
5	Life in a Strange Town	21
6	Footprints in the Snow	26
7	Trials in Saragossa	30
8	'Lord, What is it you want of me?'	38
9	The Telegram	42
10	Relations with the Archdeacon	48
11	The Slums of Madrid	57
12	The Vision as the Bells Ring Out	66
13	The Chance Meeting in the Street	73
14	Mobs Go on the Rampage	81
15	The Man Dying in a Brothel	88
16	Invocations on a Tram	94
17	The Antechambers of Death	100
18	'Father Josemaría is here!'	106
19	'Simple' Henrietta's Intention	112
20	The Devil and the Mangy Donkey	116
21	The Stabbed and Dying Gypsy	125
22	Prisoners of the Cárcel Modelo	131
23	The Class of Three	139
24	Tortured by Doubt	146
25	'The Ravings of a Madman'	152

	26	'Josemaría, I've fooled you again!'	158
	27	Enter Alvaro and Pedro	169
	28	The Man with a Beard	175
	29	Alvaro's Decision	184
	30	Dangerous Journeys	192
	31	'Woman is Stronger than Man'	195
	32	Terror Outside, Tea and 'Cakes' Within	204
	33	The Special Guest	213
	34	The 'Poisoned Sweets' Rumour	218
Part II	THE HUNTED PRIEST		
	35	'A Crime Punishable by Death'	229
	36	The Wedding Ring	236
	37	The Door the Militia Failed to Open	241
	38	The Key Thrown Down the Drain	246
	39	Refuge in an Asylum	253
	40	Life in the Consulate	267
	41	In Workmen's Overalls	280
	42	The Plan of Escape	291

Sources	302
Bibliography	303
Notes	305

PART I

PRELUDE TO CIVIL WAR

CHAPTER 1

The House Facing the Barracks

It is Sunday 19 July 1936. Civil War is about to engulf the Spanish nation. The battle for Madrid, which will be swiftly decided and bloodily concluded, is only a few hours away. On the eve of the battle, a young priest, Father Josemaría Escrivá, and a group of university students helping him with his work, have suddenly found themselves in one of the most perilous spots in the strife-torn city. It is a house they moved into a few days earlier to turn into a residence for students. The house stands facing the Montaña army barracks, which has become the nerve centre for the Madrid uprising. From the window of their balcony they have a grandstand view of the preparations for the battle. Early in the afternoon the Red guard and militia units surround the whole area and seal off the streets leading to the barracks. Checkpoints are set up and more and more armed units arrive to take up positions in preparation for an attack on the barracks.

Because of the house's strategic position, the occupants fear the militia may burst in on them at any moment. And this would inevitably lead to the arrest of Father Josemaría and his followers because of the Christian work they have been doing among their friends and fellow students. Father Josemaría's end would be swift and brutal. Being a priest he would receive the treatment being meted out to all priests discovered by the Communists at that time. He would be taken outside and shot on the spot.

For more than six years Catholics and the Catholic Church in Spain had been under constant attack. As early as 1931 a well orchestrated hate campaign was launched against religion. Its aim was to destroy the Catholic Church throughout Spain. Mob violence, intimidation and murder became part of the escalating terror and on the last day of May of 1931 organized gangs suddenly went on the rampage throughout Madrid. Churches and convents were burned down and priests and nuns murdered. So great was the fear these attacks and killings engendered that it was considered too dangerous for priests and nuns to walk the streets of the capital.

The outbreak of civil war would mark the beginning of an even bloodier episode in the religious reign of terror. Special militia units and sections of the security police would begin mercilessly hunting down priests, nuns and even ordinary lay Catholics. To be found wearing a religious medal was often sufficient reason for a person's arrest and execution. By the end of the war the Communists and other extremist groups would have slaughtered 13 bishops, 4,184 diocesan priests, 2,365 priests and brothers of religious orders and 283 nuns.

CHAPTER 2

Boyhood Memories

Father Josemaría featured high on the priest hunters' wanted list. To understand why he was the kind of priest the Communists gave such a high priority to capturing and killing, it is important to go back to the beginning, to a Spain that was such a far cry from the Spain of the hatred and class warfare promulgated in the 1930s and culminating in civil war.

Josemaría Escrivá was born on 9 January 1902, in the Spanish town of Barbastro, which lies in the foothills of the Pyrenees of Aragón. At the turn of the century it had a population of around 7,000. The ancient town, steeped in history, has been the centre of many conflicts. Barbastro was well known back in Roman times when an uprising by the inhabitants after the death of Julius Caesar ended with an assault by the Sixth Legion. When the Moors invaded Spain, Barbastro was captured by them and became a Moorish stronghold until King Pedro I of Aragón drove them out in 1101. The French invaded in the fourteenth century and their troops sacked the town on 2 February 1366 and burnt to death three hundred people who had taken refuge in the cathedral tower. In more recent times, during the Napoleonic wars, the French established their headquarters in the town and, in the process of subduing the area, committed more atrocities. And ninety-five years later, at the time of the birth of the Escrivás' baby boy, bitter memories of the last war against the French still lingered. The new baby was born into a family linked with both countries. The Escrivás had come from Narbonne, France in the twelfth century and settled in Balaguer, northern Spain, as landowners. They had moved into the professional classes in the seventeenth century and the new baby could list among his ancestors, doctors, teachers, a Bishop of Avila and even a saint. He was St Joseph of Calasanz, who founded the Piarist order in the sixteenth century to educate the poorest of children. The Escrivás could also boast of a famous Protestant ancestor, Michael Servatus, who had been burnt to death by his fellow Protestants in their Inquisition in Geneva. Josemaría in later years would joke that despite his ancestry he was neither of the stuff of saints nor heretics. The baby boy was baptized on 13 January, four days after his birth, at the ancient stone baptismal font of Barbastro Cathedral. He received four names: José (Joseph) after his father and grandfather; María (Mary) in honour of Our Lady; Julián, whose saint's day it was the day of his baptism, and Mariano, the name of his godfather. Early in life he joined his first two names together to make Josemaría. This was to show his great devotion to Our Lady, the mother of Jesus, and to St Joseph, head of the Holy Family on earth. The ancient stone baptismal font, three decades later during the Civil War, would also fall foul of the anti-religious regime. When churches were being systematically desecrated, the font of Barbastro Cathedral was smashed to pieces and thrown into the river. All the pieces, however, were later recovered and the old font lovingly and painstakingly restored.

Three months after being baptized, baby Josemaría received the sacrament of Confirmation on 23 April, the feast of St George.

Josemaría was the second child and the eldest son in what was to become a family of six children.

Five years earlier, on 19 September 1898, Don José Escrivá had married a local beauty, María de los Dolores Albás y Blanc, the thirteenth of a family of fourteen children. The Albás were a well-known family in Barbastro and the large house they lived in was referred to locally as 'the house full of children'.

Dolores was of medium height and was noted for her attractive and elegant appearance. She was strong-willed but very kind and gentle and had a good sense of humour. Josemaría's father, José, was a prosperous textile merchant, one of the partners of the firm of Juncosa and Escrivá.

José was quite handsome and distinguished and had a large moustache, curled and waxed at the ends. He was always smartly-dressed in the fashion of the time. He wore a top hat and invariably carried a cane. He had, in fact, a small collection of canes so that he was able to sport a different one every day. José was also an enthusiastic hunter and loved to go out shooting quails and partridges. He was so keen on the sport that in the courtyard of their house decoy birds were kept in a cage with a floor that could be removed so that the birds would walk around and feed themselves from the ground. Like all hunters, José liked to tell stories of his exploits.

But, above all, José Escrivá was noted for his honesty and integrity. He gave generously to the poor and was always willing to help anyone in need.

The couple's first child, Carmen, was born on the feast of Our Lady of Mount Carmel, 16 July, 1899. The name Carmen is the Spanish equivalent of Carmel. Then came Josemaría in 1902 followed by María Asunción in 1905, María de los Dolores in 1907, María del Rosario in 1909 and Santiago in 1919.

When he was about eighteen months old, Josemaría became seriously ill. Two doctors were called but little Josemaría failed to respond to any medical treatment and his condition continued to deteriorate until he could hardly breathe or speak. He was covered in sweat and shivering with fever.

The family doctor, Dr Ignacio Camps, was a close friend of José Escrivá, and as a good friend used to address him by the more familiar name 'Pepe', the equivalent of calling him Joe instead of Joseph.

Dr Camps, after doing all he could for the sick little boy, turned to his father and said, 'Look, Pepe, I have to tell you the truth. Your little boy is going to die. He won't last the night.'[1]

All that was left for his parents to do was to pray. So José Escrivá and his twenty-four-year-old wife, Dolores, stayed by their son's cot and prayed fervently for a cure. They also asked for the help of Our Lady, the Mother of Jesus, and they made her a promise that if their little boy were cured they would take him to her at the nearby shrine of Torreciudad. The name Torreciudad means Tower City, for the shrine, perched on a mountain top, towers over the surrounding countryside. For nearly a thousand years pilgrims have struggled up the steep slopes from the valley of the River Cinca to honour Our Lady at her shrine of Torreciudad.

The morning after predicting the child would not last the night, Dr Camps returned to the Escrivá home and asked, 'At what time did the baby die then?'

His father José replied with delight, 'He didn't. Not only that, he's now bouncing up and down in his cot, fit as a fiddle!'

And when Dr Camps went into room where he thought he had left a dying little boy, he found what the father had said was perfectly true. Little Josemaría was in fact holding on to the bars of his cot, jumping up and down and shouting his head off. And so proficient did little Josemaría become at leaping up and down in that cot of his that on one occasion he managed to reach such a height that he somersaulted right over the cot rails and down on the floor![2]

A few days after Josemaría's remarkable recovery, the Escrivás kept their promise and made the perilous journey to the mountain shrine of Our Lady of Torreciudad. Dolores, holding her son in her arms, rode side-saddle on a horse led by her husband, José. First they had to cross the River Cinca and then make their way along a dangerous path winding up the steep mountainside. In places the path ran along the edge of cliff faces where there were precipitous drops to the river below. And their journey was made all the more hazardous by boulders and overgrown brambles. But frightened though they were, they courageously pressed on and finally reached the shrine of Our Lady of Torreciudad and offered their son to Mary the Mother of God. Josemaría would sum it up in later years by saying. 'My mother carried me in her arms to Our Lady. She was on horseback ... and she got quite frightened because the road was very bad.'

Little Josemaría grew up in a very happy home with parents who were devout Catholics. The children prayed daily with their mother and father and on Saturdays the whole family would go to the local church of St Bartholomew's to say the Rosary and sing the Salve Regina. A friend described them as a marvellous family and a very united couple. José Escrivá, it was said, was a man very much in love with his elegant and beautiful wife.

It was Josemaría's mother and father who taught him his first prayers, which he continued saying all his life. Until his dying day he never missed saying the morning offering his parents had taught him, 'O my Lady, O my Mother, I offer myself entirely to you, and as proof of my loyal affection, I give you my eyes, my ears, my tongue, my heart, my whole being without reserve. Since I am your own, keep me and guard me as your property and possession ...'

Even after he had turned seventy he could still vividly remember those prayers of childhood and things connected with them. 'I remember a little boy,' he said, 'who, when reciting the act of contrition, instead of saying "resolve to amend" (in Spanish, propósito de la enmienda) would say "resolve to almond" (propósito de la almendra). He didn't know what "amendment" was, but he knew well enough what almonds were, because he liked them so much. That child was myself. And that prayer did show a real willingness to please God and to act well: to offer the "almond" of not sinning any more.' And he added that his parents must have begun to teach him that prayer when he was about three years old.[3]

It was his mother who prepared Josemaría for his first confession. She fixed the day with her own confessor, a Piarist priest, and, after giving him some last-minute instructions, took him to the church.

Josemaría later recalled, 'I was very happy after I made my First Confession – I was six or seven at the time – and I always look back on it with joy. My mother took me to her confessor, and ... do you know what he gave me as a penance? ... Even now I still hear the chuckles of my father, who was devout but never sanctimonious. The good priest – he was a really kind little Friar – could think of nothing else to say than: "Tell mama to give you a fried egg." When I told her this she exclaimed, "Good heavens, he could have told you to eat a sweet ..." Obviously he was very fond of fried eggs, that priest. But isn't it wonderful for a child, who still knows nothing about life or about its sorrows, to be told by his mother's confessor that she is to give him a fried egg? It's marvellous! That priest was worth his weight in gold.'[4]

The love of confession was to remain with him and grow with the years. Towards the end of his life he would travel literally thousands upon thousands of miles talking to Catholics of all races and nationalities about the joy and happiness the sacrament of forgiveness brought with it. He would write, 'It is in the sacrament of penance that you and I put on Jesus Christ and his merits.'[5] And he would say, 'Our Father in heaven pardons any offence when his child returns once more to Him, when he repents and asks for pardon. Our Lord is so much a Father that He anticipates our desires to be pardoned and comes forward to us, opening His arms with his grace ...'[6] And he would tell people, 'Those who haven't approached the confessional for some time will see how happy they are when they're cleansed; they will understand that life has a different meaning, that they are on earth for something greater.'[7]

He also learned from his parents to have recourse to his Guardian angel. They taught him that God places an angel besides each and every human being to help him or her along the road of life. And it was this devotion to the Guardian angels that would on several occasions during the bloodbath of the Spanish Civil War result in the saving of his own life and the lives of those with him.

CHAPTER 3

Cops and Robbers

It was his mother who also first taught him about Jesus in the Blessed Eucharist. In Barbastro Cathedral the Blessed Sacrament is placed in an oval aperture in the centre of the great altar, surrounded by flickering lights. After pointing out to him the Blessed Sacrament, his mother, explained that Jesus was always mysteriously present there, waiting for people to come and talk to Him.

In a side chapel of the cathedral is the shrine of The Dormition of Our Lady, or the Falling Asleep of the Mother of Christ. It depicts Our Lady falling peacefully asleep, hands joined in prayer, just before being taken from earth into heaven by her son Jesus, the Assumption of Our Lady into Heaven as it is more commonly called. Years later in a short book of meditations on the Rosary, and perhaps with this image of his childhood in mind, he wrote, 'The Mother of God has fallen asleep. Around her bed are the twelve Apostles ... But Jesus wants to have His mother, body and soul, in heaven. And the heavenly court, arrayed in all its splendour, greets Our Lady ...'[8]

Josemaría made his first Holy Communion on St George's Day, 23 April 1912, when he was ten years old. But just before the big occasion he was made to suffer a little. The hairdresser who came to curl his hair was using old-fashioned metal curling tongs which had to be heated beforehand until they were very hot. During the curling process the hot tongs caught Josemaría's scalp and burned him. He, however managed to stop himself crying out in pain and then he kept quiet and hid what for a time was intense discomfort. He did this so as not to worry his mother and also because he didn't want to get the hairdresser into trouble.

One of his teachers at the local Piarist school, an old, devout priest, Father Manuel Laborda de la Virgen del Carmen, known affectionately by his students as Padre Manolé, taught him the beautiful spiritual communion prayer he was to say all his life and was to encourage so many other people to say. It has now spread all over the world and is prayed by people of all races and nationalities, 'I wish, Lord, to receive You with the purity, humility and devotion with which Your most Holy Mother received You, with the spirit and fervour of the saints.'

As a young boy Josemaría was cheerful, mischievous and full of life. The family home overlooked the market square and when the weather was fine he used to like playing cops and robbers in the square with his friends, running in and out of the colonnade surrounding the square. He also enjoyed playing with toy soldiers. He had two kinds, lead soldiers and soldiers painted on sticks that he and his friends threw balls at to knock them over. Josemaría was a strong, healthy lad. He played boisterous games with his companions and did his share of getting into fights, but he could never do anything cruel. Some of the children in Barbastro would catch bats and pin them to a wall, and then kill them by throwing stones at them. One day Josemaría witnessed one of these brutal rituals. He remembered it for the rest of his life. From this incident, he gained an insight into how far human cruelty could go.[9] On the other side of the square was his father's store Juncosa y Escrivá which, as well as selling textile materials, made very good chocolate in the basement, as did many other shops in the town. The shop was a fascinating place for Josemaría and his friends. There were stacks of wooden shelves and drawers and a spiral staircase that led up to the storeroom. And next door there was his uncle's shop where, if they *were lucky*, he and his friends might be given sweets.

Holidays were spent at Fonz, at the home of his paternal

grandmother. Fonz was a short drive from Barbastro through a countryside dotted with olive and almond trees. Also at Fonz was a small estate owned by his uncle, a priest, Father Teodoro Escrivá and his sister, Aunt Josefa. Vines and olive trees surrounded the old house, called El Palau, and stretched as far as the eye could see.

Stubbornness is an Aragónese trait and Josemaría as a boy had a certain stubborn streak in him. Once, he recalls, 'I hid under the bed and stubbornly refused to go out into the street when I was wearing in a new suit ... until my mother gave a few taps on the floor with one of my father's walking sticks. I came out then because of the walking stick, and for no other reason. She then affectionately told me: "Josemaría, the only thing to be ashamed of is sin." Many years later I realized what a depth of meaning these words contained.'[10]

There were the usual brother and sister quarrels which sometimes ended with Josemaría pulling the pigtails of his elder sister Carmen. He had a quite a temper and could be rebellious at times. Once when his mathematics teacher had him go to the blackboard to answer a question that had not been covered in class and insisted he answer it, the duster and the chalk Josemaría was using ended up being thrown at the blackboard. And on his way back to his desk he loudly protested, 'We've never had that question!' For many years Josemaría had to struggle hard to master his temper.

The family kitchen was another place that fascinated him. Even though his mother discouraged the children from going into the kitchen, he would sneak in when she wasn't watching. He later recalled, 'There were two wonderful things in that kitchen, a cook called María, who was very good and who knew how to tell a story. It was always the same story about some very likeable robbers. And on top of that there were the most delicious fried potatoes you could imagine ... We never asked her to tell us a story. No, it was, "Come on, María, tell us THE story." We knew she didn't know any other, but she told it so well that it always seemed new.'[11]

The observant young Josemaría also noticed how the cook boiled an egg. She would calculate the time for hard-boiling it by reciting the Creed twice.

He also enjoyed seeing bread being made at the bakers. He would watch and note how a little yeast was added to the dough, which was vigorously kneaded before being put inside the hot oven with long wooden shovels. And when the bread was baked and the oven doors were opened he and the other children would often be given a cockerel-shaped pastry that had been made specially for them and put in with the bread.

Between father and son there developed a deep understanding and friendship. Father and son prayed together and played together. His father not only joined in Josemaría's games, he would also sometimes take him with him when he went shooting. They would often go for walks together and have friendly chats.

In autumn, chestnut-roasting time, his father would buy hot chestnuts and put them in his pocket and little Josemaría would stretch up on tiptoe and dip his hand into the pocket to reach them. Then, he would find his hand being lovingly squeezed by his father.

Talking of his father and his happy childhood, he once said, 'I do not remember my father hitting me except on one occasion. I was very, very small. It was on one of those few occasions when I was at table with the grown-ups, on one of those high chairs. It must have been something to do with my stubbornness he gave me a ...' (and he imitated a slap). 'Never again in all his life did he lay a hand on me. Never. He was always gentle with me, and it did me a world of good. I have the most wonderful memories of my father, who was my friend. And that is why I recommend what I have experienced. You must become friends with your children.'[12]

And about his stubbornness he said, 'I am very stubborn. I come from Aragón' (people noted for their stubbornness). And he added, 'If this (stubbornness) is taken to the supernatural plane, it is of no consequence. On the contrary, it can be good, because in the interior life one has to keep insisting ...'[13]

Though his father was a great almsgiver and was always willing to help the poor, he and his wife deliberately gave their children very little money. He used to like to say how his parents kept him short of money, 'very short, but free.'[14]

The changing patterns of the seasons also became a part of his boyhood memories. In summer when the grass yellowed and withered the shepherds would move their flocks up the mountain passes to greener pasture. Then, when the weather turned cold and the first snows arrived, they would bring them back to the lower land. He would say, 'I remember as a child having watched the shepherds, wrapped up in their sheepskin cloaks, during the bitter winter days of the Pyrenees, filing along those narrow mountain passes with their most faithful dogs at their heels. Invariably, there was a donkey heavily burdened with all the shepherds' gear. On the top would be a large basin in which the owner prepared his meals and also mixed the various concoctions for healing the sheep's wounds and sores. If a sheep had a broken leg I have seen the shepherd take the injured sheep on his shoulders and carry it like the good shepherd of the Gospel. On other occasions I have seen a shepherd lovingly carry a new-born lamb in his arms.'[15]

The image of the donkey carrying its burden was later to have great spiritual significance for him. He would often tell God he considered himself to be just a little, mangy donkey trying to do his will. All his life Josemaría would have a great eye for detail.

Growing up in Aragón in those days was to experience the grandeur of the Church's feast days and changing seasons. There was the great, joyous celebration of Easter when the bells would ring out over the hills and across the valleys. Then, during May, the month of Mary, while there was still snow glistening on the mountains of the nearby Pyrenees, there would be processions of Our Lady with great displays of spring flowers. June would bring devotions to the Sacred Heart of Jesus when the roses and the other flowers would be in full bloom. Spring, summer and autumn, there was always some great feast. And when the days grew shorter it would be time to prepare for Christmas. This was an exciting time for the Escrivá children. At home they would all be involved in making the crib and placing in it the central characters of Mary and Joseph and the baby Jesus. And round the manger in which Jesus lay would be placed the sheep and oxen, not forgetting the little, faithful donkey that was such a common sight in Aragón. The crib would also have cardboard mountains as a backdrop, like the mountains of the Pyrenees. And then there came the time when the children were allowed to go to the Christmas Midnight Mass with their parents. On Christmas Eve they would walk in the cold night air through the ancient town and then, with a certain awe, hear the joyous Christmas Mass ring out under the towering roof of the great Cathedral.

And in summer, when the nights stayed light, Josemaría, long after his mother had called him in to go to bed, would sit with his legs stuck through the railings of the balcony, watching his friends who were still playing in the market place below.

Winter too had its special attractions. On dark winter nights the children would listen open-mouthed with excitement to stories the servants sometimes told them. They were tales of ancient Spain, of great deeds of chivalry or of ghosts or of strange and terrible happenings. Josemaría's years of childhood were filled with such details and incidents. They seemed to be times of constant joy and expectation.

Early in life Josemaría showed he had a talent for storytelling. He used to enjoy sitting in a big rocking chair telling his friends horror stories he had made up. This was perhaps the first hint of the vivid, incisive style of writing he would develop and of the great gift he would have of being able to communicate with people of all ages and from all walks of life.

CHAPTER 4

Tragedies in the Family

Josemaría attended the school in Barbastro run by the Piarist Fathers, the order founded by his ancestor, St Joseph of Calasanz whose original aim had been to educate street urchins and the poorest of the poor.

One of the sayings of his saintly forebear was, 'If you want to be holy, be humble, if you want to be more holy, be more humble; and if you want to be very holy, be very humble.'[16] Josemaría would in later years change it slightly and advise people that if they wanted to be happy they should strive to be holy and if they wanted to be more happy, they should be more holy and if they wanted to be very happy while they were still on this earth they should be very holy.[17]

When Josemaría was eight years old the family began to suffer a series of tragedies. One by one his three younger sisters died in the space of four years and about the same time his father's business started to fail. Josemaría's youngest sister, Rosario, died on 11 July 1910 before she was one year old. Then, two years later, on July 10 1912, his sister Dolores died at the age of five. The following year, his sister María Asunción, who was nicknamed Chon, died on 6 October 1913, just after her eighth birthday.

After Chon's death Josemaría and Carmen were the only surviving children. Josemaría was eleven years old and Carmen was fourteen and both were deeply distressed by the deaths of their younger sisters. Chon, a very pretty, fair-haired girl, was Josemaría's favourite sister. Her death hurt him deeply. When she died he was playing in the market square. He was suddenly overcome with a sense of foreboding and decided to hurry home to see how Chon was. His mother saw him and came out to meet him.

He anxiously asked her, 'How is Chon?'

His mother quietly replied, 'Chon is very well, Josemaría. She is now in heaven.'

In a flood of tears he threw himself into his mother's arms. Seeing how miserable and unhappy he was his mother said to him, 'Now, now, Josemaría, don't be like that. Don't cry. Can't you see that Chon is already in heaven!'

She also told him that he should be happy because he now had three sisters in heaven, close to God and the Blessed Virgin.

Since his sisters had died in order of age, from the youngest upwards, Josemaría began to think that he would die next and he would say, 'Now it's my turn.' To stop him worrying about this, his mother one day explained to him what had happened when he was eighteen months old and had been given up for dead by the doctors and how she and his father had prayed to Our Lady and he had been cured.

'Don't worry,' she told him, 'You have been offered to Our Lady of Torreciudad. You will be all right.' And later she said to him, 'My son, the Blessed Virgin must have kept you in this world for something very special. Because that time you were ill, you were more dead than alive!'

It was about the time Chon was dying that the family business began to run into financial difficulties. When the business finally closed in 1914 Josemaría was twelve years old. The general opinion in the town was that his father, José Escrivá, was a good man and that some business associate had played a dirty trick on him. It was said that his business had gone under because advantage had been taken of his trust and good will. To the last, José Escrivá acted in a way he believed an honest, Christian gentleman should. He saw to it that every creditor was paid in full, even when there was no legal obligation for him to do so. The extra money needed to pay these people came out of his own pocket. He sold all that he had to pay his creditors. When the business was finally wound up there wasn't a debt unpaid, but the Escrivá family was left virtually penniless.

At nearly fifty years of age José Escrivá had to pick up the pieces and try to begin again from scratch. The once well-to-do businessman had to go cap-in-hand looking for a job. The family also had to endure the humiliation caused by gossip. In a small town like Barbastro the speculation as to how and why such a prosperous business had failed became the topic of many conversations.

There was also criticism of José Escrivá from people within the family. His brother in law, Father Carlos Albás, Archdeacon of Saragossa, in fact reproached him for what he considered was his bad business sense. And he accused him of being more concerned about paying his creditors than the welfare of his family. 'Pepe has been a fool,' he would say. 'He could have retained a good financial position, and instead he's reduced himself to misery.'

In later life Josemaría would agree that his father after losing his business could have remained in a comfortable financial situation 'Had he not been a Christian and a gentleman.' And he would also say, 'Now I love my father all the more, and I give thanks to God that my father's business didn't go at all well, because that is how I came to learn what poverty is. If not, I would never have known. I feel a holy pride: I love my father with all my heart, and I am sure he is enjoying a very high place in heaven because he managed to bear in such a dignified, marvellous Christian way all the humiliation that came from finding himself out on the street.'[18]

José Escrivá eventually found work in the town of Logroño, as a shop assistant in a clothing store called 'The Great City of London'. Alone in Logroño, he quietly and conscientiously settled into his new job and at the same time searched for somewhere he and his family could live. He soon won the respect and trust of the other members of the store's staff. They noticed that he went regularly to morning Mass but would always be at the door of the shop prompt at 9 o'clock. His punctuality became a by-word. The shop staff also noted how well he looked after customers and how courteous and helpful he tried to be to everyone.

Dolores and the children, Carmen and Josemaría, spent that summer at Fonz. Then they returned to Barbastro for the last time to collect their personal belongings. Afterwards they took the early morning horse-coach to Huesca, leaving behind their old home and their friends. Ahead of them lay a strange town, a poorer way of life and a precarious future.

CHAPTER 5

Life in a Strange Town

The year was 1915, the second year of what was being called the First World War. Even in neutral Spain the war was sending prices spiralling. The steep rise in the price of food and other commodities was causing great hardship for the ordinary wage earner. For the Escrivá family, it made their life even more of a struggle. The first few months in Logroño had been difficult enough. Their first home was a fourth floor flat just under the roof loft. It was stifling hot in summer and freezing in winter. They found a better flat which Dolores soon made into a very pleasant and attractive home for her family. A friend from those days, Sofia Miguel, remembers, 'One day I arrived when they were eating and I noticed how beautifully the table was laid. They were real gentlefolk.' Sofia couldn't understand why 'such a cultured and intelligent gentleman' which is how she described José Escrivá, was working as a shop assistant in a clothing store. Many years later she still had a vivid mental picture of Dolores from those days, 'She had very bright eyes, not very big, but slanting. And she always wore her hair in a bun, pinned up high.'

Another woman friend remembered what a united couple they were and the teas Dolores prepared. 'She did things so well and with such great care.' This way of doing things well and with great care Dolores passed on to her children.

One of the family's chief worries at the time was the

break in Josemaría's education and they carefully looked into what was the best they could do for him with their limited finances. They finally decided to send him as a part-time student to Logroño Institute, which was the state school. Josemaría attended classes there from 9 a.m. to 1 p.m. each day. Then in the afternoon, he went to St Anthony's College for study and revision classes, sometimes until 8 o'clock at night. St Anthony's was run by laymen but had a priest as spiritual director to teach religion and encourage spiritual devotion. Josemaría worked very hard and was awarded a distinction with honours for literary interpretation and composition. A free scholarship for the next twelve months went with the award and helped ease the family's financial burden. In many Spanish schools at this time, the students who got the highest marks were placed in the first row and had the responsibility of answering the teachers' questions when the other students were unable to do so. In his fourth and fifth years of secondary school, Josemaría was in the first row in three of his classes: algebra, trigonometry and literature.

Another bright student at the Institute was Josemaría's good friend, Isidoro Zorzano. Isidoro's parents had some years earlier emigrated to Argentina and Isidoro was born in Buenos Aires, which made him an Argentina citizen. But when Isidoro was still very young his parents returned to Spain.

Isidoro was working very hard at his studies. His ambition was to be an engineer.

And he was determined to be a very good engineer.

At the beginning of September 1916, Josemaría applied to enrol at the Institute as an official student for the fifth year of the Baccalaureate. His application in his own handwriting and in the rigid, formal style of those days reads, 'Having obtained, in the examination taken this past June, the evaluation of "Outstanding with Prize" for the subject of Literature and Composition, and having, in accord with current regulations, the right to a scholarship for one subject, I ask that you deign to grant this to me and apply it to the subject of General History of Literature. It being a fair thing to ask, this petitioner has no doubt of obtaining it thanks to the right judgement of yourself, whose life may God safeguard for many years. Logroño, 1 September, 1916.'[19]

Josemaría was developing a great love of literature that was to remain with him all his life. He read widely, and his reading took in the English classics. He was fascinated by poetry, history and philosophy. He loved especially the poetry of the Middle Ages, the authors of the Spanish Golden Age and the writings of the great Castillian mystics. He read and re-read Cervantes, especially Don Quixote. One poetic image that implanted itself in his mind was that of El Cid. In heroic verse the knight is depicted praying at Burgos cathedral before setting off into exile. Then,

> Having prayed, he then rode off
> Through the great gate,
> Spurred on through Burgos;
> Then he unsaddled;
> Prayed with all his heart.
> He then rode on
> And crossed the Arlanzón.

After re-reading the poem after a gap of many years he realized that his memory had played him false with one of the verses. He had thought there was a verse that said, 'And the prayer rode on horseback to heaven.' But on re-reading the poem he saw that the true verse was 'Having prayed, he then rode off.' And in a letter he wrote on 7 June 1965 he would comment that the original verse was so much better than what he had incorrectly remembered. The original, he said, 'is more realistic ... "Having prayed, he then rode off." First you pray, then you ride. Riding means working, fighting, getting ready to fight. And working and fighting, for a Christian, are praying. I understand this verse from the epic poem as fitting in very well with our epic of ordinary contemplative Christians ...'[20] And Josemaría would always advise people 'Action is worthless without prayer ... First prayer, then atonement; in the third place – very much in "third place" – action.'[21] He would also say that 'the Christian vocation consists in making heroic verse out of the prose of each day.'[22]

Young Josemaría finished the academic year of 1917

with good marks in all his subjects. That year he not only gained an excellence in literature but also did well in mathematics. No one who knew him at this time ever thought he would become a priest. He himself didn't think so either. He later said of those years, 'I remember when I was in secondary school we studied Latin. I did not like it ... I used to say, "Latin is for priests and monks"'[23] – meaning he certainly didn't think it was for him. But not only did Josemaría become a devout priest, he also discovered he had a great love for Latin, which for him was, and always would be, the language of the universal Catholic Church. He would also say in later years, 'I can never be thankful enough for the good they did me in school, when they made me study Latin.'[24]

He would also say, 'I had never thought of becoming a priest, or of dedicating myself to God. I had been taught to respect and venerate the priesthood. But it was not for me. It was for others.'[25]

At that time, he, Josemaría Escrivá, knew exactly what he was going to do in life. He was going to be an architect. He was inclined to this choice by his interests in the arts and humanities, as well as by his aptitude for mathematics and design. His parents were pleased with his choice of career, though his father would sometimes gently tease him about it, saying he was going to be just a 'glorified bricklayer'.

As Josemaría grew into a fine young man, his mother Dolores kept a watchful eye open for possible girl friends. And as there was nothing at this stage to indicate he wouldn't get married, she gave him this piece of advice about the choice of a wife: 'Ni guapa que encante, ni fea que espante.' (Neither so pretty she ensnares you, nor so ugly that she scares you.)[26]

The great issue on everyone's lips at this time was the terrible war that was tearing Europe apart and would go down in history as the First World War. The adolescent Josemaría would often discuss the war situation with his father and his friends. Every day the Spanish nation learned from their newspapers about the dreadful carnage. They read about hundreds of thousands of men who were being thrown into inconclusive battles and blown to pieces by high explosive shells or slaughtered by machine guns.

Little did they realize that their own country within the space of twenty years would itself become a modern battleground and a place of slaughter.

Spain was also informed by its newspapers at this time of the Irish Rising, which the Spanish people saw as Irish people fighting for their freedom and for their religion after centuries of persecution.

Josemaría would later say, 'I was then about 15 and I eagerly read in the newspapers everything about the events of the First World War. Most of all, though, I prayed a lot for Ireland. I wasn't against England. I was for religious freedom.'[27]

For young and old there seemed so much to discuss: so many evils, so many conflicts and so many contradictions. And, as in all ages, so much seemed wrong with the world of their day.

CHAPTER 6

Footprints in the Snow

On one bitter-cold day, just before Josemaría's sixteenth birthday, around the end of the year of 1917 and the beginning of January 1918, he came across some footprints in the snow – footprints that would change his whole life and outlook. The Logroño region at the time was in the grip of a very hard winter and there had been some very heavy snowfalls. According to the local newspaper, then called *La Rioja*, the snow had kept falling for about a month.

Temperatures plunged to 1.4 degrees Fahrenheit, or minus 17 degrees Celsius. Rivers froze, ponds and lakes were covered with thick ice. It turned out to be one of the coldest winters on record and so severe that several people died. Josemaría was out walking one morning after a fresh fall of snow had spread an immaculate white layer over town and surrounding countryside. As he trudged through the snow, he suddenly saw the footprints. He stopped to examine them. Someone had been walking in the bitter, freezing snow in bare feet! Josemaría stared in amazement at the glistening footprints and as he did so realized that the person who had been walking barefoot in the snow must have been doing it as a small sacrifice, as an offering to God. He discovered the footprints had been made by a Carmelite priest, Father José Miguel. The footprints immediately awakened in Josemaría's soul what he called 'premonitions of Love'. (He always used this expression, 'barruntar el Amor'.) At the same time he also felt a profound uneasiness in his soul. And he began to ask himself, 'If others are capable of such sacrifices for the love of God, can't I offer Him something?'[28]

From out of the deep disquiet he was experiencing there came the feeling that Our Lord was asking something special of him. Then this feeling turned into a certainty. God was definitely asking something of him. But what that something was, he had no idea.

'I began to have,' he says, 'intimations of Love, to realise that my heart was asking for something great, and that it was love ... I didn't know what God wanted of me, but it was evident that I had been chosen for something. What this was would come later ... Realising at the same time my own inadequacies, I made up that litany, which is a matter not of false humility but of self-knowledge: "I am worth nothing, I have nothing, I can do nothing, I am nothing, I know nothing ..."'[29]

He decided to pray more and go daily to Mass and receive Holy Communion. He also sought the help of Father José Miguel, the priest who had made the footprints in the snow and started going to him for spiritual direction. The devout priest realized that the Lord was calling Josemaría to a life dedicated to God and suggested that he become a Carmelite. But Josemaría, after calmly praying and thinking about it, and also taking into account his family responsibilities, came to the conclusion that this was not what the Lord wanted of him. He then came to understand that whatever it was that Our Lord wanted, he could best make himself available for it by becoming a diocesan priest.

He spoke to his father about it. For José Escrivá, what his son was telling him seemed to be yet another test of his trust in God. The family was just getting back on its feet after the collapse of his business and he was making plans for the future, plans that involved his son. But this son was now telling him he wanted to become a priest! José Escrivá's immediate response was that if Josemaría wanted to become a priest, he should become a priest. And these plans of his, these dreams for the future, would have to be abandoned.

'It was the only time I ever saw him cry,' Josemaría later recalled. 'He had other plans for me but he did not object. He told me, "My son, think it over carefully. A priest has to be a saint ... It is very hard to have no house, no home, to have no love on earth. Think about it a bit more, but I will not oppose your decision." And he took me to speak to a friend of his who was a priest ...'[30]

In fact his father took him to see two priests, Father Antolin Oñate, the Abbot of the collegiate church in Logroño, who encouraged his vocation and Father Albino Pajares, a military chaplain, who gave Josemaría further help with his spiritual and intellectual preparation. At this time Josemaría was going to confession to Father Ciriaco Garrido, canon of the collegiate church and parochial vicar of the Church of Santa Maria de la Redonda, the church where he usually went to pray. This priest, who was about forty-five, was known affectionately as 'Don Ciriaquito' 'Little Ciriaco,' partly because of his short stature, but mainly because he was very much loved in Logroño. In fact so great was the people's affection for 'Don Ciriaquito' that after his death in 1949 they named one of the town's streets after him. 'Don Ciriaquito' also helped and encouraged Josemaría's budding vocation.

Josemaría began his studies for the priesthood as a non-resident student at the local seminary in Logroño. Known as the 'Old Seminary' it was in a dilapidated building which dated back to 1559 when it first opened as a Jesuit school. It first became a seminary in 1776 but from 1808 to 1815 Napoleon's occupying troops used it as a barracks and stables and later it was turned into a military hospital and prison. Then once more it returned to being the local seminary.

Before he could be accepted by the seminary Josemaría learned he would have to sit a special examination. On 6 November, 1918, just a few months after talking with his father about becoming a priest, he wrote to his local bishop saying, 'Since I feel that I have a Church vocation and since I have completed my secondary-school examinations, I request that Your Excellency design to allow me to take the examination in Latin, logic, metaphysics and ethics that is a prerequisite for first-year theology.'[31]

He took the exams and passed them, but because of the terrible killer flu epidemic which was sweeping Europe in 1918 and which had then reached the Logroño area, the seminary did not begin its new term on 1 October as it usually did. It was not able to open its doors to students until 26 November when the epidemic had subsided. As a non-resident student, or day student, Josemaría had to rise very early each morning to be at the seminary before 6.30 a.m. when the seminary day began with a period of private prayer and Mass. After Mass Josemaría would go home for breakfast and return to the seminary for classes until 12.30 p.m., when he would again go home for lunch. He would return to the seminary in the afternoon for another class, which would be followed by a period of free time. The seminary day ended with the saying of the Rosary and either spiritual reading or a talk, after which Josemaría would return home for his evening meal and to sleep.

Resident students at the seminary had to undertake tasks that the day students were not required to do, such as giving catechism classes on Sundays. But Amadeo Blanco, a resident student, would always remember Josemaría as the only day student who turned up on Sundays to help them.

Now that Josemaría had decided to become priest, it left his father with a problem. There would be no wage earner to look after the family if he, the head of the family, died. And he began to worry about what would become of the family if such a thing happened. Realizing how disappointed his father was and the problem he faced, Josemaría began to pray fervently to God to give his mother and father another son to take over from him.

A few months later, in autumn of that year, his mother Dolores called Josemaría and his sister Carmen together. She said she had some good news to tell them. They would soon have another brother or sister.

Once Josemaría had recovered from his surprise he was sure the baby was going to be a boy. 'I felt I had touched the grace of God,' he said. 'I saw Our Lord's hand in it.'[32] The baby was born on 28 February 1919 and was a boy. Josemaría would later say, 'Our Lord God (just nine or ten months after I asked him) saw to it that my brother was born ...'[33] The baby boy was christened Santiago Justo and his arrival brought great joy to the whole family. Josemaría's mother at the time was forty-two years and his father was fifty-two.

CHAPTER 7

Trials in Saragossa

After spending two years as a day student at the Logroño seminary Josemaría decided he would transfer to a major seminary and chose San Carlos in Saragossa, which was also known as the San Francisco de Paula. One of his reasons for deciding to go to Saragossa, the capital of Aragón, was that his father from the beginning had wanted him to take a civil law degree as well as studying for the priesthood. Josemaría was now of the same mind as his father. He also felt he would be better prepared to fulfil whatever it was God wanted him to do if he had a degree in law. At Saragossa he would be able to read law at the university.

On 28 September 1920, at the age of eighteen, Josemaría left home for the first time and travelled to Saragossa. He was by this time a smoker, a pipe smoker. But as he entered San Carlos he gave his pipes and tobacco to the doorman and for the rest of his life was a non-smoker.

Seminary life at San Carlos ran to a strict timetable. The seminarians rose at 6.30 a.m. and had half an hour to wash and dress. At 7.00 a.m. there was a meditation in a private chapel on the third floor and afterwards they went down to the chapel of San Carlos' seminary to hear Mass. Afterwards they ate breakfast in silence listening to a reading from some spiritual book. Immediately after breakfast, the seminarians, accompanied by a Superior, walked in double file to the Pontifical University in the Square of La Seo. Normally there were three periods of lectures in the morning and then they would return to the seminary for lunch. In the afternoon they went back to the university for more lectures. They returned to the seminary for a period of recreation, study and saying of the Rosary. Between supper and bedtime they prayed and listened to a short talk which outlined some points for the following day's meditation. On Thursday afternoons they went for walks, keeping all together and in line, through the quiet districts of Saragossa or out in the countryside. On feast days, however, the seminarians rose half an hour later, had no classes and were able to go out for walks. There was also a very good meal that day with extra food and wine on the table. Moving to the San Carlos seminary must not have been an easy transition for the teenage Josemaría. Most of Josemaría's companions at the seminary came from a poor, rural background and were of a rough and ready sort with a very elementary education. A former student is on record as saying that most pupils had 'a certain contempt for appearances due to a misguided notion of sincerity, and a disregard for personal hygiene.'

Josemaría once commented, 'There were no washbasins in the rooms, so in order to wash myself from head to toe, I had to fetch three or four buckets or water. Perhaps this is what some of them found scandalising!'[34] One of the more aggressive fellow students who hadn't much time for soap and water used to taunt him and say, 'You ought to smell more like a man.' And one day dripping with sweat he rubbed his sleeve on Josemaría's face. Josemaría managed to control his anger and replied, 'Being dirtier doesn't make you more of man.'[35]

From childhood his parents had instilled in him a great devotion to Our Lady of Pilar. And in Saragossa is where the great shrine of Our Lady of Pilar is to be found, in the basilica of El Pilar. Josemaría began visiting the shrine every day – to honour 'my Mother,' as he would later say. And with his keen interest in Spanish history he was fascinated by the story of the shrine, which goes back to Apostolic times. According to popular tradition Saint James, the son of Zebedee and brother of Saint John, journeyed to Spain following Christ's command to his Apostles to, 'Go and preach to all nations'. At first, the Apostle James had little success in converting the people of the Iberian peninsula. He was in fact on the point of giving up when, tradition has it, Mary, the mother of Jesus with the child in her arms, appeared to him on the banks of the Ebro river, standing on a small pillar. James recognized her as the same Mary who prayed with him and the other Apostles in the upper room after her son's crucifixion and resurrection, as the Gospels relate. Our Lady's message to James was that he should stay and persevere with his preaching. He did. And the result was a barbaric people became a great Christian nation.

The small pillar that Saint James saw Mary standing on has been reverently preserved by the people of Spain down through the ages. A church, and later the present basilica, was built on the site of the apparition. The place where the pillar was kept soon became a place of popular pilgrimage. And that's how it came to be called the Shrine of Our Lady of the Pillar, or Pilar as it is written in Spanish. Many families to this day choose the name Pilar for their daughters in Our Lady's honour.

The Pilar, or Pillar, is now swathed in beautiful tapestry. On it stands a statue of Our Lady holding the child Jesus in her arms. History records that Saint James returned to Jerusalem and was condemned to death by Herod Agrippa and beheaded in the year forty-four. He was the first Apostle to be martyred. His body was recovered by the early Christians and returned to Spain and according to tradition was buried at Compostela. The present cathedral of Compostela is believed to have been built above the grave of St James, or Santiago as he is called in Spanish. Since then Santiago's final resting place has been called Santiago de Compostela (St James of Compostela) and has become a place of pilgrimage for people from all over Europe down to the present day. Our Lady of Pilar is now the national shrine of Spain and St James is the country's patron saint.

When some of Josemaría's fellow seminarians found out about his daily visits to the Shrine they started teasing him by nicknaming him 'Mystical Rose.' Although Josemaría did his best not to stand out from the other seminarians he wasn't afraid of living up to the counsel he would later give to others: 'Don't be afraid if your effort to be devout is noticed.'[36]

He also spent many hours, and sometimes the whole night, praying before the Blessed Sacrament in the seminary chapel of San Carlos. And these long visits, no matter how careful he was, did not go unnoticed either. Some of his fellow students began to say, loud enough for him to overhear, 'Look, here comes the dreamer!' (This was a reference to Joseph in the Old Testament where this expression is used by Joseph's brothers, just before they sell him as a slave to the Egyptian merchants.) And because Josemaría tried to wash thoroughly every day from head to toe and keep his shoes and clothes clean he was contemptuously referred to as 'el senorito' ('the little gentleman' perhaps the English equivalent of 'Little Lord Fauntleroy'). He was also called by the coarser Aragónese expression, 'pijaito' ('pampered little daddy's boy').

Josemaría ignored their jibes and provocations but the nickname 'Mystical Rose' did hurt him, mostly because it showed – even if this was unintentional – a lack of reverence for Our Lady. It also saddened him to have his friends make fun of behaviour that he felt should have been seen as completely normal, not just for someone studying for the priesthood, but for any Christian.[37]

The seminarians' overall Christian virtues, however, seemed to have made up for these defects. And whenever Josemaría recalled his days in the seminary, all that he would mention about his companions were their virtues and their desire to serve the Church. Many of them would later die as martyrs for their priesthood just over a decade later during the civil war.

Josemaría, however, faced a much more serious problem than the jibes and torments of some of his fellow seminarians. In that first year the Rector of the seminary Father José López Sierra began to have serious doubts about Josemaría's suitability for the priesthood, possibly based on reports of the various clashes of personality he was having with some of the other seminarians. In fact the Rector at one stage became convinced that Josemaría did not have the qualities to persevere in his vocation and tried to persuade him to give up his idea of becoming a priest.

At the end of the first year, in the summer of 1921, he wrote his views of Josemaría in the seminary record book. In the section headed 'De Vita et moribus' 'Of the life and customs of the students') he wrote, 'Character: Inconstant and haughty, but well-mannered and courteous' and under Vocation wrote 'He seems to have one'. The Rector himself seems very uncertain. And one wonders whether this was written before or after the Rector tried to get him to abandon his vocation?[38]

In October, at the beginning of Josemaría's second seminary year, the Rector wrote to the Rector of Josemaría's previous seminary in Logroño: 'Please be so good as to inform me, as briefly as possible ... as to the moral, religious and disciplinary conduct of a former non-resident student of the seminary that you so worthily direct: José María Escrivá ... Please also mention anything else you consider relevant concerning his vocation to the priestly state and his personal qualities, returning this communication with the corresponding report. God grant you a long life. Saragossa, 17 October, 1921. José López Sierra, Rector.' By return of post came this short and to the point reply: 'During his stay in this seminary I saw his moral, religious and disciplinary conduct as being beyond reproach and as giving clear proof of a vocation to the ecclesiastical state. God grant you a long life. Logroño, 20 October, 1921. Gregorio Fernández, Vice-rector.'[39]

Father José López Sierra would completely change his mind about Josemaría and become his great supporter.

And Josemaría, when in later years looking back at the people who helped his 'incipient vocation' would write, 'In Logroño ... there was that holy priest, the Vice-Rector of the seminary, Father Gregorio Fernández. In Saragossa, Father José López Sierra, the poor Rector of San Francisco whom Our Lord changed in such a way that, after really doing everything he could to induce me to abandon my vocation (he did this with the best of intentions) he was my one and only defender against everyone else.'[40]

What is also quite clear is that Josemaría himself was so troubled by doubts about his vocation that at one point he considered giving up studying for the priesthood and leaving the seminary. During a retreat he was making in 1934, as he was looking back on his priestly vocation, he would write in a note that was not to be read until after his death, 'Had You [Lord] not prevented my leaving the seminary of Saragossa when I believed I had mistaken my path, I would perhaps be traipsing around the Spanish parliament, as some of my classmates from the university are doing ... and not exactly on your side, since ... there was a point when I felt profoundly anticlerical – I who love my brothers in the priesthood so much!'[41]

During this time he suffered not only from the taunts of some of his fellow seminarians and the doubts about his vocation but also from a series of strange temptations against purity. He always tried to live the virtue of purity as he advised others to do, 'Never talk of impure things or events, not even to deplore them. Look, it's a subject that sticks more than tar. Change the conversation, or if that's not possible, continue, but speak of the need and beauty of holy purity – a virtue of men who know what their souls are worth.'[42]

The temptations came from some women he did not know from Adam who tried to attract his attention as he walked with the other seminarians in double file to and from the Pontifical University. These women would wait for him out on the street, clearly intent on trying to seduce him. When he passed by with the other seminarians, they would brazenly stare at him, and make their intentions obvious through unmistakably provocative words or gestures. Another strange thing about these incidents was that the women made it quite clear that Josemaría was the only one they were interested in. He, for his part, never so much as looked at them. He placed himself under the protection of Our Lady; and from the outset he notified the superiors of the seminary and kept them fully informed of the situation.

But it didn't stop there. Garbled versions of what was happening to him even spread as far as his home town of Logroño. One day, his father, José Escrivá, happened to be in the barber's shop in Logroño when he heard someone remark that some women were after his son. José was so worried that he immediately went to Saragossa to see him. His intention was to go and point out to his son that it would be better for him to become a good father of a family than a bad priest. But as soon as they met Josemaría was able to set his father's mind at rest. He explained that he didn't know the women who were trying to seduce him and that he had never given them the least encouragement. His father then clearly saw that nothing had weakened his son's determination to become a priest and to live up to all that it would entail.[43]

It was while Josemaría was a seminarian that he began his corporal mortifications. He used the discipline and at times wore a cilice, a tight metal band worn on either an arm or a leg and which bites into the skin.

It was also at this time that the great persecution of the Catholic Church in Mexico was taking place. It was this persecution which was later to inspire Graham Greene to write what he always considered was his greatest novel, *The Power and the Glory*. The sufferings of the Church and its people in Mexico deeply touched Josemara's heart. He prayed a great deal for the Church in Mexico and offered many sacrifices all the time he was a seminarian. And when he later became a priest he continued with his prayers and sacrifices for Mexico. In his prayers he commended her especially to Christ the King and to Our Lady of Guadalupe.

CHAPTER 8

'Lord, What is it you want of me?'

About this time, Josemaría began making visits at night to the seminary church of San Carlos to spend hours in prayer. After the lights of the seminary had gone out he would make his way to the upper level of the church and would kneel in the balcony to the right of the altar. From there he would look down on the Tabernacle. Alone with Our Lord in the silence of the night and the flickering light of the sanctuary lamp he would have long, deep conversations with Jesus in the Blessed Sacrament.

Prayer, sacrifice and hard work. These filled Josemaría's days. He would later write, 'Study. Study in earnest if you want to be salt and light ...'[44] He certainly studied in earnest. In the year 1920–21 he was awarded meritissimus in four subjects and in the following years meritissimus in every one of his subjects. His qualities soon began to be noticed. Cardinal Soldevila, the Archbishop of Saragossa, used to single Josemaría out in front of the others and ask him how he was and how he was getting on with his studies. Then Cardinal Soldevila showed his high regard for him by personally appointing him a seminarian Superior when he was just twenty years old. Seminarian Superiors or Inspectors – official documents use both terms – were chosen from among the more promising and pious pupils. Their job was to direct studies and see that discipline and rules were observed. The Superiors always accompanied pupils when they walked between seminary and university. Although still seminarians they had to be obeyed and respected by the other seminarians. Superiors also had certain privileges such as a room of their own and an attendant or servant. These were scholarship seminarians whose tasks including cleaning the rooms of the Superiors and serving the other seminarians at table. The Superior's job, an old boy of the seminary later said, 'was difficult because the young boys used to give a lot of trouble, as could be expected from boys of that age. Josemaría never lost control or became flustered. He was always kind, prudent and well-mannered.'

The Rector of the seminary, Father José López Sierra, who had by this time completely changed his mind about Josemaría put on record that he was chosen to be a Superior 'because of his exemplary conduct, no less than his application'. It was also the Rector's opinion that he stood out among the other seminarians 'for his refined manners, his kindness and simplicity in his dealings with others, and marked modesty.'[45]

To be a Superior the seminarian had to be a tonsured cleric. This meant that the clerical tonsure had to be granted to Josemaría ahead of schedule. Cardinal Soldevila conferred the tonsure on him on 28 September, 1922 in a chapel of the Archbishop's House in Saragossa.

The following year, Cardinal Soldevila would meet a violent death. On 4 June, 1923, he was shot down by anarchists as he was visiting a school, one of the first signs of the hatred and bloody persecution that was soon to engulf the country.

After receiving the tonsure, Josemaría in 1923 enrolled as a non-resident student in the law school of the University of Saragossa. Being a non-resident student meant he was exempt from having to attend lectures. This would enable him to pursue both his clerical and his legal studies. His plan was to work on his ecclesiastical studies during the normal academic seminary year, from October to June, and on his law studies during the summer vacation, from June to September.

It was around this time that he was involved in an ugly incident with another seminarian which led to blows being exchanged. In the seminary record book, the Rector wrote on Josemaría's page: 'He (Josemaría) had a row with Don Julio Cortés and received due punishment, the acceptance and fulfilment of which was to his credit. In my opinion it was his opponent who attacked him first and hardest, uttering against him coarse words improper for a cleric, and insulting him in my presence in the Cathedral of La Seo.'

Julio Cortés, the other seminarian, was a late vocation and over forty years old at the time. He had lived for some years in Argentina and claimed to have been the secretary to the Governor of Buenos Aires. One seminarian says he could be insolent and describes him as 'capable of getting anyone angry.'

Josemaría must have poured out his sadness about the confrontation to his old spiritual director at the Logroño seminary, Father Gregorio Fernández, for on 26 October 1923 Father Fernández sent him the following reply: 'I feel very badly about your encounter with Julio – not so much for him since he has very little to lose, as for you. I realize that it was unavoidable on your part, but I wish you had never had to find yourself in the position of having to defend yourself with such forceful arguments. I know the nobility of your sentiments, and I'm sure that by now you do not hold in your heart the slightest trace of resentment ... You should not discuss this matter with anyone other than God.'

Josemaría took his advice and would no doubt not only have forgiven Julio but prayed for him. There is a happy ending to the incident. Julio became chaplain to a Tuberculosis hospital in the south of Spain. And, after Josemaría's death, among his papers was found a card, on which was the printed heading,

Julio María Cortés
Chaplain of the Tuberculosis Hospital
'El Neveral'
Jaén

Below Julio had written:

'Repentant, and in the most humble and absolute way possible. Mea culpa!'

It was dated 8 October 1952

Josemaría concluded his ecclesiastical studies in June of 1924 and he then presented himself for the examination in Spanish history as part of his law exams. He had always had a great love of history and it was a subject he knew well from his secondary school courses and from his wide reading. However, as he had not attended classes during the year because he had been doing his theological studies, the history professor let him know, by way of a common acquaintance, that he might as well not show up for the examination. The professor said he intended to fail him.

Josemaría was taken aback, especially as he knew that he was not required to attend classes. So, in order to defend a right which was his by academic regulations, and feeling confident of his knowledge of history, he still showed up for the examination despite the professor's warning. The professor promptly failed him without asking him a single question.

After some calm reflection, which no doubt was accompanied by much prayer, Josemaría decided to write a letter to the professor. In it he explained, as politely as he could, that he thought the professor had committed an injustice and had a moral obligation to make up for it. He then added that he wanted to take the examination again in September, and that he would like to be sure of receiving fair treatment. It was a very daring and courageous thing to do. In those days professors enjoyed complete autonomy and had full responsibility for making up the examinations and grading them, so it was not easy for students to defend their legal rights, even if they did so in the most respectful manner. But Josemaría's letter achieved the desired result. When September came, the professor acted very properly. He acknowledged his error, and Josemaría took his history examination and passed it.

A fascinating account of the way Josemaría passed his canon law and Roman law exams about this time has been left to us by one of the professors at the university, Professor Sánchez del Rio. He says, 'I remember that at the start of the exam in canon law, Professor Juan Moneva, the teacher of this course, asked him in Latin if he wished to take the exam in that language. Without a moment's hesitation he answered yes, and so he did. His answers were very good, very specific and concise. He answered quickly in correct Latin, in a clear and brief manner; it was a brilliant examination. And the one in Roman law showed the special liking he had for this discipline.'[46]

The theme of Josemaría's prayer at this time never varied. He was always asking how he could fulfil God's will. He felt he was going about 'half blind, always wondering why. Why, why am I becoming a priest?' He knew the Lord wanted something of him, but what was it?[47]

He read the Gospels every day and tried to imagine himself being actually present in the particular scene being described, either as a passer-by or one of the crowd. One day he was reading the passage where Jesus asks the blind man Bartimeus, 'What do you want Me to do for you?' and Bartimeus replies, 'Lord, may I see!' The words seemed to strike a chord within Josemaría so that he began using the same words in his prayer, 'Lord, what do You want me to do for You? What is it?' And Bartimeus' plea would echo back to him, 'Lord, may I see!' From then on Josemaría bombarded heaven with those words of the blind man Bartimeus, 'Lord, may I see! May I see! Let me see what it is You want of me. And may this thing You want me to do, but which I don't know what it is, come about!'[48]

He later said, 'Almost without realising it, I kept repeating, "Domine, ut videam! Domine, ut sit!" ("Lord, let me see! Lord let it come about!"). I did not know what it was He wanted, but I went on and on, without fully corresponding to God's goodness, waiting for what I was later to receive: a succession of graces, one after another which I did not know how to describe and called them operative, because they so dominated my will that I hardly needed to make any effort. I carried on, without doing anything unusual, working with just average intensity ... Those were the years in Saragossa.'[49]

CHAPTER 9

The Telegram

Just a few months before he was to be ordained Josemaría received a telegram. It said his father had been taken ill and asked him to return home.

With the rector of the seminary's permission he caught the first train for Logroño. Waiting for him at the station was Manuel Ceniceros, who worked with his father at 'The Great City of London' clothing store. It was Manuel who had sent the telegram. He at once told Josemaría that his father had died.

Josemaría learned that his father had got up at his usual time and appeared his normal self. If he was ill, he hadn't said anything about it. After breakfast he had knelt and prayed in front of a statue of Our Lady of the Miraculous Medal that was in the house at the time. It was the custom to take this particular statue from house to house, and it was the turn of the Escrivá home to have it. Then, his father, as he always did just before leaving for work, stopped to play with his little boy, Santiago, who was then five years old. Afterwards, as he was leaving and had reached the front door of the house, he felt faint. He leaned against the door post and then suddenly toppled on to the floor unconscious. Hearing him fall, his wife, Dolores, and his daughter Carmen ran to help him. They immediately called the parish priest and the doctor and then carried him into a bedroom. The doctor told them nothing could be done. Two hours later José Escrivá, having received the Last Sacraments, died without recovering consciousness.

Grief-strickened, Josemaría hurried home. As he went he kept praying for the repose of his father's soul. And he immediately began to worry how he, a student priest, would ever be able to support his family. He realized there was only one answer. It was to place himself and his problems in the hands of God, which he did.

He later said of his father, 'He died worn out. He was just 57 years old, but was always smiling. I owe my vocation to him.'[50]

Josemaría took charge of all the preparations for the funeral. In the process he discovered that the family had not enough money to pay for the funeral. A priest and family friend, Father Daniel Alfaro, who was a military chaplain, lent him the money and saved the family from what would have been a terrible embarrassment. As soon as he possibly could Josemaría repaid the loan. And he never forgot the generosity of that priest. After his ordination Josemaría prayed for him and for his intentions every day in the Memento of this Mass. And years later when he came to hear of Father Alfaro's death, he commended his soul to the Lord in every one of his daily Masses, up to and including that of 26 June 1975, the last Mass he would say on this earth. The burial of Josemaría's father took place the following day. The cemetery of Logroño was then on the other side of the Ebro River, on the road to Mendavia. On his way home, crossing the bridge over the river, Josemaría was absorbed in his grief and was thinking how the weight of responsibility for the family now rested entirely on his shoulders. Then he suddenly remembered that he had in his pocket the key to the coffin. It had been given to him by the undertaker as a keepsake. He thought, 'What am I doing with this key, which for me could turn into an attachment?' So he took the key and threw it into the Ebro river, offering to God the separation from his father. God, he reasoned, had decided to take his father to himself. And he, Josemaría, had to accept, without any reservations, being left on earth without the support which his father had provided. He also saw the hand of God in the fact that he had already received the subdiaconate when he had promised he would serve the Lord with priestly celibacy for the rest of his life. He felt he was thus bonded forever to God. He would, he resolved, put all his trust in the divine will – especially now, when the whole responsibility of looking after this family fell upon him, the eldest son.[51]

After thinking about the problem of caring for his family while he was still a student and not yet ordained, he came to the conclusion that the best thing he could do for his mother, his sister Carmen and his brother Santiago, was to find somewhere for them to live in Saragossa so that he could be near to them. Then, after comforting them in their sorrow, he returned to Saragossa to continue with his studies and find a new home for them.

Three weeks later, on 20 December 1924, in the chapel of the San Carlos seminary he received the diaconate from Bishop Miguel de Santos. Carrying out the duties that came with the diaconate made a great impact on him. Such was his great reverence for Jesus in the Blessed Sacrament that when he touched the Sacred Host, his hands, and sometimes his whole body, would tremble. This happened to him when he was assisting at Benediction for the first time and the moment came when had to put the small class case containing the Sacred Host in the monstrance. His immediate response was to ask Our Lord never to let him get used to handling the Blessed Sacrament.[52] And years later he would relate how one day at Mass, when it came to the washing of the priest's hands, his hands had trembled at the thought that they would soon be touching the consecrated host. Then he remembered the first time he had touched Our Lord during Benediction and from deep within him came the plea: 'Lord, let me never get used to being close to You. Let me always love You as I did that time when I touched You trembling with faith and love.'[53]

At the beginning of 1925, he was able to move his family from Logroño to Saragossa, having found a small flat for them not far from the seminary.

Josemaría was ordained priest on 28 March 1925, still not knowing what it was that God wanted him to do. His first Mass he said at the shrine of Our Lady of Pilar on 30 March, which was the Monday of Passion Week. He offered his first Mass for the repose of his father's soul.

That same day, 30 March, he was given his first priestly assignment. He was asked to go to a village called Perdiguera, on the slopes of the Alcubierre mountains about fifteen miles from Saragossa. There was a difficult situation in the village. The priest there had abandoned his parish under circumstances that were never to be fully explained. The reason officially given was that he been taken ill. There could have been some truth in this official explanation for the priest died suddenly a month later, in May.

The people of Perdiguera (population 870) lived in humble houses clustered around the church of the Assumption. They gave a warm welcome to Father Josemaría, the newly ordained priest who had come to help out. And Father Josemaría responded with all the priestly zeal he could muster. When he inspected the church he was sad to find the interior looked neglected and dirty. So before saying Mass there the following day he swept and cleaned it as best he could, even getting down on his knees to give parts of it a good scrubbing. He said Mass daily and prayed the Rosary with them every afternoon. He also held catechism classes and gave talks on the basic teaching of the Church to anyone who was interested, to children and adults, either in groups or, when necessary, on a one-to-one basis. He also prepared children for their First Holy Communion. He took special care of the sick, visiting them as often as he could. No matter what time of day or night it was, he would always take the Sacraments to any sick person asking for them. He also went from house to house visiting his parishioners. Within less than two months he had met all the families of the village. He spoke a great deal to all of them about going to Confession, which he called 'the sacrament of joy' because he would say, 'it brings us back to God'. In this way he succeeded in getting practically all the inhabitants of the village to Confession. He would later exhort priests to make the ministry of Penance the dominant passion of their lives and he would also advise priests, 'Sit down in the confessional every day, or at least two or three times a week, waiting for souls the way the fisherman waits for the fish. To start with, perhaps nobody comes. Take the breviary with you, or a book for spiritual reading, for your meditation. In the first days you will be able to do so. Then some little old woman will turn up, and you will teach her that it is not enough for her alone to be good, that she must bring her little grandchildren with her next time. Four or five days later two young girls will come, and then an older boy, and then a man, in an offhand sort of way ... After two months, they'll hardly let you draw breath. You will not be able to pray at all in the confessional, because your anointed hands, as those of Christ, confused with His because you are Christ, will be too busy saying: "I absolve you".'[54]

At that time it was the custom in small villages like Perdiguera for the parish priest, once his day's duties were finished, to get together with the local 'powers that be' – the mayor, the doctor, the pharmacist and the town clerk – and play cards. But Father Josemaría found he had so many things to do that he had no time to take part in the leisure activities with the 'powers that be'. During all the days he spent in Perdiguera he clearly felt that the Lord was wanting something special of him, even if that something was still wrapped in obscurity. When the people of the village were taking their siesta and it was not possible to do any pastoral visits, he made good use of the time by praying or taking long walks in the country. On these walks he would sometimes take with him Teodoro Murillo, one of the altar boys and use it as an opportunity to teach Teodoro some aspect of Christian doctrine. Teodoro noticed that while they were walking along Father Josemaría would often stop, pick up a pebble and put it in his pocket. But he would never say a word in explanation. To Teodoro it was a complete mystery. And this pocketing of the pebbles would remain a mystery for many years, and only be revealed after Father Josemaría's death.

In Perdigera, Father Josemaría stayed in the home of a poor peasant family, Santurnino Arruga and his wife

Prudencia. Their son took the goats out every morning and Father Josemaría recalled later, 'I felt sorry for him, seeing him spend all day out there with the herd. I did my best to give him a few catechism lessons, so that he could make his first Holy Communion. Little by little I taught him a few things.

'One day, to see how much he was learning, it occurred to me to ask him: "What would you like to do if you were rich, very rich?"

'"What does being rich mean?" he answered.

'"To be rich is to have a lot of land, and instead of goats, very big cows. And to go to meetings, change suits three times a day . . . What would you do if you were rich?"

'His eyes opened wide and then at last he said: "I would like to have lots of bowls of wine soup!"'

Josemaría never forgot that reply. He said, 'It struck me and it made me think: Josemaría, it is the Holy Spirit speaking. The wisdom of God did it to teach me that the things of the earth, all of them, add up to that. Very, very little.'[55]

Father Josemaría's priestly efforts in Perdiguera did not find favour with everyone. The nickname 'Mystical Rose' that had been given to him in Saragossa somehow reached Perdiguera. And because of his priestly activity some of his fellow priests in the region began to call him 'The Mystic'. But he never protested or ever showed any resentment.

He returned to Saragossa on 18 May 1925. His short stay in Perdiguera had left a deep and permanent impression on his soul. He would do a second spell in a country parish at Fombuena during Holy Week of 1927 and would say in later years, 'I have been in country parishes on two occasions. What a joy when I recall those times . . . They did me an immense amount of good, immense, immense! How delighted I am when I think back on them.'[56]

CHAPTER 10

Relations with the Archdeacon

On his return to Saragossa he was, somewhat surprisingly, not offered any position by the diocesan authorities and as a result received no money from them either. Father Josemaría, with his mother, sister and brother to provide for, was living in a modest apartment in Rufas Street. To keep the roof over their heads he immediately had to set about looking for something that would bring him some remuneration. After a month or more searching, the only priestly work he could find was that of assistant priest at the Jesuit church of St Peter Nolasco, which was also known as the Church of the Sacred Heart. He took up the post of assistant priest in April or May of 1925 and in September was offered a contract. This contract makes interesting reading:

DUTIES AND RIGHTS OF THE ASSISTANT PRIEST AT SAINT PETER NOLASCO CHURCH:
On feast days, First Fridays, and other solemn days, he is to be at the service of the church from 6.00 to 10.30 in the morning; on other days, from 7.00 to 9.30 or 10.00 in the morning.
Whenever there is a sung Mass, and also during Holy Week, he is to be on hand to help out as needed.
On First Fridays, during Forty Hours Devotion, on every

day in the month of June, and on any other occasion that includes exposition of the Blessed Sacrament, he is to show up punctually at the time of the service to do the exposition and to help out in any way needed.
When necessary he will wash the purificators.
He will say Holy Mass at the assigned times.
He will receive a fixed stipend of 3 pesetas for each Mass.
For the other services described above, he will receive 2 pesetas a day.
On feasts days he will have breakfast in the sacristan's office.
On days when for any reason he does not fulfil his duties, he will not receive either stipend unless he sends a substitute who fulfils all of those duties.
The father superior of the church can, if he sees fit, appoint a different assistant priest, giving the undersigned eight days' notice.
Agreeing with these conditions, I accept them, in Saragossa, on 10 September, 1925.
It is signed, José Maria Escrivá, Priest.

These meagre earnings would hardly have kept the wolf from the door. In these years the income of an average middle-class family was around 7,500 pesetas a year. A labourer earned six pesetas a day. And on a labourer's pay in those days it was very difficult to support a family. Father Josemaría's stipends amounted to five pesetas a day, one peseta less than a labourer received. And, as he had in Perdiguera, he spent many hours in the confessional, something not listed among the duties of an assistant priest and presumably something for which there was no extra remuneration.

His efforts to find other priestly work were unsuccessful. Twice he was recommended for posts as chaplain to orders of nuns but each time was turned down by the Archbishop of Saragossa. On 19 December 1925 the Archbishop wrote to the president of the Provincial Assembly who had recommended Father Josemaría:

My dear and distinguished friend:
In answer to your esteemed letter recommending Father José Escriba [surname mis-spelt] for the chaplaincy of the Reparatrix nuns, I must with great regret inform you that this position was offered a week ago to Father Manuel de Pablo, and he has accepted it.
I will be most happy to serve you on another occasion. You know you can always feel entirely free to count on your good friend and Prelate, who blesses you.

A few months later the 'opportunity to serve on another occasion' arose when another order of nuns needed a chaplain. But on 3 April 1926 the Archbishop wrote this time to say:

My dear and distinguished friend:
By the time I received your esteemed letter recommending Father José Escrivá (this time spelt correctly) for the chaplaincy of the nuns of the Incarnation, I had already signed the letter of appointment. I am truly sorry not to be able to oblige you in this matter. You must understand that it is not for lack of good will.

There was a feeling in certain informed circles in the Saragossa diocese that there indeed was a lack of good will towards Father Josemaría on the part of the diocesan authorities. It was thought that someone very influential was doing his best to get Father Josemaría out of the diocese.

This influential person turned out to be none other than Father Josemaría's uncle, his mother's brother, Father Carlos Albás, who was the Archdeacon of Saragossa. At the time of the failure of Josemaría's father's business it was the Archdeacon who had disapproved of his sister's husband paying off the debts he was not legally obliged to and had remarked, 'Pepe has been a fool. He could have retained a good financial position and instead he's reduced himself to misery.'[57]

The Archdeacon, however, had been very helpful and friendly towards Josemaría at the beginning. When Josemaría wanted to transfer from the Logroño seminary to Saragossa the Archdeacon had used his considerable influence to get him a place in the San Carlos seminary together with a half scholarship. And while Josemaría was at San Carlos seminary his uncle had taken him under his wing. The Archdeacon liked talking to his nephew and would invite him to his home for an afternoon snack. He even took care of Josemaría's washing, which was collected from the seminary and washed at his home. It was his uncle too who gave him help and good advice about how and when to start his legal studies. But relations between uncle and nephew began to deteriorate when Josemaría would not agree to the Archdeacon's plans for his future. His uncle, who could be quite domineering, wanted him to abandon his legal studies and take a clerical post as soon as he was ordained so that he could then look after his family. No doubt the Archdeacon would have used his influence to get him a good well-paid post and would have helped him to get ahead in his clerical career. But Father Josemaría was not interested in a clerical career and he had not become a priest 'to get ahead'. He was also very conscious of the fact that he had promised his father that he would take a law degree and he felt deep in his soul that this was what God wanted of him. Time would later clearly prove this to be the case. In the years to come his legal knowledge would be an invaluable instrument and help in finding a place for the work God had given him to do within the legal framework of the Church. For these reasons Father Josemaría felt he could not abandon his law studies and fall in with the Archdeacon's plans for him. This decision must have upset Archdeacon Carlos Albás.

The Archdeacon had also taken great exception to the Escrivá family moving from Logroño to Saragossa so that they would all be together. After the family settled in Saragossa, Josemaría and his sister Carmen went to visit their uncle and got a very bad reception. He greeted them by asking them point blank if the reason they had come to Saragossa was to parade their poverty.

Carmen's immediate response was, 'Josemaría, let's get out of here, since we are not approved of in this house.'

Another occasion when the Archdeacon behaved badly

towards the family was shortly after Father Josemaría returned from Perdiguera. His mother went to see her brother the Archdeacon because she was worried that her son might be given another assignment away from Saragossa and the family would be separated again. She took with her Santiago, who would never forget the visit. He says, 'Once he (Josemaría) was ordained a priest my mother wanted him to be allowed to stay in Saragossa with us. She went to ask this of her brother Father Carlos who had a lot of influence in the Chancery.'

'But,' says Santiago, 'her brother Father Carlos treated her very badly. In fact, he threw us out of his house.'[58]

Father Josemaría never complained about the treatment he and his family received at the hands of his uncle, the Archdeacon, and his feelings towards him were always exceptionally charitable. Several times he tried to approach him to settle their differences but to no avail.

After the Spanish Civil War, however, early in 1940, he made a visit to Saragossa to see his uncle because he did not want him to think he was harbouring any resentment. He found his uncle after the horrors of the civil war a changed man. Their friendship was renewed and Father Josemaría was very happy with the outcome of that meeting. Eight years later, on January 6 1948, when Father Josemaría received news of Father Carlos' death he immediately wrote a short letter to his sister, Carmen and his brother Santiago: 'I hear that Father Carlos has died. I ask you to pray for his soul, especially since he acted so badly towards Mama and us – I feel this obliges us to pray all the more for him. If you do, you will please Our Lord God and I will be grateful to you.'[59]

The news of the Archdeacon's death, however, was incorrect. His uncle did not die for another two years, but the letter shows the loving concern that Father Josemaría always had for him.[60]

In the months following his return from Perdiguera, Father Josemaría and his family did their best to hide their poverty. But life was becoming more difficult by the day. Making at that time, an inventory of their resources he wrote, 'I don't know how we are going to live ... Really –

I'll spell this out when I have more time – we have lived in this way since I was fourteen, but the situation has got worse since Papa's death.'[61] He realized that it was imperative that he should get his law degree as quickly as possible. On 25 April 1926 he wrote to the head of the law school requesting to be allowed 'to take, the next time they are given, the examinations in the following subjects: political law, penal law, administrative law, public international law, business law, and judicial procedures ...'[62]

His plan proved to be a little too ambitious. His duties as assistant priest at St Peter Nolasco's didn't leave him with much free time. And he was also carrying out extra pastoral initiatives. One of these was getting a group of young men together, mostly students, and on Sundays going with them to give catechism classes to poor children in deprived areas on the edge of the city, such as the Casablanca district on the old road to Teruel.

When the time came to take his law examinations in June he had to put off taking two of the subjects until later in the year. For the exams he managed to take he gained one 'Special Honours,' two 'Notables' and one 'Pass'. The two remaining subjects, penal law and judicial procedures, he took and passed in September. This left him only one more examination, which was in Forensic Practice, to complete his law degree.

When attending law lectures at the university Father Josemaría always wore his cassock but got along very well with his university colleagues. Sometimes, when classes were over, his fellow students would invite him to go for a drink at the Abdón Bar in Constitution Square which was very popular with students. Occasionally he accepted because he found it a very good way to get to know them better. He formed several deep friendships, some with non-believers opposed to the Catholic Church. One such student who became a very good friend was Pascual Galbe. Years later during the civil war their paths would cross again when Galbe held an important legal position in Communist controlled Barcelona. The two friends would face each other on opposite sides of the political divide, the powerful lawyer and the hunted priest. And it was then that the good friend from his University of Saragossa days, at considerable risk to himself, would put their deep friendship before his political doctrines and loyalties and do all he could to help his friend the hunted priest.

Soon after taking his September exams father Josemaría found a way to earn a little more money to help the family finances. A former infantry captain with a degree in science, Santiago Amado, for some time had been planning to open a school preparing students for various careers, concentrating especially on those wanting to enter military academies. The school, which he named the Amado Institute, opened in October of 1926 and Father Josemaría was given a post in the law department teaching Roman law and Canon law. As well as teaching law he must also have tried, whenever he could, to help his students spiritually. For in May of the following year one of his students, Nicholís Tena, wrote to him a very cheerful letter telling him how he did in his Canon law exam. The letter ends happily with the words, 'Father, I have gone to Confession and received Communion – I'll have to write you a very long letter about this.'[63]

Father Josemaría was having to make use of every minute of the day to carry out all his numerous and varied tasks. He was meticulously fulfilling all his duties as assistant priest, caring for his family, studying hard for his final law exam and teaching at the Amado Institute.

And as he immersed himself in his work it seemed as if he was being more and more isolated by the Diocesan authorities.

Dr José Pou de Foxá, a well-known professor of Canon law, was one of Father Josemaría's teachers in the university law department. He also took it upon himself to help him in his first steps in the priesthood and Father Josemaría would always consider him a 'good, loyal, noble friend'.

Father José Pou was convinced there was 'no future' for him in the Saragossa diocese and advised him to go to Madrid. Father Josemaría would later describe what was happening to him in Saragossa at that time as 'some providential injustices' and he sensed that in this way God was leading him step by step to where He wanted him to be.[64]

In 1926, he decided to make a special trip to Madrid to

look at the possibility of taking a doctorate in law. The University of Madrid, then known as the Universidad Central, was the only university in Spain where law doctorates could be taken. He believed that a doctorate in law would not only be the ultimate fulfilment of his father's wishes but would also make it easier for him to find work as a teacher and provide for his family.

There was, however, one great problem about being a priest and going to Madrid. To work in another diocese a priest has to receive 'faculties' from the bishop of that diocese. These faculties give the priest the right to say Mass, to hear confessions and to preach. Without them a priest cannot work as a priest.

But the Bishop of Madrid, Leopoldo Eijo y Garay, had too many priests from other dioceses in Madrid already. This was also the opinion of the Holy See in Rome. In a handwritten letter some years later Bishop Leopoldo would clearly and forcefully spell out his views on the subject. The letter was to a cardinal, a member of the Roman Curia, who was interceding on behalf of a priest from another diocese who was wanting to stay in Madrid and whom we will call 'Father M'.

The bishop writes, 'I received the estimable letter of Your Eminence ... and am honoured to be able to provide the following information.

'It has always been the wish of a great part of the Spanish clergy to come and live in Madrid. There is no need for more priests here. In fact, there are already more than there should be.

'In fulfilment of my duty to comply with the wishes of the Sacred Congregation, which does not want a crowding of extra-diocesan priests into the great capitals, I have always taken the utmost care to avoid granting faculties to those who want to move to Madrid without sufficient canonical reason to do so.

'This constitutes a real cross in this diocese, where almost every day we have to turn down four or five similar petitions ... Father M. of the diocese of Avila, is in that situation. The Count of Santa Engracia brought him here to be his chaplain, and when he asked me to grant faculties to this priest, I told him that I could not do so because the Holy See forbids me to ... Now, then, my humble request to the Sacred Congregation is that in the case of Father M. as in that of all others who ask for the same thing the Sacred Congregation would deign to answer non expedire (do not proceed). Otherwise, all of the extra-diocesan priests aspiring to live in Madrid will direct their petitions to the Holy See, and if they are granted, half the clergy of Spain, especially in these times we are living in, will come here, with really serious detriment to the diocese and the Church.'

Father Josemaría would no doubt have been aware of the bishop's views on extra-diocesan priests like himself when he visited Madrid. Getting to Madrid must have seemed to him to be an almost impossible task at this time.

Still in the dark about what God wanted of him, he continued to work, study and teach. And as he walked about Saragossa he would continually pray, 'Lord, what is it you want?' And visiting the shrine of Our Lady of Pilar he would kneel and plead, 'Domine, ut sit! Domina, ut sit ... Lord, may it come about. Our Lady, (whatever it is your Son wants me to do) let it be done!'[65]

CHAPTER 11

The Slums of Madrid

Father Josemaría took and passed his final law examination, Forensic Practice, in January 1927. He now had his degree in law. The next step was to get his doctorate in law. But to do this he would have to go to Madrid and he was immediately faced with the problem. How could he work as a priest in a diocese where the Bishop didn't want any more priests from outside his diocese? For some time Father Josemaría had been in correspondence with a Claretian priest, Father Prudencio Cancer, who was a good friend of the Escrivá family. Father Cancer had been busy looking for some way that Father Josemaría could work as a priest in Madrid and was doing all he could to help him. But he didn't seem to be having much success finding a way round the problem. He persevered and one day suddenly stumbled on a solution. In a letter dated 9 March, 1927, he joyously writes, 'My dear friend: Can we now sing the Te Deum? (a hymn of praise and thanksgiving) I think we can! So you can understand what I'm saying, I will tell you that I accidentally found out that Saint Michael's Church in Madrid – which is near Calle Mayor, is under the jurisdiction of His Excellency the Nuncio (the Pope's representative) and is run by the Redemptorists, who have a house there – has an opening for someone to say Mass there every day at 5.50 a.m., and to obtain this position you only need the permission of His Excellency the Nuncio. I saw the heavens open when I learned this, because the great difficulty, as I see it, in getting you into Madrid, even with good recommendations, is to get permission from this bishop. Look how Our Lord is smoothing your path!'

Father Cancer also enclosed in the letter a note that the rector of St Michael's had sent him. This gave more details about the position and showed that Father Cancer had already recommended Father Josemaría for it. The note says, "The priest you recommended will, of course, be able to get permission of the Papal Nuncio to celebrate Mass in this church ... This position is not a chaplaincy, but it does assure that he can continue celebrating Mass and receiving the stipend for as long as he remains in Madrid.

'To obtain faculties from the Nuncio, he must have in order the ministerial licences from his own prelate and must also present a document authorising him to live in Madrid with that prelate's blessing. His Excellency the Nuncio also wants the prelate to say in that same document at least a word testifying to the priest's good conduct. This is what is always required, and with this it's no problem – he can come.'

Now all that remained was for Father Josemaría to get permission from the Archbishop of Saragossa to go to Madrid to study for his law doctorate together with the necessary letters of recommendation. In his application to the Archbishop he made it quite clear that while he was in Madrid he would put his priestly obligations before all else. On 17 March, eight days after Father Cancer wrote his last letter, he received permission to study for two years at the University of Madrid. Five days later he received the letters of recommendation.

Almost immediately another problem arose. The Rector of St Michael's, Madrid, wanted him go to the capital as soon as possible so that he would be there for Passion Week and Holy Week, because, as the Rector explained, 'this is the time we need priests most.'

But out of the blue the Saragossa chancery office suddenly notified Father Josemaría that he had been assigned to the parish of Fombuena for Passion Week and Holy Week.

He was now faced with a dilemma. He would either have to turn down the chancery assignment, which might cause further ill-will, or disappoint the Rector of St Michael's, who might then appoint someone else. His mother advised him to do what the chancery had asked him to do and go to Fombuena, and he accepted her advice. He wrote to the Rector of St Michael's explaining what had happened and that he wouldn't be able to go to Madrid until after Holy Week. The Rector replied, 'I would appreciate it very much if you do not delay your coming beyond the time that you indicated, because we need your Mass. We expect you, then, during the first days of Eastertide.'

All was now set fair for him going to Madrid. He fulfilled his priestly assignment in Fombuena and returned to Saragossa on Easter Monday, 18 April.

The following day, Easter Tuesday, 19 April, he travelled to Madrid and immediately on arrival presented himself at St Michael's.

He found a place to stay in a boarding house in Farmacia Street, which was within walking distance of St Michael's. The boarding house charged him seven pesetas a day. As his Mass stipend was five and a half pesetas, this meant he would be ten and a half pesetas down by the end of the week. So he had to search for more modest lodgings. He found what he was looking for at a recently opened house for priests in Larra Street run by a congregation of nuns known as the Damas Apostólicas del Sagrado Corazón, the Apostolic Ladies of the Sacred Heart. One of the Damas Apostólicas' bulletins about this time notes that their Priests' House was functioning very well and goes on to say, 'The priests residing there seem very happy with it ... They pay five pesetas, the usual stipend for Mass and enjoy excellent treatment in terms of meals, cleaning services etc ... The Bishop was so kind as to inaugurate it himself, and the Vicar General, who so much appreciates this endeavour, has offered to say Mass for us so that we can have the Blessed Sacrament reserved in the very lovely chapel ...'

Ten priests lived in the residence and, as Father Josemaría was one of the youngest he took on the job of doing errands for the older priests.

Doña Luz Rodríguez Casanova, daughter of the Marchioness of Onteiro and described as 'a very enterprising woman with a deep spiritual life,' had founded the Damas Apostólicas in Madrid three years earlier in 1924. By 1927 they were running a great many schools and charitable organizations throughout the city. One of them was the Foundation for the Sick, which cared for the sick and the dying all over Madrid, especially those in the poorest and most deprived areas of the city.

In the late twenties the hospitals of Madrid were grossly overcrowded and overworked and many of the poor were left to die in their homes. The Damas, and the women who helped them, sought out these abandoned sick and dying and as a result cared for thousands of people every year. They offered to all in need, food, medicine, clothing, companionship and spiritual comfort. But the sisters' charitable works were then turning into dangerous undertakings. The first campaigns against religion, aimed particularly at priests and nuns, had begun to spread the venom of hate throughout the city, especially in the poorest areas.

Doña Luz, the foundress, soon heard about the zeal of a young priest called Father Josemaría, who was staying in their Priests' House. He had been there for only about a month when Doña Luz asked him if he would be chaplain to their church of the Foundation for the Sick. Father Josemaría agreed to do so. In return, it was this remarkable lady Doña Luz Rodríguez Casanova who requested from the Bishop of Madrid that he should grant Father Josemaría his faculties. And Father Josemaría's faculties were duly granted.

Of these faculties he would later write, 'The first time they were granted me in the diocese of Madrid, at the request of Mother Luz Casanova they were general, if I remember correctly: to celebrate, to absolve, and to preach.'[66]

Doña Luz died with a reputation for sanctity in 1949 and her Cause of Beatification was opened in 1958.

Father Josemaría's job as chaplain to the Damas Apostólicas was to say Mass for the congregation, take Holy Communion to any of the Damas who were ill and give Benediction.

He said Mass early each morning at the church of the Foundation for the Sick. Pedro Rocamora, a law student, sometimes served his Mass and remembers that there came about Father Josemaría what he called 'a kind of transfiguration.'

'I'm not exaggerating,' he says. 'For him the liturgy was not a formal act but a transcendent one. Each word held a profound meaning and was uttered in a heartfelt tone of voice. He savoured the concepts. At that time many of us knew the Latin Mass by heart and so I could follow one by one the words of the liturgy. Josemaría seemed detached from his human surroundings and, as it were, tied by invisible cords to the divine. This phenomenon peaked at the moment of Consecration. At that instant something strange happened in which Josemaría seemed to be disconnected from the physical things around him (the church, the sanctuary, the altar) and to be catching sight of mysterious and remote heavenly horizons.'[67]

One of the Damas Apostólicas, Maria Vicenta, tells us he said Mass 'thoughtfully and devoutly, taking up to three quarters of an hour.'

Later because he thought this was too long for his congregation he cut the time to half an hour and would place his watch on the altar to help him keep to this time limit.

Father Josemaría was soon doing far more for the Damas Apostólicas than was required of him as chaplain. He began travelling all over Madrid visiting the people the sisters were caring for. He heard their confessions, took them Holy Communion and gave them the Last Rites. An indication of the immense task he took on, and the unrelenting work it required, can be seen in the records the sisters kept at the time. These show that in his second year as chaplain, the year 1928, the sisters visited more than 4,000 sick people. More than 3,000 confessions were heard and a similar number of sick people received Holy Communion.

One of the sisters, Asunción Muñoz, recalling the apostolic activities of those days wrote, 'We could not have managed without Father Josemaría. He was under no obligation to get involved in our charitable work. Yet he devoted himself totally to the huge numbers of poor and sick people he saw could be reached by his priestly heart. And so, when we came across a sick person who seemed likely to die without the Sacraments, we put him under Father Josemaría's care and were absolutely sure he or she would be well looked after.

'I don't recall a single case where a sick person under Father Josemaría's care died without receiving the Sacraments. He worked very hard and kept up a constant rhythm of work. Yet he looked after each person unhurriedly, as if he had all the time in the world.'

And she also adds that the difficult and tricky cases were always turned over to Father Josemaría because the Damas knew 'he would gain the good will of each person and open to them the gates of heaven.'

Each day the Damas sisters would give Father Josemaría a list of the sick to be visited. One day the Damas were deeply concerned about a dying man who was known to be rabidly anti-clerical. The man had refused to go to Confession and had relapsed into a coma but they hoped Father Josemaría would be able to help him. 'When I got near the house of this poor man as I got to his street (Cardinal Cisneros),' Father Josemaría writes in his notes, 'I remembered how, when they gave me the note about him, I protested saying, "It's crazy to think I can do anything. If he's delirious what chance is there that I'll find him in any condition to go to Confession? But, all right, I'll go and I'll give him conditional absolution."'

As Father Josemaría was on his way to see him he followed his usual custom when going to visit a sick person of asking Our Lady's help and he said a Memorare that the dying man would be able to receive conditional absolution.

When he arrived at the house, however, the neighbours told him there was nothing he could do. A priest from the parish had been, but had left unable to hear the man's Confession because he had not regained consciousness. Undeterred, Father Josemaría carried on and went to the man's bedside and called his name, 'Pepe!'

'Immediately he gave me a very favourable response,' the note continues, '"Would you like to go to Confession?" "Yes," he told me.

'I threw everybody else out. He went to Confession – with me helping him a lot, naturally – and received absolution.'[68]

Father Josemaría also records another occasion when a dying, stubborn sinner was refusing to see a priest. 'I came to the man's house,' he writes. 'With holy, apostolic shamelessness I sent his wife outside and was then alone with the poor man. "Father, those women from the Foundation are such nuisances, so impertinent. Especially one of them . . ." (He was talking about Pilar, who could be canonised!) "She told me I should go to Confession . . . because I am dying. Well, I will die, but I will not go to Confession!" Then I said, "Up to now I haven't said anything about Confession, but tell me, why don't you want to go to Confession?" "When I was seventeen I swore that I would never again go to Confession, and I have kept that promise." That's what he said. And he told me also that not even when he got married – the man was about fifty years old – had he gone to Confession . . . About fifteen minutes after saying all this, he went to Confession, in tears.'[69]

Father Josemaría also helped the Damas Apostólicas in their schools. The sisters provided 'free schools' in the poorest areas of the city. Over the years they had established more than sixty of them. He visited these schools, said Mass for the children and heard their confessions. He also helped to prepare thousands of children for their First Confession and First Holy Communion. In one year alone, about 4,000 children made their first Holy Communion in the chapel of the Foundation.

Father Josemaría was to say in the last years of his life, 'I have it upon my conscience – and I say it with pride – that I spent many, many thousands of hours hearing children's confessions in the poorer districts of Madrid. I would have liked to have gone to hear confessions in the saddest and most abandoned slums of the whole world.'[70]

There was an assistant chaplain at the Foundation, Father Norberto Rodriguez, who was then nearly fifty years old. Thirteen years earlier Father Norberto had had a nervous breakdown and had later suffered a relapse, which for quite some time made it impossible for him to hold any ecclesiastical position. Father Josemaría seems to have taken him under his wing. The two would go together to visit the sick and to the Damas' schools. Sister Asunción Muñoz at that time was convinced the main reason Father Josemaría took Father Norberto along with him was to help Father Norberto. 'It was so that he would feel useful and appreciated,' she says.

In November of 1927, so that he could be reunited with his family, Father Josemaría rented a small apartment in Fernando el Católico Street, not far from the Foundation for the Sick. His mother, his sister Carmen and his brother Santiago then travelled to Madrid and they all lived as a family in the apartment. To earn more money and provide for his family he found a teaching post similar to the one he had in Saragossa, teaching Roman law and Canon law at the Madrid Cicuéndez Academy.

This academy occupied the first floor of a building at 52, San Bernardo, close to Madrid University and was well-known by the university students. Its aim, it proclaimed, was 'to be a private school of juridical studies, providing painstaking preparation for the legal profession.' Father Josemaría was a good, conscientious teacher and was well-liked by the students. One of them, Julián Cortés, says that the students 'felt drawn to this professor because he was such a good teacher and because he was so human and priestly.' And another student, Manuel Gómez-Alonso, remembers, 'It was quite easy to make friends with him and so, quite often, when classes were over, I would walk with him part of the way back to his home.'

Among Father Josemaría's students was an older man, the father of a family, who was trying to get a university degree in his spare time so that his family would be better off. But the man had to spend long hours working in a very demanding job and as a result was often exhausted. His work left him little time for his family or his studies. Father Josemaría felt very sorry for him and gave him free extra tuition. His reward was the satisfaction of seeing him get his degree.

To augment his meagre income he also gave private lessons for which he charged fees. Father Josemaría's brother Santiago says, 'Josemaría gave several private classes, some in the apartment on Fernando el Católico. A girl came there for a class and Josemaría saw to it that my mother was always present, sewing. He also gave lessons to some boys older than me.'

One day another professor at the Cicuéndez Academy happened to mention to the students that their lecturer in Roman and Canon law spent a great deal of time working in the slum areas of the city. The students found that hard to believe. They couldn't imagine their dignified law lecturer in the appalling slums and shanty towns that were springing up in the outskirts of the city. Bets were made and the students decided they would follow Father Josemaría. They would then see where he went and what he was up to. As a result they found themselves in some of the meanest and most appalling slums of the city. These middle-class students had their eyes opened by what they saw. They discovered that some of the people Father Josemaría cared for didn't even have a roof over their head, but lived in holes in the ground. And the students also discovered that Father Josemaría was not only spending many hours a day in the slums, but was walking miles upon miles a day, often Rosary in hand, to all parts of the city. Constantly on the move, he seemed to be going everywhere, visiting the sick and the dying and the poorest and most abandoned souls. And to all of them he was offering the joy of Christ's teachings and the comfort of the Sacraments.

CHAPTER 12

The Vision as the Bells Ring Out

The year was 1928. And Father Josemaría still had no idea what God wanted of him. He had now been in Madrid for eighteen months and more than ten years had passed since he had come across the footprints in the snow and had felt the first inklings of a Divine calling. As he went about through all parts of the capital he continued to pray, 'Lord may I see! May I see! May I see what it is You want of me!'

Then, suddenly, God surprised him and let him 'see' exactly what it was He wanted him to do.

It happened on the morning of 2 October, the feast of the Guardian Angels, when he was on a retreat at the central house of the Vincentian Fathers in Madrid. Between talks he returned to his room and began rereading and trying to put into some kind of order the notes he had been making of the inspirations he had been receiving from God over the last ten years. Then, all at once as the bells of the nearby church of Our Lady and the Angels joyously rang out, he 'saw' – he always used the verb see on the rare occasions he spoke about it – the mission God was entrusting to him. What he saw and clearly understood was that he was to open up a new way of holiness in the middle of the world. He was to teach ordinary men and women of all nations and all races how they could become saints doing their ordinary work and living their everyday family lives. Many years later his successor at the helm of Opus Dei, Bishop Alvaro del Portillo, would explain that in the vision Father Josemaría saw 'opening before him the horizons to which the Lord was calling him ... This was the mobilisation of Christians in every part of the world, Christians of every social class, who, by way of carrying out their professional work, would seek their own sanctification while sanctifying from within all their temporal activities in a daring movement of evangelisation aimed at bringing all souls to God.'[71]

And Father Josemaría would later say, 'The ordinary life of a man among his fellows is not something dull and uninteresting. It is there that the Lord wants the vast majority of his children to achieve sanctity.

'It is important to keep reminding ourselves that Jesus did not address himself to a privileged set of people ... God loves all men, and he wants all to love him – everyone, whatever his personal situation, his social positions, his work. Ordinary life is something of great value. All the ways of the earth can an opportunity to meet Christ, who calls us to identify ourselves with him and carry out his divine mission – right where he finds us.

'God calls us through what happens during our day: through the suffering and happiness of the people we live with, through the human interests of our colleagues and the things that make up our family life. He also calls us through the great problems, conflicts and challenges of each period of history which attract the effort and idealism of a large part of mankind.

'It is easy to understand the impatience, anxiety and uneasiness of people whose natural Christian soul stimulates them to fight the personal and social injustice which the human heart can create. So many centuries of men living side by side and still so much hate, so much destruction, so much fanaticism stored up in eyes that do not want to see and in hearts that do not want to love!

'The good things of the earth, monopolised by a handful of people; the culture of the world confined to cliques. And, on the outside, hunger for bread and education. Human lives – holy, because they come from God – treated as mere things, as statistics. I understand and share this impatience. It stirs me to look at Christ, who is continually inviting us to put this new commandment of love into practice.'[72]

And Father Josemaría also came to understand that with the birth of Jesus, all good human realities were raised to the supernatural order. Working, studying, smiling, crying, getting tired, resting, developing friendships – all of these things, among so many others, became divine actions in the life of Jesus Christ.

'I was moved,' Father Josemaría wrote after having the vision, 'and knelt down and gave thanks to God.'[73]

He then realized how little he had to begin such a vast undertaking 'I was 26 years old. I had God's grace and a good sense of humour and nothing else,' he said.[74] And years later he would add, 'If I had known in 1928 what was in store for me, I would have died.'[75]

He began by praying and undertaking severe corporal penances. From then on every step of his pastoral and apostolic activity would be preceded and accompanied by severe mortifications. His mother and brother and sister would later recall that during those years in Madrid he would shut himself up in the bathroom of the apartment where they lived and would turn on the taps to muffle the sound of the discipline. But they would still be able to hear it. And, even though he very carefully washed the walls and floor afterwards, his mother and sister would discover with dismay drops of blood which had escaped his notice.[76] But he would always insist, and he underscored this with his own example, that the best mortification consisted in the faithful fulfilment – down to the last detail – of the ordinary duties of one's own state in life. And he strove to practise small mortifications in what he called 'the little things of each day' which he maintained ought to be constant, like the beating of one's heart. Among his notes discovered after his death is this one dated 3 November, 1932:

1) I mustn't ever 'look.'
2) I mustn't ask questions simply out of curiosity.
3) I mustn't sit down unless it is unavoidable, and must never use the back of the chair.
4) I mustn't eat anything sweet.

5) I mustn't drink water, except that used for the ablutions at Mass.
6) After lunch (the main meal) I mustn't eat any more bread.
7) I mustn't spend even five cents that a poor beggar wouldn't spend if he were in my position.
8) I mustn't complain to anyone about anything, except to seek direction.
9) I mustn't flatter or criticise. Deo omnis gloria![77]

'Action is worthless without prayer,' he would later write in *The Way*, adding, 'Prayer is worth more than sacrifice,' and 'First, prayer. Then atonement. In the third place – very much "in the third place" – action.'[78]

In September of 1929 the Escrivá family left their apartment on Fernando el Católico Street and moved into the apartment for the chaplain to the Foundation for the Sick. They most probably did this because they were so hard up. The apartment, which came with the chaplaincy, would have been ideal for one person but for a family it was small and cramped. It did have the advantage, however, of being connected with the main building so the chaplain could go into the church without having to go outside.

At this time Father Josemaría was all too conscious of his inadequacy for the task God had set him and would often repeat in his prayers, 'I am worth nothing, I have nothing, I can do nothing. I know nothing. I am nothing, nothing!' Before God he considered himself to be nothing more than 'a mangy donkey'. He prayed to be a faithful instrument so that he could open up the divine paths of the earth as God had shown him.

At the start he believed his work would be only with men and at the beginning of 1930 he wrote, 'Never – no way – will there be women in this work!'[79]

But God soon changed his mind. A short time later, on 14 February, 1930, while he was saying Mass, God suddenly made him see that, contrary to what he thought and had recently written, women would be very much a part of the work he had shown him.

Father Josemaría would later say, 'I used to go to the house of an old lady of eighty, who came to me for

Confession, to celebrate Mass in the small oratory she had. And it was there, in the Mass, after Communion, that the Women's Section came into the world.'[80]

The old lady was the Marchioness of Onteiro, the mother of Doña Luz Rodríguez Casanova, the founder of the Damas Apostólicas. Sick and housebound she had asked her daughter to see if a priest could say Mass for her in her private oratory and Father Josemaría had agreed to do so. The Marchioness died less than a year later on 22 January, 1931.

'That February 14, 1930,' he would later say to some of women members of Opus Dei, 'Our Lord made me feel what a father experiences when he isn't expecting another child, and God sends him one. Since then I feel as it were obliged to have more affection towards you. I see you as a mother sees her smallest child.'[81]

He would write in his notes, 'I always believed, and I still believe, that Our Lord, as on other occasions, "managed" me in such a way that there would be a clear, external, objective proof that the Work was his. I said, "I don't want women in Opus Dei!" and God said, "Well, I do."'[82]

Up to that time, Father Josemaría, had had little success finding men to help him with his work. Now he had to find women which, he realized, was going to be even more difficult.

One of the first people to know about this work God had given him to do was Dr José Pou de Foxá, his 'good, loyal, noble friend' and his professor of Canon law in Saragossa. In the thirties this priest wrote to him: 'Tell me what's going on – why I find you so changed. You always write with a lot of joy, and I see that you are still happy, but you seem now to be rather reserved. Something has happened to you. Are you suffering some sorrow?' Father Josemaría must then have told him something of what had happened for in his next letter Dr Pou says that after learning the news, he understood very well why his friend seemed to be immersed in God and so eager to fulfil His most holy will. He adds: 'You say you are a useless and inept instrument. It is not so bad if you say that, because otherwise you would be doing your own thing and not

God's. Since you are disposed to consider yourself inept, God will do everything, and everything will be of God.'[83] Father Josemaría did not speak to anyone else about the mission he had received from Our Lord, except for those who came close to the Work, and about the middle of 1930 to his spiritual director. His search for a spiritual director led him to Father Valentín Sánchez, a Jesuit held in high esteem. At the beginning of July 1930 he went to the Jesuit residence on De La Flor Street to ask Father Sánchez to be his spiritual director. He would later write of this meeting, 'Slowly, I revealed to him my soul and told him all about the Work. Both of us saw in all of it the hand of God. We agreed that I would bring him some papers – a packet of note-size sheets, it was – where I had written out the details of the whole endeavour. I brought them to him. Father Sánchez went to Charmartín for a few weeks. When he returned, he told me that the enterprise was from God and that he would have no problem being my confessor.'[84]

As his spiritual director the Jesuit would assure him many times that what he was doing was all from God. From then on Father Josemaría carried out, in a great spirit of obedience, the plan of mortification that was approved by his confessor.

And it was Father Sánchez who later helped confirm the name for the work God had given Father Josemaría to do. Describing this incident, which took place towards the end of 1930, Father Josemaría wrote: 'One day I went to have a talk with Father Sánchez in one of the rooms of the residence at La Flor. I spoke to him about my personal affairs (I only spoke to him about the Work insofar as it related to my own soul) and at the end the good Father Sánchez asked me, "How is that Work of God coming along?" Afterwards, as I walked along the street, I began to think: "Work of God. Opus Dei! Opus, operatio ... God's handiwork. This is the name I have been looking for!" And after that it was always called Opus Dei.'[85]

A little later, he realized that he himself had called it that in his notes. On 9 December 1930 he wrote, 'The Work of God: today I asked myself why do we call it that? And now I will answer myself in writing ... Father Sánchez, in the course of conversation, referring to the unborn family of the Work, called it "the Work of God". Then, and only then, I noticed that in my notes I had called it that. That name – the Work of God!! – which seemed like an impertinence, something presumptuous, almost an impropriety, was something that Our Lord had me write the first time without knowing what I was writing. He put it on the lips of the good Father Sánchez so that there could be no doubt that the Lord himself was directing that his work bear that name: the Work of God.'[86]

Later Opus Dei, the Work of God, came to be shortened and referred to simply as 'the Work' by its first members and then by all those who were to follow them.

CHAPTER 13

The Chance Meeting in the Street

Once it was confirmed for him that the work he was doing had been given him by God, Father Josemaría went about with a new vigour looking for people who would be willing to bring God into their ordinary everyday lives and their work.

But the universal call to holiness which Father Josemaría saw with such clarity, thanks to the divine illumination he had been given, seemed for many too revolutionary and too outrageous.

In the 1960s he gave this explanation for it: 'When some forty years ago a young priest of twenty-six started to say that holiness was not just for friars, nuns and priests, but that it was for all Christians, because Jesus Christ Our Lord said to all, "Be holy as My heavenly Father is holy" – whether one is single, married, or widowed makes no difference, we can all be saints – they called that priest a heretic.'[87]

Others said he was crazy, a madman. What today is the teaching Church seemed at that time, to all the world, like sheer nonsense. Father Josemaría coined his own expression for it: 'un disparaton' ('a mega folly').[88]

Years later, when he was asked who had called him a madman and why, he said 'Don't you think it is madness to say that here right where you are, you can and should be a saint? That a man who sells ice cream can and should be a saint, and so can a woman who works in the kitchen all the day, and a bank manager and a university lecturer, and a farm labourer ...?' All are called to sanctity! This has now been included in the last Council [the Second Vatican Council] but at that time – in 1928 – it didn't enter into anybody's head. So that ... it's only natural they should think that I was mad.'[89]

To Father Josemaría the way of life he was teaching was in some ways reverting back to early Christianity, to those first Christians who were married or single, centurions, taxmen, tentmakers, doctors, lawyers, fishermen, freemen or slaves. He wrote, 'The spirit of Opus Dei reflects the marvellous reality, forgotten for centuries by many Christians, that any honest and worthwhile work can be converted into a divine occupation. In God's service there are no second class jobs. All of them are important.'[90]

He also accepted that by carrying out the task God had set him he would be confronted by many problems. 'All the theological and ascetical doctrine had to be created,' he said. 'I found before me a break in continuity, a gap of centuries; there was nothing. Humanly speaking the whole Work was a crazy venture ...'[91]

He kept wondering how he could possibly accomplish all God was asking of him. At one stage he became, to use his own words, 'a beggar of prayers'. He would ask for prayers from as many people as he possibly could, even from people he didn't know, priests he met on the street, or people he saw in church who seemed to be specially recollected in their prayer. This is how he met Father Casimiro Morcillo, who in later years became Vicar General of Madrid, then Archbishop of Saragossa, and finally Archbishop of Madrid. For a time in the early thirties, father Josemaría used to come across this priest very early in the morning. And the priest always seemed recollected. So one morning Father Josemaría stopped him and asked, 'Are you going to say Mass? Would you pray for an intention of mine?' Father Casimiro was surprised by the request but promised to pray for the intention, and did so. Soon afterwards they got to know each other and became friends.

Recalling the incident in later years, Father Josemaría said to the future archbishop, 'When I stopped you in the street when I didn't know you, you must have taken me for a madman.'

Father Casimiro laughed and replied, 'I have to admit, the thought did cross my mind, because up till then nobody had ever stopped me in the middle of the street to ask for my prayers.'[92]

In his own prayers Father Josemaría would ask, 'What can a creature do if he has to carry out a mission and has neither means, nor age, nor knowledge, nor virtues, nor anything?'

And the answer he says that came to him was, 'He has to go to his Mother and his Father, he has to turn to those who can do something, he has to ask help from his friends ...' And he added, 'This is what I did in the spiritual life.'[93]

He prayed constantly to God the Father. He developed a deep and tender devotion to Our Lady, to St Joseph, and the Holy Guardian Angels. He liked to call Our Lady, 'Mother of God and our mother', and would say, 'I went to seek strength in the Mother of God, like a young son, following the paths of childhood.' St Joseph he called, 'My father and lord, head of the Holy Family on earth, whom God Himself obeyed ...'

He turned with great confidence to the angels for their intercession.

'I had devotion to the Holy Guardian Angels,' he explained, 'because it was on October 2nd, the Feast of the Angels, when those bells rang out ... the bells of Our Lady of the Angels. I turned to the Holy Angels with confidence, like a little child, without realising that God was leading me along paths of spiritual childhood ...'[94]

His penances now became ever more severe and intense. On 22 June 1933 after a retreat he wrote to his spiritual director Father Sánchez, 'Our Lord is undoubtedly asking me to toughen up my penance. When I am faithful in this matter, it seems the Work flies higher.'[95]

And among the notes found among his papers after his death there is one that reads, 'Since Saturday, February 17, 1934, Father Sánchez has advised me to follow this easier plan: 'Every day without exception, apart from Sundays: in the morning for four hours, two cilices. Monday – discipline – thee Misereres.' (Every discipline, would last as long as it took to recite three Misereres, or three Laudates, or whatever prayer he chose) 'Tuesday – three – Laudates. Wednesday – three Benedictuses. Saturday – three Magnificats. Friday – discipline – three Te Deums, three Magnificats, and three Benedictuses.'[96]

These notes known as 'Intimate notes' (Apuntes intimos) he had been writing since he was about eighteen years old when he says, 'I felt impelled to just start writing without rhyme or reason.'[97]

He stipulated that the notes, all hand-written, were not to be read until after his death. He also explains in another of them, 'These are candid notes – "Catherines", I called them, in honour of the saint of Siena – which for a long time I wrote kneeling down, and which served me as reminders and calls to wake up. I think that as a rule, when I was writing with that childlike simplicity, I was praying.'[98]

The first notebook and the early loose notes Father Josemaría destroyed. And the reason he did it was that he was afraid that if anyone read them they might think he was a saint when he himself was convinced that he was nothing but a sinner. He would also say, 'I would have burned them all if someone with authority and later my own conscience, hadn't forbidden me to do so.'[99]

The notes that have survived therefore begin in March 1930 when he started the second notebook.

And when Father Sánchez became his spiritual director Father Josemaría used the notebooks as a way of opening up his soul to him. At the end of February 1931 a note says, 'When I write these Catherines (That's what I always call these notes), I do so because I feel urged to preserve not only the inspirations of God – I very firmly believe they are divine inspirations – but also other things in my life that have served, and could serve, for my spiritual benefit and help my father confessor get to know me better. Otherwise I would have torn up and burned these sheets and notebooks a thousand times, out of self-love (the child of my pride).'[100]

It is also clear from these notes that his spiritual director, Father Sánchez, was curbing his more severe mortifications for Father Josemaría notes, 'He will not let me undertake any heavy penances. He will only let me do what I was doing before, no more, and two fasts (on Wednesdays and Saturdays), and six and a half hours sleep, because he says that if I do any more, I'll be of no use to anyone in two years' time.'[101]

And about his fasting another note says, 'Lord, what a struggle fasting is for me! ... If I'm not up to a battle that small, how hard would a Lepanto be for me?' [Lepanto was the naval battle that decided the fate of Christian Europe in 1571. The Christian forces, greatly outnumbered by what seemed an invincible Turkish fleet, won an amazing victory.] And in another note he writes, 'Yesterday I was brought to tears because Father Sánchez would not let me fast this week. I believe it is precisely against gluttony that I must fight hardest! But yesterday, on the bus, I got dizzy; that's why he won't let me fast.'[102]

It was about this time that Father Josemaría experienced a serious setback that made him angry. What this setback was has not been revealed but as a result of it he learned a very good lesson, 'I was angry,' he explained years later, 'and afterwards I was angry at myself for having become angry,' Then, as he was walking along a street in that angry state of mind he came upon an automatic-camera booth, which for a few coins provided instant passport-type pictures. It was then that the Lord gave him to understand that he now had a good opportunity to humble himself and receive an ascetic lesson in cheerfulness. He went into the booth and got himself photographed, and found, 'I looked really funny with that angry face!' Afterwards he tore up all the snapshots but one, 'I carried it in my wallet for a month,' he said. 'From time to time I would look at it, to see that angry face, humble myself before God, and laugh at myself. I would say to myself, "You fool!"'[103]

He would later write this advice in The Way, 'Serenity. Why lose your temper if by losing it you offend God, you trouble your neighbour, you give yourself a bad time ... and in the end you have to set things aright anyway.'[104]

Keeping a cheerful face, he continued doing as best he could the Work God had set him. But even with all the prayers he said and sought and his personal mortifications he seemed to be having little success in finding people who would join him. One person who came to mind about this time as someone who might understand the Work was his good friend from his schooldays in Logroño, Isidoro Zorzano. He hadn't seen Isidoro for many years but hadn't lost touch with him. Isidoro had qualified as an engineer in Madrid and, after finishing his studies, had moved south to Cádiz to work at the naval shipyard in Matagorda. From there he went to Málaga to work for the Andalusian Railway Company. At the beginning of the summer of 1930 Father Josemaría wrote to him saying, 'When you come to Madrid, don't fail to look me up. I have some interesting things to tell you ...'

A few weeks later, on 25 August, Father Josemaría writes in his notes about his providential encounter with Isidoro in Madrid. 'Yesterday, the feast of Saint Bartholomew, I was at the Romeos' house and I felt restless – for no apparent reason – and left earlier than expected; normally I would have waited for Don Manuel and Colo to get home. Just before arriving at the Foundation I ran into Zorzano, on Nicasio Gallego Street. When told that I was not at home, he had left Casa Apostólica (the Foundation) with the intention of going to Puerta del Sol, but the CERTAINTY of running into me – that's what he told me – made him turn into Nicasio Gallego.'[105] Isidoro was delighted to meet him in the street he had turned into. What he actually said to Father Josemaría was, 'I've just been to your flat and found you weren't home. So I decided to take a tram, find a restaurant and have a meal. Then I was going to catch the next train North and join my family on holiday.

'But a strange thing happened to me, Josemaría. While I was waiting for a tram I all at once experienced an overwhelming urge to walk down this street. And somehow I knew that I would bump into you if I did walk along it. And that is exactly what has happened. I walked down the street and I met you.'

They returned to Father Josemaría's flat where Isidoro told him the reason for his visit, 'I came to see you because I wanted to ask your advice on something.'

Isidoro then went on to explain that he was a little unsettled. 'I feel God is asking something of me, that I've got to do something for Him. But I really don't know what it can be. I have an interesting job as an engineer and I'm very happy doing it. And I feel no attraction to the priesthood or the religious life.'

Isidoro then said that he wondered if this was because he was being too worldly or too cowardly. And he ended by saying, 'I don't know what to think, Josemaría. You'll have to point me in the right direction.'

Father Josemaría could hardly believe his ears. 'You remember my letter?' he asked. 'Well, it was precisely because I wanted to talk to you about the work I am now doing.' He then explained how he believed a man or a woman could get to heaven and become a saint doing his or her ordinary job. How the little things of everyday life could be turned into an encounter with God. How an engineer could become a saint by being a good engineer.

Isidoro's response was immediate, 'This is for me. I can see the hand of God in the way we met in that street, Josemaría. You can certainly count on me.'

But Father Josemaría felt that Isidoro had decided too quickly. He told him that he should think about it more carefully before committing himself.

But Isidoro insisted. 'As far as I'm concerned, my mind's made up.'

Isidoro, however, did agree to give it a little more thought. He said he wouldn't catch the next train north as planned, but the train after that. He would think about it again and come back after dinner. Then he would let Father Josemaría know what he had finally decided.

When Isidoro returned he was still of the same mind. From that moment on, he said, he would consider himself bound irreversibly to Our Lord, to serve Him in this Work of God.[106]

Father Josemaría sums it up in the note he wrote about their meeting, 'In the evening Isidoro came over. We spoke. He is very happy. He sees, as I do, the hand of God. "Now I know," he said, "why I've come to Madrid."'[107]

Isidoro was true to his word. He dedicated himself totally to the Work and remained faithful for the rest of his life, throughout the years of terror and suffering brought about by civil war and ferocious religious persecution.

Isidoro always believed that his meeting in the street with Father Josemaría had been providential. During the civil war Isidoro's Argentine citizenship proved invaluable. It allowed him to move freely about Communist controlled Madrid and do much heroic work. He died with a reputation of holiness aged forty-one in 1943. The process of the beatification and canonization of Isidoro Zorzano, the man who has been called 'God's engineer', began five years after his death in 1948.

CHAPTER 14

Mobs Go on the Rampage

The vast political upheaval that would convulse the Spanish nation and lead to civil war really got underway early in 1931 after the king, Alfonso XIII, had dismissed General Miguel Primo de Rivera, the dictator who had governed the country for the last seven years, from 1923 to 1930. Municipal elections were held throughout Spain on 12 April 1931, and resulted in a victory for the Republicans. Immediately after the results of these elections the national government collapsed and the king fled. Just two days later, on 14 April, Spain was declared a Republic. Perhaps the best summary and analysis of the situation and how it all turned so vicious is that given by Father Josemaría himself who lived through this critical period of history. Explaining the historical background and how events developed he wrote this for the benefit of Pope Paul VI (a personal friend from the 1940s) in 1964:

> In 1923, General Primo de Rivera carried out a coup d'etat and, with the consent of King Alfonso XIII, set up a dictatorship that lasted until 1930. Although on the whole the action of Primo de Rivera was rather beneficial to Spain, in many respects it wounded the liberty of Spaniards, as any other dictatorship would. The fact that such a lack of freedom was sanctioned or at least tolerated by the king provoked a strong reaction against the monarchy: a movement led by some noted anti-Catholic

intellectuals, some members of the National Association of Catholic Propagandists (directed by a journalist by the name of Herrera), and the leaders of anarchist and Marxist unions. Thus began a pendulum swing that swept the masses from one extreme, a lack of freedom, to the opposite, licence. This kind of swing of the pendulum is always potentially dangerous, but in a passionate people it is extremely so, and it continues to hang menacingly over Spain.

(This could only be a reference to the dictatorship of Franco following the Civil War and clearly shows what he thought of it.)

The letter continues:

On 14 April 1931, as a result of the state of tension created especially in Madrid by the Republican victory in the administrative elections in some of the most important cities of Spain, and fearing a possible civil war, Alfonso XIII decided it was best for him to leave the country, and thus the Republic was proclaimed.[108]

The new Republic provided an ideal opportunity for antireligious extremists to proclaim their views and plans for the future. One of their demands was that the new republic should be an atheistic state where God and religion should be outlawed. Vicious, virulent hate campaigns were launched against the Catholic Church including organised public demonstrations against religion, which often turned violent and led to bloodshed.

On 20 April 1931 Father Josemaría makes this entry in his journal:

May the Immaculate Virgin defend this poor Spain! God confound the enemies of our Mother the Church! The Spanish Republic: Madrid, for twenty-fours hours, was one huge madhouse ... Things seem to have calmed down. But the Freemasons are not sleeping ... The Heart of Jesus is also awake! That is my hope ...[109]

On 11 May, gangs suddenly appeared in all parts of Madrid and began looting and burning down churches, monasteries and convents and schools run by religious orders. One of the first buildings to go up in flames was the Jesuits' house on De La Flor Street where Father Josemaría went to see his confessor, Father Sánchez. As the mob attacked the building the police just stood and watched and refused to intervene. They had in fact had advanced warning of the riots but the day before they began a circular signed by Madrid's chief of police was sent to all police stations prohibiting the use of anything but verbal persuasion in dealing with the rioters. So as the police stood by churches, monasteries and convents were burned down and priests, monks and nuns attacked. Many priests and nuns had to flee for the lives and some of them were murdered. The next day and the day after, as a result of the non-intervention policy by the authorities and in what seems to have been a well-orchestrated plan of destruction, similar gangs appeared on the streets of other cities and towns and throughout Spain burning and looting and desecrating churches and other buildings connected to religion. The destruction of churches and religious institutions in Madrid was on such a vast scale and created so much fear and anxiety that three months later in the oppressive heat of August people still felt a sense of foreboding. It was as if the smoke and smell of the burning buildings continued to hang over the city.

The day the mobs began their rampage through Madrid and as thick columns of smoke were billowing into the sky from the blazing buildings, Father Josemaría's immediate concern was to prevent the profanation of the Blessed Sacrament in the tabernacle of the church for the Foundation for the Sick.

He decided to remove the Blessed Sacrament as quickly as possible and find a new home for it. With this in mind he went to see an army officer, Colonel Manuel Romeo, whose family the Escrivás had known in Saragossa. Colonel Romeo was living in officers' quarters at Cuatro Caminos not far from the church for the Foundation of the Sick and Father Josemaría asked him if he could bring the Blessed Sacrament to his house. Colonel Romeo willingly agreed and also lent Father Josemaría a suit belonging to his son, Colo, to protect him from the priest-hunting mobs. Then Father Josemaría accompanied by the colonel and his brother Santiago went to the church. In a journal entry for May he writes:

> On Monday the 11th, accompanied by Don Manuel Romeo, after dressing up as a layman in one of Colo's suits, I consumed the large host for the monstrance, and then, with a ciborium filled with consecrated hosts and wrapped in a cassock and paper, we left the foundation through the back door, like thieves.[110]

His brother Santiago, who was twelve at the time, also remembers that as well as being dressed as a layman Father Josemaría also wore a beret 'which covered the large priestly tonsure he had at the time.'

As the small group made their way along Santa Engracia street towards Cuatro Caminos Father Josemaría tightly clutched to him Jesus in the ciborium and prayed, 'Jesus, may each sacrilegious fire increase my fire of love and reparation.'[111]

Two days later Father Josemaría had to flee with his family from the chaplain's house at the Foundation for the Sick. 'On the third we learned that they were planning to burn down the Foundation,' he writes in his Intimate notes, 'So at four o'clock that afternoon we went, with our belongings, to 22 Viriato Street, to a run-down apartment – one with no windows facing the street – that I found by God's providence.'[112]

Everywhere in the capital the atmosphere was tense. Priests and ordinary Catholics, men and women, young and old, all felt in danger, not knowing where the next outbreak of violence would suddenly erupt. Many priests began to dress as laymen but Father Josemaría, after wearing a suit to rescue the Blessed Sacrament, went back to his cassock. And on top of his cassock he wore a cape, which made him even more conspicuous as he walked along the dangerous, violent streets of Madrid.

In the no-holds-barred campaign against the Church new newspapers were set up and had powerful backers and great amounts of money. These newspapers were ferociously anti-religious. Filled with hate and intolerance, they incited people to harass priests and nuns on every possible occasion. Father Josemaría was soon experiencing these harassments. He writes at this time:

> Yesterday, at the barber's shop I gave some people a talking to. I was tired of hearing them take as infallible the opinions of those obscene pieces of trash El Sol and La Voz. Well, today, I was coming back from Chamartín. Father Sánchez had just told me, with regard to what I just mentioned, that since it's for the good of my neighbour, I should not keep quiet but should speak in a pleasant way, without harshness or anger.

Then there was another incident. Not far from the barber's shop, as he was walking along Fernández de la Hoz Street towards the Foundation, he was faced with what could have turned into an ugly encounter. 'I came across a group of bricklayers. One of them in a mocking tone of voice shouted, "Black Spain!" The instant I heard that, I resolutely turned around and faced them. I remembered what Father (Sánchez) had said, and I spoke calmly, without anger. They all agreed that I was right, including the one who had done the shouting. He, and also another of them, shook hands with me. Now these men will not, I feel sure, insult another priest.'[113]

Later, in another of his notes he writes:

> In this campaign that has been and is being waged against religious orders, priests and the Church, I have been confirmed in the opinion – already expressed in these notes – that there is a secret organisation that is moving people (always a child) via the press, pamphlets, cartoons, calumnies, spoken propaganda. Later they will lead it where they wish: to hell itself.[114]

Throwing stones at priests became a popular pastime. On the last day of July 1931 Father Josemaría began making a novena, nine days of prayer, at the grave of one of the Damas Apostólicas, Mercedes Reyna, who had died with a reputation for holiness. He was with her during the last days of her illness up to the very moment of her death and at one point had said to her, 'Mercedes, ask Our Lord from heaven that if I am not going to be a priest who is not just good, but holy, that he take me young, as soon as possible.'

Father Josemaría's nine days of prayer were from 31 July to 8 August. Each day he went to the Este cemetery and on his knees before her tomb said the Rosary asking for her help from heaven.

> On one of those days, [he writes] a group of children was next to one of the two fountains on the road that leads from Aragón Road to Este. They were with some women who were standing in line, waiting to fill their pitchers, jars, cans ... From the group of children arose a shout: 'A priest! Let's throw stones at him!' Without even thinking about it, I shut my breviary that I was reading, looked straight at them and said, 'You brats. Is that what your mothers are teaching you!' I also added some other words.[115]

And every day he was making the novena, apart from the last day, there was a strange confrontation as he was leaving the cemetery:

> I found waiting for me a devil in the guise of a boy of about twelve to fourteen [he writes in his intimate notes]. When I got a few paces past the cemetery gate he would start singing in a bugle-like voice, that pierced to the marrow, the nastiest verses of the Riego hymn.

This is a typical verse of the Riego hymn:

> If the priests and friars knew
> The beating they are going to get,
> They would join the chorus singing
> Freedom, freedom, freedom.

Father Josemaría's note continues, 'And what looks I then got from a labourer who was working with some others in that little plaza in front of the cemetery. If looks could kill, I would not now be writing my Catherines. I remember being looked at that way one day when I was making my rounds. My God, why this hatred for those who are yours?'[116]

And there was yet another incident during the days he was making the novena. He records in his notes, 'Lista Street, at the end. This poor priest was coming back tired from his novena. A bricklayer turned aside from his work and said, insultingly. "A cockroach! It should be stepped on!" Often I turn a deaf ear to such insults, but this time I could not. "How courageous of you," I said, "to pick on a gentleman who walks by you doing nothing to offend you! That's freedom?" The others made him shut up, indicating, without openly saying so that I was right. A few steps further on, another bricklayer tried to give me a reason for his colleague's conduct. "It's not right," he said, "but you have to understand he hates priests." And he said it so matter-of-factly.'[117]

Shortly afterwards he made a resolution not to respond to the insults but instead to say Hail Marys. He writes, 'The barrage of insults against priest continues ... I made the resolution – I am renewing it – of keeping quiet when they insult me, even if they spit on me. One night, in Chamberí Plaza when I was going into the building someone threw at my head a handful of mud that almost blocked up my ears. I didn't say a word.

'Even more: the resolution I am talking about includes pelting those poor haters with Hail Marys. I thought that my resolve was very strong, but the day before yesterday I failed twice, kicking up a fuss instead of being meek.'[118]

CHAPTER 15

The Man Dying in a Brothel

Father Josemaría's workload at this time could only be described as horrendous. As chaplain to the Foundation for the Sick he now had to run the gauntlet of abuse as he visited the thousands of sick and the dying the Damas Apostólicas were caring for all over Madrid. He also faced the same dangers going to the Damas' schools which were also mainly in the poorest areas of city. And as he made his way through these deprived areas having stones thrown at him, some of which found their target, threats and insults became part of his everyday existence. The Damas Apostólicas and their women helpers, or auxiliaries, faced great dangers and showed remarkable courage as they continued to carry out their charitable works. It was around this time some of them were badly hurt as they were leaving the Tetuán quarter. They were attacked, dragged through the streets and hit on the head with a shoemaker's awl. One of their helpers, Margarita Alvarado tells how one of the sisters, Amparo de Miguel, heroically tried to defend the others. The mob then set about Amparo. They tore off part of her scalp and beat her so badly that she was permanently disfigured.

One day about this time the Damas told him about a young man who was dying of tuberculosis in the brothel where his sister was a prostitute. Could he do anything for him? Father Josemaría wanted to help the man but it posed a problem. How could a priest go into a brothel without risking a scandal, especially when the Church and its priests were under so much scrutiny and attack?

For Father Josemaría the primary concern was that a man's eternal destiny was at stake. Without the sacraments and final repentance, the dying man could be facing eternal damnation.

Father Josemaría asked permission of the Vicar General of Madrid, Father Francisco Morán, to enter the brothel to hear the young man's confession and give him the Last Sacraments. Permission was given. Father Josemaría then received a promise from the madam who ran the brothel that no one would offend God there that night. Next he contacted a well-known and highly respected and dignified elderly gentleman, Don Alejandro Guzman who sported a short beard and usually wore a cape. He asked him to go with him. The following morning Father Josemaría, with Don Alejandro acting as his altar boy and chaperone, went to the brothel. Father Josemaría heard the dying man's Confession and gave him the Last Rites and Holy Communion. He had arrived just in time. The man's life was rapidly drawing to a close. With his dying breaths he prayed the short prayers. Father Josemaría taught him, finding hope, comfort and peace in his final moments on earth.

On top of all the work he was doing, Father Josemaría had to make time for what for him was the most important work of all – to find people to help him with the specific task God had given him to do, to open up paths of holiness for ordinary men and women the world over. And at this time it became crystal clear to him that this special task God had entrusted to him, this Work of God, would have to be given priority before everything else. He prayed a great deal about what to do and came to the conclusion that he would have to give up being chaplain to the sisters of the Foundation for the Sick.

In June 1931, he resigned but offered them his services until they could find another chaplain. He writes in his journal at this time:

> I am leaving the Foundation I am leaving with pain and

with joy. With pain, because after four long years of working in this apostolate, and of putting my soul into it each day, I know very well that I have a good part of my heart invested in this apostolic centre ... With pain, too, because another priest in my situation during these years would have become a saint, whereas I, on the other hand ... With joy, because I'm exhausted! I am convinced that God does not want me involved with the Foundation any more; there I am getting destroyed, wiped out. I mean physically – at that pace I would end up getting sick, and, of course, incapable of intellectual work.[119]

Because the Damas Apostólicas had great difficulty finding a replacement, Father Josemaría continued working as chaplain for the Foundation for the Sick for another four months, until October. During this time he continued to visit the sick and the dying in the Damas' care.

But, hardly had he resigned from being chaplain to the Foundation of the Sick when he heard of the plight of some enclosed nuns, the Augustinian Recollect nuns of the Foundation of Santa Isabel. The Foundation of Santa Isabel was a royal foundation named after Queen Elizabeth of Hungary, which had been set up in 1595. The Foundation consisted of the convent of Augustinian nuns, the chapter house, a public church, a school dedicated to the Assumption, and the Rector's house, where the Father would later move with his mother, his sister Carmen and his brother Santiago. But in that year of 1931 the Republican government had taken over the administration of all royal religious foundations and claimed for themselves the right to appoint rectors and chaplains. Shortly afterwards, the Rector of Santa Isabel, Father Buenaventura, was removed from the staff list by government decree. The head chaplain of Santa Isabel had then been taken ill and the assistant chaplain had moved to a new post. The Augustinian nuns were now left without a priest. And with no priest the enclosed nuns were unable to hear Mass or receive the sacraments. To make matters worse the area around Santa Isabel was considered to be too dangerous a place for priests to pass through. This is confirmed by one of the nuns, Sister Maria del Buen Consejo, who says, 'As things got worse in the country, especially after the Republic was proclaimed, it was dangerous for a priest to walk down the street to come to our convent.'

So Father Josemaría immediately offered his services.

For the nuns of Santa Isabel Father Josemaría's appearance on the scene was like manna from heaven. They decided they would try to get Father Josemaría appointed as their chaplain as quickly as possible.

On 13 August – while he was still helping the Damas Apostólicas at the Foundation for the Sick – Father Josemaría wrote in his notes, 'These days the little nuns of Santa Isabel, which used to be a royal foundation, are trying to get me appointed chaplain of that holy house. Humanly speaking, even in relation to the Work, I think it would be good for me. But I am not doing anything about it. I am not even seeking a recommendation. If my heavenly Father sees that it will all be for his glory, he will take care of the business.'[120]

A little later, however, his spiritual director, Father Sánchez, advised him to drop his passive attitude to the appointment and to get actively involved in the negotiations. As always he was obedient to his spiritual director and on 21 September he was able to write, 'Feast of Saint Matthew, 1931: I have for the first time celebrated Mass at Santa Isabel. All for the glory of God.'[121]

He was now chaplain in the eyes of the Church but not in the eyes of the State. Getting the approval of the civil authorities would be a much more difficult and prolonged procedure. But his confessor, Father Sánchez, urged him to do it.

Sister Maria del Buen Consejo remembers the day the Mother Prioress of Santa Isabel called the community together and told them the good news: a priest from Saragossa would be saying Mass for them every day. Mass was at eight o'clock sharp and Father Josemaría heard confessions before and after Mass. If any nun was sick he took Holy Communion to her and Sister Maria says that every day for two months he took Communion to one sick nun.

Father Josemaría was, she states, 'an exemplary priest who was very devout, with a great spirit of recollection, which he made compatible with naturalness and cheerfulness.'

There was something else that Sister Maria vividly remembers about Father Josemaría in those dangerous and troubled times. It was, she says, 'his way of laughing, which made the atmosphere peaceful by making light of things.'

A few weeks later Father Josemaría learned how becoming chaplain to the nuns of Santa Isabel had saved him from being expelled from the Madrid diocese. As the Santa Isabel foundation was a royal foundation their chaplain came under the Patriarch of the Indies or the ecclesiastical palace jurisdiction and he had accordingly been transferred to this jurisdiction.

He wrote in his notes. 'Another caress from Jesus for this donkey ... I now belong to the jurisdiction of the Patriarch of the Indies. Well, now it turns out that the bishop of Madrid is making all the priests in the capital sign some papers which, he has publicly stated, have no other purpose than to send back to their respective dioceses all the priests who are not from this one, of Madrid-Alacalá. Of course, such is the way God has taken care of things, this does not affect me at all.'[122]

And it was in the Church of Santa Isabel, while he was making his thanksgiving after Mass, that he conceived the idea for a booklet about the Rosary which would bring to life the scenes that make up the Joyful, Sorrowful and Glorious Mysteries. He completed the booklet in what must have been record time. He wrote it from start to finish in one go, sitting before the altar, putting himself in the gospel scenes as an onlooker and trying to see all that was happening in the scripture narrative. The words flowed on to the page. He portrays the scene, 'Don't forget, my friend, that we are children. The Lady of the sweet name, Mary, is absorbed in prayer. You in that house, can be whatever you wish: a friend, a servant, an onlooker, a neighbour ... For the moment I don't dare to be anything. I hide behind you and, full of awe, I watch what is happening ...'[123] And he also advises, 'The beginning of the way, at the end of which you will find yourself completely carried away by love for Jesus, is a trusting love for Mary.'[124] This booklet, he called *Holy Rosary*, but he was not able to publish until 1934. It is now a spiritual best-seller.

He was also finishing in that year of 1931 a book of meditations to help people pray and meditate and keep in daily contact with God. For some time he had been in the habit of carrying around a little notebook inside his cassock. When anything caught his attention or struck a chord in his memory, he would jot it down. It could be anything: a passage from scripture, some personal experience, snatches of conversation, or extracts from a letter he had received. All went into his notebook. Then when he had a few moments to spare, he would develop the notes into thought-provoking reflections. 'They are,' he would later write by way of explanation, 'things that I whisper in your ear – confiding them – as a friend, as a brother, as a father ... so that some thought will arise and strike you; and so you will better your life and set out along ways of prayer and of Love.'[125] When completed the book had 438 points for people to meditate on and was called *Consideraciones Espirituales (Spiritual Considerations)*. The first copies were run off on a stencil mimeograph which was at that time all he could afford. He then expanded the book. The 438 points for meditation were increased to 999 and the book was then given its definitive title, *The Way*. The first edition of *The Way* was published in 1939 and was an immediate success. The early editions rapidly ran out of copies and reprint followed reprint. Over the years millions of people of all races and cultures have found in the words of *The Way* light and strength to help them recognize God and give meaning to their lives. *The Way*, which has been described as 'à Kempis for modern times' has been translated into almost every language on earth. It has not only become a global best-seller but is also now considered a classic of spiritual literature.

CHAPTER 16

Invocations on a Tram

Amid all the political upheaval and violence of the year 1931, Father Josemaría was granted important new divine insights. The first was on 7 August, which was the feast of the Transfiguration in the diocese of Madrid. The same day he wrote in his journal about what happened while he was saying Mass on a side altar at the Foundation for the Sick. 'The time for the Consecration arrived. At the very moment I elevated the Sacred Host ... there came into my mind, with extraordinary force and clarity, those words of Scripture: "Et Ego, si exaltatus fuero a terra, omnia traham ad meipsum" (And when I am lifted up from the earth, I shall draw all things to myself – John 12:32) ... Ordinarily, before the supernatural, I feel afraid. Then comes, the "Ne timeas," "Do not be afraid, it is I." And I understood that there will be the men and women of God who will lift the Cross with the teachings of Christ to the pinnacle of all human activities. And I saw Our Lord triumph, drawing to Himself all things.'

And he continues, 'In spite of feeling myself devoid of virtue and knowledge (humility is truth ... without exaggeration) I would like to write books of fire – books that will race across the world like burning flames and set people ablaze with their light and heat, turning poor hearts into red-hot coals to be offered to Jesus as rubies for his royal crown.'[126]

And explaining this light God had given him he would

say, 'I understood it perfectly. Our Lord was telling us: "If you place me in the very heart of human activities, fulfilling your duty at each moment, being my witnesses in what seems great and in what seems little ... then, omnia traham ad meipsum! (I will draw all things to myself) My Kingdom among you will be a reality!'[127]

Later in a letter to members he would say:

> United with Christ through prayer and mortification in our daily work, in the thousand human circumstances of our simple life as ordinary Christians, we will work that miracle of placing all things at the feet of the Lord lifted up on the cross, on which he has allowed himself to be nailed because he so loves the world and us human beings. Thus simply by doing with love the tasks proper to our profession or job, the same ones we were engaged in when he came looking for us, we fulfil that apostolic task of placing Christ at the summit and in the heart of all human activities, since no upright activity is excluded from the sphere of work that can be made a manifestation of the redemptive love of Christ. Similarly work for us is not only our natural means of meeting financial needs and maintaining ourselves in a reasonable and simple community of life with other people, but also – and above all – the specific means of personal sanctification that God Our Father has indicated to us, and has put in our hands to make the order that he wants shine forth in all of creation.[128]

A second divine insight was given to him exactly a month later and once again it happened in the church of the Foundation for the Sick. On 8 September, 1931, the Feast of the Birthday of the Blessed Virgin Mary he wrote in his journal:

> Yesterday, at three in the afternoon, I went to the sanctuary of the church of the Foundation to pray for a little while in front of the Blessed Sacrament. I didn't feel like it, but I stayed there, feeling like nincompoop. Sometimes, coming to, I thought, 'Now you see, good Jesus, that if I am here, it is for you, to please you.'

Nothing. My imagination ran wild, far from my body and my will, just like a faithful dog stretched out at the feet of his master sleeps dreaming of running around and of hunting and of friends (dogs like himself), and gets fidgety and barks softly ... but without leaving his master. That's how I was, exactly like that dog, when I noticed that, without meaning to, I was repeating some Latin words which I had never paid any attention to and had no reason to recall. Even now, to remember them I have to read them off the sheet of paper I always carry in my pocket for writing down whatever God wants. (Right there in the sanctuary, I jotted down that phrase instinctively on that sheet of paper out of habit, without attaching any importance to it.) The words of Scripture that I found on my lips were 'Et fui tecum in omnibus ubicumque ambulasti, firmans regnum tuum in aeternum.' ['And I have been with you everywhere, wherever you went ... your throne shall be established forever' (2 Sam. 7:9, 16)]. Repeating them slowly I applied my mind to their meaning and again today, when I read them again (for – I repeat – as if God was taking pains to prove to me that they were his, I can't recall them from one moment to the next), I well understood that Christ Jesus was telling me for our consolation. The Work of God will be with him everywhere, affirming the reign of Jesus Christ forever.[129]

Then on 16 October 1931 was a third divine insight. He had just said Mass for the Augustinian nuns at the church of Santa Isabel. In his notes, describing what happened that day, he says;

Feast of Saint Hedwig, 1931: I wanted to pray after Mass in quiet of my church. I didn't succeed. On Atocha Street I bought a newspaper (ABC) and got on the tram. Up to the moment I am writing this I have not been able to read more than one paragraph of the paper. I have felt flowing through me a prayer of copious and ardent feelings of affection. That's the way it was in the tram and all the way home. What I am doing now, this note, is really a continuation. I only interrupted this prayer to exchange a few words with my family (and all they can talk about is the religious question) and to kiss My Lady of the Kisses ... [This was a statue of Our Lady and the Child Jesus which he always used to kiss before leaving the house and on his return.][130]

Giving more details of this prayer on the tram he writes:

> I felt the action of the Lord. He was making spring forth in my heart and on my lips, with overriding force, this tender invocation: Abba! Pater! I was on the street, in a tram. Probably I made that prayer out loud. And I walked the streets of Madrid for maybe an hour, maybe two, I can't say; time passed without my being aware of it. They must have thought I was crazy. I was contemplating, with lights that were not mine, that amazing truth. It was like a lighted coal burning in my soul, never to be extinguished.[131]

He was also made aware that the word Abba, which Christ called his Father, had a much more affectionate and loving meaning than the formal English word Father. Abba was the way a little child would call out to his Father and was more like Dad or Daddy. He began to think about all God's many kindnesses to him and couldn't stop himself repeating, 'Abba, Father! Abba, Father!' And with great inner wonder he also kept exclaiming, 'A son of God, I am a son of God!'

In his intimate notes he writes:

> I was considering God's kindnesses towards me and, filled with inner joy, I would have cried out in the steet, so that the whole world might know of my filial gratitude: Father! Father! And – if not shouting – at least to myself, I went about calling him that way (Father!) many times, quite sure that I was pleasing him.[132]

From that time on the deep awareness of being a son of God was engraved in his soul. And he understood with utter clarity that this was the foundation of the spirit of holiness that God was asking him to spread.

Following this divine insight on the tram he wrote in his book, *The Way*:

> It's necessary to be convinced that God is always near us. Too often we live as though Our Lord were somewhere far off – where the stars shine. We fail to realise that He is also by our side – always. For He is like a loving Father. He loves each one of us more than all the mothers in the world can love their children, helping us and inspiring us, blessing ... and forgiving ... We have to be completely convinced, realising it to the full, that Our Lord, who is close to us and in heaven, is a Father, and very much OUR Father.[133]

He summed up his experience in two words, Divine Filiation, meaning that all human beings are daughters and sons of a God who loves us more than we will ever be able to understand!

And in energetic handwriting he also notes:

> Precisely because we are children of God this reality also leads us to look at all the things that have come from the hands of God the Father and Creator with love and wonder. And that is the way we become contemplatives in the midst of the world, loving the world. Getting to know Jesus Christ. Getting others to know him. Taking him everywhere we go.[134]

Father Josemaría believed that these insights, in which God made things plain to him, constituted one of the means chosen by Our Lord to form his soul. He called them interior locutions. These locutions, he once said, were 'intellectual, without the noise of words, but they remained as if branded by fire on my soul.'[135]

Many years later Bishop Alvaro del Portillo, his successor, would explain:

> Often this kind of inspiration would consist of an unusually profound understanding of a scriptural text. This is what would happen: suddenly a verse of a psalm

or some other scriptural text, a passage which up until that time he had never dwelt upon with special attention, would come irresistibly to his lips. Afterwards, in the same sudden and irresistible way, without his seeking it, there would come to him a completely new spiritual interpretation, one which raised the level of his contemplation still higher. The Holy Spirit was taking him by surprise and showing him, beyond the shadow of doubt, that all this was the work of the Lord.[136]

And Bishop Alvaro also says that Father Josemaría told him that 'in the midst of the great difficulties at the beginning, the Lord had made him see how utterly powerless he was, but at the same time did not fail to keep alive in him the serene certainty of divine assistance.'[137]

This serene certainty that came from having been shown how much God loves all human beings, that we are his sons and daughters, this sense of Divine Filiation, couldn't have been given to Father Josemaría at a more crucial time. As the religious persecution in Spain grew daily more vicious leading inevitably to the bloodbath of civil war, he needed as never before this comforting, sure knowledge that God, his loving father, was constantly watching over him and helping him.

CHAPTER 17

The Antechambers of Death

It was a great wrench for Father Josemaría to leave the Foundation for the Sick. He had lavished so much priestly care on the sick and the dying he had visited in their homes and the children he had prepared for their First Confession and Holy Communion in the Damas Apostólicas Schools. He felt a terrible spiritual emptiness as he said his final goodbyes to the Damas Apostólicas and left the Foundation for the Sick for the last time on 28 October 1931. 'It was at the foundation for the Sick,' he writes in his intimate notes, 'That the Lord wanted me to find my priestly heart.' And he would later add, 'I think that some of those sick people I assisted before their death, during my apostolic years, have a lot of influence with the Heart of Jesus.'[138]

But the very day of his departure the Lord pointed him in the direction of other sick and dying people he could help, the patients who were in the appalling hospitals of those times. He writes in his notes on 27 October, 'Another favour from Our Lord. Yesterday I had to definitively leave the Foundation, and therefore all those patients. But my Jesus does not want me to leave Him. He reminded me that He is nailed to a hospital bed.'[139]

What had happened was that from the sacristan at Santa Isabel, Antonio Díaz, Father Josemaría had learned about the work of the Congregation of St Philip Neri of the Lay Servants of the Sick, known as the Philippians. Antonio was one of the Philippian Brothers. These were laymen who went to look after the sick at the General Hospital of Madrid with the aim of 'seeing in each of them a living image of Christ Our King, reflecting on His saying that whatever one does for them He will take as done to Himself ...'

The Brothers met at four o'clock on Sunday afternoons, put on their black gowns and then went into the Congregation's chapel to pray. Then after being assigned their tasks they picked up what they would need from their store room: towels, washbowls, soap, bandages, scissors and anything else that was necessary.

The Congregation's constitution laid down the specific tasks the Philippian brothers would undertake, which included among many other things, 'that they make the beds of the poor,' 'that they take special care of the very weak,' 'that they wash the feet and cut the hair and nails of the poor,' 'that when necessary they clean the bedpans ...'

Shortly after hearing about the work of the Philippians, a medical student, Adolfo Gómez, also told Father Josemaría about the appalling conditions in the General Hospital. This started Father Josemaría thinking about how he might be able to collaborate with the Philippians and so gain admission to the hospital to take care of the sick. After consulting with Father Sánchez his confessor, he got in touch with the Philippians and a little later wrote in his notes, 'Beginning next Sunday I will start taking part in that beautiful work.'[140]

On 8 November 1931 he took part in their activities for the first time and went with them to Madrid's General Hospital.

At the time the General Hospital was so crammed full of sick and destitute people that there were not enough beds for all the patients. Many were left lying on the floor in corridors, huddled in a few blankets.

Looking after the sick and the dying and trying to lift their spirits was a hard and thankless job. The anti-Catholic propaganda urging people to hate priests and anyone or anything connected with religion had even invaded the hospital wards. As the Philippian brothers and Father Josemaría went about trying to help the patients they found anti-religious sentiment everywhere. Many of the patients insulted them. The hospitals were desperately short of staff and the brothers made themselves useful taking on some of the jobs the hospital staff hadn't had time to get round to doing. These included washing and shaving the patients, cutting and combing their hair, trimming their nails and emptying the bowls they had spit into and their chamber pots. Sometimes they left the hospital feeling physically sick and with insults ringing in their ears.

Among the group of Philippians were two young men, Jenaro Lázaro who became a well-known sculptor and Luis Gordon, young businessman. They both joined Father Josemaría in his Work. Luis Gordon had recently qualified as an engineer and had started a small malt business just outside Madrid. It was of Luis Gordon that Father Josemaría spoke many years later when he described this incident:

> He was one of the first members in those earliest years ... He took a chamber pot from the bedside of a tuberculosis patient. It was ... well ... But I told him, 'Go ahead and clean it.' But then, because the look of revulsion on his face made me regret what I had said, I followed him out of the room. And I found him cleaning the pot with his bare hands, his face beaming wonderfully.[141]

Father Josemaría also referred to this same incident in his book, *The Way*. 'Isn't it true, Lord, that You were greatly consoled by the childlike remark of that man, who, disconcerted by having to obey in something unpleasant and repulsive, whispered to You, "Jesus, may I put on a good face"?'[142]

After working in the General Hospital, Father Josemaría began going to the other hospitals in Madrid. At King's Hospital he found men and women with diseases such as malignant typhus, smallpox and tuberculosis. In 1928 King's hospital had 1,971 patients with the numbers rising to 2,666 by 1936. The patients were kept in complete isolation to prevent the spread of these killer diseases, which accounted for the deaths of thousands upon thousands of people each year. In those years before the discovery of antibiotics, the mortality rate for typhus and smallpox was around twenty per cent. But tuberculosis had a mortality rate of almost 100 per cent and one isolation ward after another was filled with TB patients. They were in reality nothing more than vast antechambers of death, where men and women spent the last days of their lives, isolated without any hope of recovery. Many of these TB patients were mothers of families and these mothers were not even allowed to see their children because the authorities considered the risk of spreading the disease was too great. The people of Madrid had their own name for King's Hospital. They called it 'the hospital for incurables'.

He also went to Princesa Hospital, which catered for the really poor who were nursed free of charge. Its 2,000 patients were housed in enormous wards each with two to three hundred beds.

Father Josemaría began going regularly to all three hospitals visiting all the patients he could, even those confined in strict isolation. He chatted to them, heard their confessions and took them Holy Communion.

'I begged them,' he used to say, 'to offer up their sufferings, their hours in bed, their loneliness (some of them were very lonely) to offer all that to the Lord for the apostolate we were doing with young people.'[143] In this way he taught them that their sufferings made them co-redeemers with Christ.

A doctor, years later recalling Father Josemaría's hospital visits said, 'He was not afraid of catching the patients' diseases. And most of them were highly contagious. More than once he was warned of the risk, but he always answered with his habitual smile, saying that he thought he must be immune to the diseases.'

On his visits to the hospitals and the poor, Father Josemaría began taking with him students from Madrid University. Many of these university students came from well-to-do families and their hearts used to sink at the sight of so much misery. In the hospitals they would move from ward to ward chatting to the patients, trying to cheer them up and taking them some small present.

The students were dismayed to find people living in such appalling conditions. Afterwards they talked about social justice and how a more just and compassionate society could be created. Father Josemaría would tell the students the best way they could help make a better world was first of all by studying hard and doing well in their university courses. 'Study.' he would tell them. 'Study in earnest. If you want to be salt and light you need knowledge and ability.' And he would also say to them, 'An hour of study for a modern apostle is an hour of prayer.'[144]

He would explain to them what their first steps towards making a better and more just world should be. They should, he said, first pass their exams well. Then they should do their work as perfectly as possible and in this way achieve professional prestige in whatever profession they had chosen. It was when they had professional prestige that people would take notice of them and their dreams of making a better and more just society would then become a reality.

Father Josemaría's move from the Foundation for the Sick to looking after the enclosed nuns of the Santa Isabel Foundation meant that he and his family were now even poorer than ever. He had in fact moved from what was a poorly paid chaplain's post to become a chaplain who didn't receive any pay at all. And he wouldn't receive any pay until he was officially recognized as chaplain by the anti-clerical government that now controlled the Santa Isabel Foundation. His only income was from his part-time job as law lecturer and from the private lessons he gave at home.

On 30 September 1931, he wrote in his notes:

> I find myself in a more difficult financial situation than ever before. But I haven't lost my peace. I have absolute trust, real confidence that God my Father will soon resolve this matter once and for all. If only I were alone! Then, I realise, poverty would be a delight. A priest and poor, lacking even what is necessary – great![145]

And a few days later, on 2 October he wrote,

> I confronted Him [Our Lord] and told Him that since Father Sánchez has forbidden me to ask Him for 'that', I was asking not for it, but that (I said it bluntly) he set things right for my family and bother only me.[146]

The 'that' his confessor had forbidden him to ask for was a serious illness, which he felt would be better for him than seeing his family suffering such poverty. His mother one day remarked, 'In this Madrid we are going through Purgatory.'

At the same time his mother was able to accept their poverty and remain at peace. At the end of December he wrote:

> I am amazed to see with what tranquillity, as though she were talking about the weather, my poor mother said last night, 'Never have we had it so bad as now,' and then how we went on to talk about other things, without losing our joy and peace. How good you are, Jesus, how good! You will know how to reward them generously.[147]

CHAPTER 18

'Father Josemaría is here!'

At this time Father Josemaría was also devoting a great deal of effort to working with priests he thought might be able to help him with the Work God had given him to do. Many of the priests were older than he was but they all trusted him because it was clear to them that he was very much a man of God.

Two priests he had great hopes for were Father José María Somoano and Father Lino Vea-Murguía who both asked to join the Work and were a great help to him. Father Somoano was the chaplain of King's Hospital, 'the hospital for incurables'. At the beginning of January 1932 Father Josemaría went to visit him to talk about the Work. But before doing so he asked the nun who was portress at Santa Isabel to offer up prayers and mortifications so that something good would result from this meeting. Father Somoano, who was from the Arriondas in Asturias, had what was described as a sturdy piety and zeal for souls. It turned out he was very interested to hear about the Work. In fact two days later Father Josemaría was able to write in his journal. 'Her (the nun's) prayer and penance was not in vain, for this friend now belongs to the Work.' Father Josemaría considered Father Somoano a first-rate vocation and a real treasure for his apostolic work. In his journal he wrote:

> With José Maria Somoano we have obtained, as they say around here, a wonderful 'connection,' because our

brother knows, admirably how to channel the suffering of the patients in his hospital so that the heart of Our Jesus, moved by such beautiful expiation, will accelerate the hour of his work.[148]

One of the patients Father Somoano was looking after in King's Hospital was a woman called María Ignacia García who was dying from tuberculosis of the stomach and intestines. She had undergone a number of operations and had sufferd very much. Father Somoano used to say to her, 'María, we have to pray a great deal for an intention of Father Josemaría's which is going to benefit everyone. Something which will do good to the whole world is involved. And it needs prayers and sacrifices, today, tomorrow and always. Please pray for it unceasingly.' And María did.

Father Josemaría in turn devoted a great deal of time talking to María. He explained to her about the Work he was doing and the way of holiness that could be lived in the middle of the world, especially by a sick person in a hospital bed.

María agreed to offer up all her pains, especially the intense pains she suffered, and her fever, for Father Josemaría's intention. She liked to write in a notebook which she kept by her. But sometimes for weeks on end she was in such agonizing pain that she was unable to write.

Referring to the Work she wrote, 'The foundations must be laid very well. We must set them in granite, so that what happened to the house mentioned in the Gospel, the house which was built on sand, will not happen to us. The foundations must be really deep; then will come the rest.'

María was determined to do all she could to help make the foundations unshakeable. Another passage of her diary reads, 'At night, when my pains do not let me sleep, I pass the time reminding Our Lord, many times, about his intention.'[149]

María asked to join the Work on 9 April 1932 and became one of the first women members. She afterwards noted, 'This 9th of April 1932 will never be effaced from my memory. Again You have chosen me, good Jesus, to follow Your divine footsteps ... From this moment on, I promise that with Your help, I promise to give You my all in the place You have put me because all the glory must be reflected back to You.' Two days later she wrote, 'A new era of Love!

But the Spanish revolutionary propagandists at that time were hell-bent on creating an era of hate. Their campaign against religion and its priests became more vicious by the day and had even infiltrated into the hospital wards. The sick and the dying were urged to have nothing to do with priests but to despise them and have only hatred for them in their hearts.

It was no doubt as a result of this campaign that Father Somoano, the King's Hospital chaplain, was murdered. He died on the night of Saturday, 16 July 1932 after two days of agony. The general opinion was that he had been poisoned. And the story that circulated throughout the hospital was that he had been poisoned by an anti-clerical fanatic. The authorities, however, refused to take any action or to investigate the mysterious death and Father Somoano was buried two days later on Monday 18 July. After returning from his funeral Father Josemaría wrote in his journal:

> The Lord has taken one of us: José María Somoano, an admirable priest. He died, as a victim of charity at King's Hospital (where he had been chaplain to the end despite all the laicist fury), on the night of the feast of Our Lady of Mount Carmel, to whom he was very devoted. He was wearing her holy scapular, and since this feast fell on a Saturday, it is certain that he entered the joy of God that same night. [This is a reference to an apparition of Our Lady when she promised to free from Purgatory on the Saturday following their death those who wore the scapular and lived this devotion to her.]
>
> His life of zeal had won him the affection of everyone who associated with him. He was buried this morning ... Today, willingly, I give to Jesus that member. He is with Him and will be a great help. I had put so much hope in his upright and energetic character. God wanted him for himself: blessed be God.[150]

Although Father Josemaría was convinced that Father Somoano was in heaven he continued to pray a great deal for him and would also for many years ask his sons to pray for him.

Father Somoano's death left King's Hospital without a chaplain. The situation was complicated even more by the fact that the Government had recently passed a series of anti-clerical laws, one of which deprived hospitals of the right to have chaplains. Father Josemaría decided to do all he could to help them. He went to see Sister Engracia Echevarria, the Superior of the Daughters of Charity, the nuns who ran the hospital, and offered his services free.

Sister Engracia said, 'He came and told me that I need not worry about not having an official chaplain. If anyone seriously ill asked for the Sacraments, I could call him any time, night or day.'

Before she died Sister Engracia wrote this testimony about him. 'Father Josemaría was the soul of a group of priests who helped at that time. You could see he was tremendously apostolic. In my opinion, a real saint ... Very courageous, at a time when courage and prudence were necessary to overcome so much opposition.

'He was very, very hard working ... It was obvious to me that his only concern was for the good of the patients' souls. He wanted to ensure that someone was with each patient caring for his or her soul right to the end.'

Father Josemaría's arrival at the hospitals brought immediate joy and happiness to the patients, especially the most destitute and abandoned. María Ignacia García's sister, Benilde, remembers the women suffering from TB like her sister, many of them mothers cut off from their children. 'No sooner did they see Father Josemaría,' she said, 'than they were filled with profound happiness. All they needed to say was, "Father Josemaría is here!" That said it all.'

People also began to realize that he seemed to have the great gift of getting to know each patient personally and of being able to give them individual help and guidance tailored to their particular needs. After he had talked with patients they could be seen facing death with peace and even joy.

He took special care of María Ignacia García who towards the end of her life was in constant pain. Her body was shrivelled and was covered with sores. Her backbone had become deformed and a segment of it stuck out. Father Josemaría spoke to her of the future apostolates of the Work she was helping to found by offering up her sufferings. It was, he explained to her, a Work that would spread out all over the world in a panorama she would soon be able to contemplate from on high.

He asked if she would like to receive the Sacrament of the Sick or Holy Viaticum and after administering the Sacrament he made one last request of her. Once she was in heaven, would she not forget to pray for this Work of God. He wrote in his journal at the time,

> Feast of Saint Isidore, May 15, 1933. Yesterday I administered Holy Viaticum to my Daughter María García. Here is a vocation of expiation. Suffering with tuberculosis, she was admitted to the Work with the blessing of the Lord. A beautiful soul. She made a general confession to me before receiving Communion ... That sister of ours loves the will of God. She sees in that long, painful, compounded illness (she has not a healthy bone in her body) the blessing and favour of Jesus and, while affirming in her humility that she deserved punishment, she sees the terrible pain she is feeling in her whole system, especially on account of the abdominal adhesions, as not a punishment but a mercy.[151]

María lived at death's door for another four months and died a very happy and holy death on 13 September 1933 with Father Josemaría at her bedside. He left hospital and wrote this obituary notice,

> On September 13, the vigil of the feast of the Exaltation of the Holy Cross, there fell asleep to the Lord this first sister of ours, of our house in heaven ... Prayer and suffering were the wheels of the chariot of triumph of this daughter of ours. We have not lost her; we have

gained her. The realisation that she has gone home should immediately turn our natural sorrow into supernatural joy, because now we are sure of an even mightier intercessor in heaven.[152]

Father Josemaría was totally convinced María was already enjoying the happiness of heaven, described in scripture as, 'The eye has not seen, nor ear heard, neither has it entered into the heart of man, what things God has prepared for those who love him.'

CHAPTER 19

'Simple' Henrietta's Intention

One of the people Father Josemaría had been helping spiritually since first becoming chaplain to the Foundation for the Sick in 1927 was a poor, mentally retarded woman called Henrietta. She had little education and she suffered from a speech defect. She would often say to him, 'Pade, le quero mucho. Pade, le quero mucho', which in English would translate as 'Fada, I lub you very much. Fada, I lub you very much'. People called her 'Simple Henrietta' but to Father Josemaría she was a good and simple soul loved by God. It was at this time that the fanatical, anti-Catholic newspaper *El Sol* was doing great harm to souls. Its pages were filled with attacks against the Church and it spread intolerance of anyone or anything connected with religion. It was a newspaper backed by many leading intellectuals and had a large circulation. It was well produced with many prestigious writers. One day Father Josemaría said to Henrietta, 'From today on, until I tell you to do otherwise, I want you to pray for an intention of mine.' The intention was that the newspaper *El Sol* would cease to be published. Henrietta who had a strong faith and great determination began to pray for Father Josemaría's intention. A few months later, *El Sol* when out of business, without any explanation ever being given, and was never published again.[153] Father Josemaría would later comment,

Within a short time the saying of Scripture was fulfilled: 'Quae stulta sunt mundi elegit Deus ut confundat sapientes' ('God chose what is foolish in the world to shame the wise.') That newspaper went under because of the prayer of a poor 'simple' woman. She went on praying for the same intention and a second newspaper [*Crisol*], succeeding the first and likewise doing great harm to souls, also went under.[154]

In his journal at this time he wrote, 'It's happened – *Crisol* is defunct. They're going to bring out another paper – *Luz* – but undoubtedly if 'Simple Henrietta' keeps praying that candle too will soon have no wick.'[155]

And 'Simple Henrietta' did keep on praying. And *Luz* went the same way as its two hate-filled predecessors and ceased publication.

The Devil began to show he was clearly very unhappy about Father Josemaría's activities and 'Old Scratch', as Father Josemaría called him, resorted about this time to physical assaults. At first Father Josemaría didn't realize that 'Old Scratch' was behind them but after suffering a series of bruising 'accidents' began to catch on as to what was happening. One Sunday, at noon, he received a very hard blow from a ball. But he went on his way not looking around 'to see if it was an accident or an act of malice'.

Ten days later on his way to hear confessions at Santa Isabel school he saw some boys with a ball playing in the street. He quickly crossed over to the other side. Then it happened again. 'A really hard kick and ... pow! on the right-hand lens of my glasses, driving them into my nose,' he writes in his notes. 'I didn't even turn my head. I got out my handkerchief and calmly kept on walking while cleaning my glasses ... At that moment I perceived the devil's rage (it is too much of a coincidence) and the goodness of God who lets him bark but not bite. One would have expected at least that the lense would have been broken, since there was nothing moderate about that blow I received. My right eye might also have been injured. Even just a broken lense would have been quite a setback, since I already have a hard time paying for the few tram rides I have to take ... The bottom line: God is my Father.'

Then came a third attack. He writes, 'Yesterday, as I was walking on Alvarez de Castro Street on the pavement reading my breviary on my way to catch the 48 to the hospital, they again hit me hard with a ball! I laughed. It upset him.'[156]

Father Josemaría was convinced that God was allowing the Devil to attack him but keeping him in check, letting 'him bark but not bite'.

Despite the ever-growing wave of anti-clericalism and the countless dangers priests faced out on the street, Father Josemaría continued to travel around Madrid helping all he could, especially the sick and the dying in the hospitals.

Dr Tomas Canales, who worked at Princesa Hospital, recalled that even at this time there was only praise for Father Josemaría from both the hospital staff and patients. 'They all loved to talk to him because he was so welcoming,' he said. 'There was something about him which was difficult to define.'

The doctor also noticed Father Josemaría's care for the sick was not confined to certain days of the week or to set hours. He saw him, he said, go several times a day to comfort a dying person and, no matter what time of day or night, he was always available to hear the confessions of the sick.

'Some days,' Dr Canales adds, 'I saw him more than once, so I reckon he must have spent three or four hours in the hospital.'

And when his work in the hospitals was over, Father Josemaría would return to the tabernacle of Santa Isabel. Before Jesus in the Sacred Host he would unburden all his troubles and concerns. He would tell Our Lord of the sick and the dying, each one by name, and plead for grace and help for every single one of them. There were deathbed conversions that surprised many. There were many untold minor miracles. The sick, in their turn, offered up all they had, their sufferings, sicknesses and their deaths, which brought down abundant blessings from heaven on the priest caring for them and on the special Work that God had entrusted to him.

'Sick people are the treasure of Opus Dei,' he would

constantly say, 'Suffering is a proof that one knows how to love, that one has a heart.'[157] And when his Work of God had spread to every corner of the world, he would insist it was 'thanks to the sick in those hospitals of Madrid.'[158]

CHAPTER 20

The Devil and the Mangy Donkey

'I have no order in my prayer life,' he wrote in his notes on 13 October 1931 and went on to say in parenthesis '(I resolve to have some starting today). I don't usually do a meditation (starting today I will do this for one hour each day). But many days I do a prayer of affection from morning to night – sometimes, of course, in a special way.'[159]

This resolution to do one hour of prayer each day became two half hours of prayer at fixed times, one in the morning and one in the evening. This way he was able to talk to God about everything, especially the ordinary things of every day. He prayed as he would later advise in his book, *The Way*:

> You write: 'To pray is to talk with God. But about what?' About what? About Him, about yourself: joys, sorrows, successes and failures, noble ambitions, daily worries, weaknesses! And acts of thanksgiving and petitions; and love and reparation. In a word to get to know Him and to get to know yourself; 'to get acquainted!'[160]

Often he would tell God that he considered himself to be a mangy donkey. In a note he made on 9 October, 1931 he wrote about his prayer of that day,

> Today, in my prayer I renewed my resolution to become

a saint. I know I will accomplish this – not because I am sure of myself, Jesus, but because I am sure of you. Then I thought about the fact that I am a mangy donkey. And I asked – and ask – Our Lord to cure the mangyness of my miseries with the sweet ointment of his Love, that his Love might be the cauterising agent that will burn away all the scabs and clean out the mangyness of my soul . . . I then decided to be a donkey, but not a mangy one. I am your donkey, Jesus, but no longer mangy. I'm saying it like this so that you'll clean me, not wanting to make a liar out of me. And with your donkey, Child Jesus, do whatever you please. Like the mischievous children of earth, pull my ears, give this stupid donkey a good whack, make him run the way you want . . . I want to be your donkey. I want to be patient, hardworking, faithful . . . [161]

In a meditation he gave in later years he would say, 'I am not humiliated to acknowledge that in the Lord's eyes I am a beast of burden. He then quoted Psalm 72; "I am like a little donkey in your presence, but I am continually with you. You hold my right hand",' and he added, 'You take me by the bridle.'

He went on to say,

Try to remember what a donkey is like – now that so few of them are left. Not an old stubborn, vicious one that would give you a kick when you least expected, but a young one with his ears up like antennae. He lives on a meagre diet, is hardworking and has a quick, cheerful trot. There are hundreds of animals more beautiful, more deft and strong. But it was a donkey Christ chose when he presented himself to the people as King in response to their acclamation.[162]

Then one day he experienced a very disturbing and threatening confrontation which involved his prayer about being a donkey. The confrontation occurred near a statue of Our Lady high up on a house in Atocha Street, which he regularly greeted as he passed by. A few days before the confrontation, there is this happy note he made that gives a wonderful glimpse into his soul and his child-like devotion to Our Lady.

Written on 3 December 1931 it says,

> This morning I retraced my steps and became a little boy, to greet Our Lady before her statue on Atocha Street, at the top of the house the Congregation of Saint Philip has there. I had forgotten to greet her. What little boy misses a chance to tell his mother he loves her? My Lady, may I never become an ex-child.[163]

Then, thirteen days later he tells in another note about the strange incident that happened in the street below the statue of Our Lady:

> Octave of the Immaculate Conception, 1931: [16 December] Yesterday afternoon, at three, when I was going to the school of Santa Isabel to hear the confessions of the girls, on Atocha Street (on the side near San Carlos, almost at the corner of Santa Ines) three young men, all of them probably thirty-something, crossed paths with me. When they got close to me one of them shouted, 'I'm going to get him!' and raised his arm in such a way that I thought for sure I would be struck. But before he could carry out his intended aggression, one of the other two said to him in an authoritative voice, 'No. Don't hit him!' And then immediately, this same man in a mocking tone of voice, bending towards me, added, 'Burrito, burrito! ('Little donkey, little donkey!')
>
> 'I crossed Santa Isabel's corner at a calm pace, and am sure that I in no way showed on the outside the trepidation I was a feeling inside. To hear myself called – by that defender! – by this name, 'little donkey,' that I use when speaking to Jesus. This really got to me. Immediately I said three Hail Marys to the Blessed Virgin, who witnessed that little event from her image on the house of the Congregation of Saint Philip.

And he adds in another note,

> 16 December, 1931: Yesterday I felt kind of tired,

undoubtedly as a result of that 'assault' I suffered on Atocha Street. I am convinced that it was from the devil. Father Norberto thinks so too. The one who tried to attack me had the ferocious face of a madman. About the looks of the other two, I find I can't remember a thing. Then, and also afterwards, I did not lose my peace. There was a physiological fear that made my heart beat faster, but I could tell that it did not show on the outside, not even on my face ... Afterwards, on my notepaper, I jotted down exactly what those people had said.[164]

Father Josemaría would always believe that his would-be assailant was the Devil. And the young man who had stopped the Devil in his tracks and had said 'Little donkey, little donkey!' words from the depth of Father Josemaría's soul, known only to God and his confessor, must have been his Guardian Angel.

God, like a good father, he realized, was leading him by the hand as if he were a little child and teaching him spiritual ways and mysteries. He was being shown that he must seek the help of his Guardian angel and teach others to do the same. It inspired him to write these passages about Guardian Angels, 'You seem amazed because your Guardian Angel has done so many obvious favours for you. But you shouldn't be. That's why Our Lord has placed him at your side.'[165]

And,

'Have confidence in your Guardian Angel. Treat him as a lifelong friend – that's what he is – and he will do a thousand services for you in the ordinary affairs of each day.'[166]

He also liked to point out how close the early Christians were to their Guardian Angels. 'Drink at the clear fountain of the Acts of the Apostles,' he advised. 'In the twelfth chapter, Peter is freed from prison by the ministry of angels and comes to the house of Mark's mother. Those inside don't want to believe the servant girl when she tells them Peter is at the door. "Angelus, eius est!" – "It's his angel!" they say. See on what intimate terms the early Christians were with their guardian angels.'[167]

In the midst of all hate and unrest Father Josemaría

continued his constant search for more people to join him in what he liked to call his 'crazy' divine venture. He prayed, 'Lord, make us crazy with a contagious craziness that will draw many to your apostolate.'[168]

At this time he used to take some university students to a small cafe he had found. It was called El Sotanillo, The Little Basement, and it had two signs outside advertising helados and chocolateria (ice cream and chocolate) In the little cafe he would talk to the young men about spiritual things. And he became so well known at the cafe that the owner's son would say as soon as he saw Father Josemaría and the young men who came with him, 'Here he is again with his disciples.'

Money, as always, was scarce. But Father Josemaría would somehow find enough to pay for what the young men had, and would find an excuse for not having anything himself. It often meant that after paying the bill he was so hard up that he would have to go without meals and walk even more miles about Madrid because he hadn't the price of a tram ticket.

He would also talk to the young men who were interested in helping him as they walked along the street or sat on a park bench. Some came closer to joining the Work and began to understand his teaching about finding God in everyday life. But many abandoned him, some as he sadly remarked, 'without even saying goodbye.' But he pressed on looking for men and women who wanted to be apostles in the modern world. And sometimes God surprised him. He found the people he was looking for not among the ones he expected might have vocations, but among those he described as people 'with big hearts, even though their weaknesses had been bigger.'[169]

On 2 October 1931, the feast of the Guardian Angels and the third anniversary of the founding of Opus Dei Father Josemaría prayed to his Guardian Angel in a special way. His entry in his journal for that day says,

> I paid him compliments and asked him to teach me to love Jesus at least – at least! – as much as he loves Him. Undoubtedly Saint Teresa [It was also the vigil of the feast of St Teresa of Lisieux] wanted to give me something in

anticipation of her feast day, for she succeeded in having my Guardian Angel teach me today how to make a prayer of childhood. What very childish things I said to my Lord! With the trustful confidence of a boy talking to his Grown-up friend, of whose love he is certain, I said, 'Let me live only for your Work. Let me live only for your glory. Let me live only for your love ...' I duly recalled and acknowledged that I do everything badly, and said, 'That, my Jesus, should not surprise you – it is impossible for me to do anything right. You help me, you do it for me, and you will see how well it turns out. So, then, boldly and without straying from the truth, I say to you: Saturate me, get me drunk, with your Spirit, and thus I will do your will. I want to do it. If I don't do it, it's because ... you're not helping me.' And I had feelings of love for my Mother and Lady and right now I feel myself very much a child of God my Father.[170]

Twelve days later, on 14 October, Father Josemaría learned that the infamous Article 26 had been approved by the Spanish Parliament that morning, which proposed the dissolution of all religious orders and the nationalization of their property. One clause stated, 'Hereby dissolved are those religious orders which juridically impose, besides the three canonical vows, a special vow of obedience to an authority other than the legitimate one of the state.' This was specifically targeting the Jesuits, for priests of the Society of Jesus take a vow of obedience to the Pope, Christ's Vicar on earth. The aim, it was stated, was the liberating of the masses from religious slavery. Marxists and anarchists intensified their campaigns against priests and Christianity in general, and openly vowed they would finish off religion once and for all.

All monasteries and convents again became targets for destruction and some Catholic students formed special defence groups and at night mounted guard over monasteries and convents to prevent them being attacked and burned down.

On 15 October, the day after the decision to expel the Jesuits and the feast of the great Spanish saint, Teresa of Avila, Father Josemaría went to reassure as best as he could the nuns of Santa Isabel who were very frightened by rumours of an imminent attack on their foundation.

Father Josemaría wrote in his notes,

> Today I went into the cloister of Santa Isabel. I encouraged the nuns. I spoke to them about love, about the cross, and about joy ... and about victory. Away with anxiety! We are at the beginning of the end. Saint Teresa [of Avila] has obtained for me, from Our Jesus, the joy – with a capital J – that I have today ... when it would seem humanly speaking, that I should be sad, both for the Church and about my own situation (which, truth to tell, is not good). We just need much faith and expiation and, above faith and expiation, much Love. Besides, this morning, when purifying two ciboriums, so as not to leave the Blessed Sacrament in the church, I received almost half a ciboriumful of hosts, even though I gave several to each sister.

Then he added,

> On my way out of the cloister they showed me, in the vestibule, a Christ Child. [This is a painted wooden carving, which the nuns of Santa Isabel still have] ... I have never seen a better Child Jesus ... He has his little arms crossed on his breast and his eyes half open, beautiful. I devoured him with kisses ... and would have loved to kidnap him.[171]

He now began to go every week to the nun on duty at the convent's window to ask her to let him hold the statue of the Child Jesus in his arms. And the nun would pass it to him. In his notes he writes,

> The Child Jesus: how this devotion has taken hold of me since I first laid eyes on that 'consummate Thief' that my nuns keep in the vestibule of their cloister! Child Jesus, adolescent Jesus – I like to see you that way, Lord because ... it makes me more daring. I like to see you as a little boy, a helpless child, because it makes me feel like you need me.[172]

He would later write a whole section about spiritual childhood in his book *The Way*, in which he says, 'The way of childhood. Abandonment. Spiritual childhood. All this is not utter nonsense, but a sturdy and solid Christian life.'[173] And he goes on to say, 'In the spiritual life of childhood the things which the "children" say or do are never puerile or childish.'[174] and, 'The great daring is always that of children. Who cries for the moon? Who won't stop at danger to get what he wants? Put in such a child a great deal of God's grace, the desire to do God's will, a great love for Jesus and all the human knowledge he is capable of acquiring, and you'll have a likeness of the apostles of today just as God undoubtedly wants them.' Then he advises, 'Before God, who is eternal, you are a smaller child than, in your sight, a two-year-old toddler. And besides being a child, you are a child of God. Don't forget it.'[175]

The Augustinian nuns to this day call the statue 'the Christ Child of Father Josemaría.' Mother St Joseph, who was the sacristan at the time Father Josemaría was their chaplain, recalls how at Christmas time when the statue was taken into the sacristy by the nuns she often saw Father Josemaría rock it in his arms as if it were a real baby, speak to it and even sing songs for it. In his booklet *Holy Rosary*, which he composed in the church of Santa Isabel, he gives us a hint of his devotion. Writing about the birth of Jesus he says,

> And in Bethlehem is born our God: Jesus Christ! There is no room in the inn; He is born in a stable. And his Mother wraps him in swaddling clothes and lays him in a manger. Cold, Poverty ... I am Joseph's little servant. How good Joseph is! He treats me like a son. He even forgives me if I take the Child in my arms and spend hour after hour saying sweet and loving things to Him. And I kiss Him – you kiss Him too! – and I rock Him in my arms, and I sing to Him and call Him King, Love, my God, my Only-One, my All ...! How beautiful is the Child ... and how short the decade.

And in his meditation he would pray the Our Father very carefully:

> I would recite, savouring them, the words of the Our Father, and I would pause, relishing the thought when I considered God is my Father, my Father, and that this makes me a brother of Jesus Christ and a brother to all men. I never got over my astonishment, contemplating that I was a son of God! After each reflection I found myself firmer in faith, more secure in hope, more on fire with love. And there was born in my soul the need, since I was a child of God, to be a small child, a needy child. That was the beginning, in my interior life, of my living whenever I could – whenever I can – the life of childhood.[176]

As the religious persecution remorselessly ground out its message of hate, Father Josemaría persisted in spreading his message of love and service to all men. He wrote this advice to priests:

> To serve is the greatest joy a soul can have, and that is what we, the priests, have to do; night and day, at the service of all, if not, one is not a priest. He must love the young and the old; the poor and the rich, the sick and the children; he has to prepare himself to say Mass; he has to receive the souls, one by one, like a shepherd who knows his flock and calls each sheep by its name.
>
> We priests have no rights: I like to feel that I am everyone's servant and I am proud of the title. We only have duties and there lies our joy.[177]

CHAPTER 21

The Stabbed and Dying Gypsy

At this time the subject of politics was on everybody's lips and the political situation dominated almost every conversation. But what impressed many people who met Father Josemaría was the fact that he never spoke about politics and never wanted to do so.

He recommended to all his followers and the young men who came to him for guidance that they should avoid talking politics completely. In a letter dated 9 January 1932 he reminds his followers that the bond uniting them was exclusively spiritual 'which consists of bringing the light of Christ to your friends, your families and those around you ...'[178]

He recognized, however, the vital need there was for Christians to take part in politics. After all there was no reason why a politician couldn't be a good politician and be a saint. Good men were needed in politics as in all professions. Years later when someone asked him what he could do to make his friends understand that the most important thing was to get to know God and that they shouldn't worry about politics, Father Josemaría quickly corrected him.

Well, you can't tell them not to be concerned about politics, because some people, precisely because they love God, do make politics their concern. But not me! That's not my subject, but it's my view that there should be people involved in it who are very honest; some leaning to the right, others to the left, others leaning another way, and none of them is wrong. They are all men of good will. I would not tell them to leave politics.

What I can and should advise is that they shouldn't make personal attacks. Let them defend their programme without offending anybody personally. And this refers both to the present day personalities and to those who belong to the immediate past. If not, there will never be any decent person in a country who is prepared to make the sacrifice necessary to be a leader. For he will think: 'If afterwards this fails, they will not only take it out on me, but also on my children and on my family and on everybody else.' And there follows one persecution after another and it becomes a madhouse![179]

In the early 1930s, many young men in Spain were attracted to the idea of direct political action, or to political solutions that promised more tangible and immediate results. One such a man was Juan Jiménez Vargas, a young medical student. Juan was very much involved in the political activities of the university. He had heard a lot about Father Josemaría from one of his friends at the university who used to go to him for confession. After meeting Father Josemaría, Juan told his friends that he was very impressed by him. But, he said he felt the message Father Josemaría was preaching wasn't what he, Juan, was looking for. When a country was on the brink of the abyss as Spain was, he thought there were more urgent and vital things to get involved in than praying and doing good.

When Father Josemaría heard about Juan's reaction, he smiled and said that considering the time of crisis in Spain, Juan's response was the natural reaction of any young man. But he added that perhaps one day, sooner than Juan thought, he would come to realize what was really the most important thing: Christians had to give priority to spiritual and doctrinal formation and to living their lives in union with Christ. Then they would transform society in a much more effective and lasting way. How accurate and prophetic Father Josemaría's words turned out to be.

On 22 January 1932, the Republican government dissolved the Society of Jesus and ordered the expulsion of all the Jesuits. This meant that Father Josemaría lost contact with his spiritual director Father Sánchez. For a time he then went to confession regularly to Father Juan Postius, a Claretian Father. However, many Jesuits remained and went into hiding and Father Sánchez was one of them. As soon as he could, Father Josemaría returned to Father Sánchez for confession and for spiritual direction. The Republican Government had also suppressed religious instruction in state schools in Spain. As a result many families approached Father Josemaría to ask him if he would teach catechism to their children. He readily agreed to do so.

A girl who worked at the home of one of these families remembers the catechism classes Father Josemaría gave to her and to eight children of the house. The girl, who became Sister Benita, a nun of the Servants of Mary, describes how from 1932 to 1933 Father Josemaría went twice a week, on Wednesdays and Saturdays between five and six o'clock, to give them their classes. 'He was very lively and cheerful,' she recalls, 'and the children, some of whom were very young, enjoyed themselves a lot during the classes and we did not want him to stop. The time flew and we complained that he had to go so soon ...

'We felt very happy by his side, and he helped us understand the catechism by means of illustrated cards. The children would gather round to get a look at them.'

In the first few months of 1932 two dying hospital patients would leave deep and lasting impressions on Father Josemaría. Both could be described as having been big sinners but sinners who had repented and were very sorry for their sins. The first reference to them can be found in Father Josemaría's notes of 14 January 1932 when he wrote, 'Blessed be pain. Loved be pain Sanctified be pain ... Glorified be pain. and the same words would also appear in *The Way*.[180] It was not until 1974 that he would explain the story behind those words, 'There was this poor woman, a prostitute who had belonged to one of the most aristocratic families of Spain. When I met her she was decomposing – decomposing in body but being healed in soul, in a hospital for incurables. She had been a "camp follower" as they say, the poor thing. She had a husband, she had children, she had abandoned everything driven crazy by passion. But then that creature knew how to love. She reminded me of Mary Magdalene: she knew how to love.'

After administering the Last Rites he whispered in her ear those words, 'Blessed be pain. Loved be pain, Sanctified be pain ... Glorified be pain' and she repeated them aloud. 'She died shortly after that, and is now in heaven and has helped us a lot,' he went on to say.[181]

Then, one Sunday in February of 1932, during another of his hospital visits, a Philippian Brother came to him to tell him about a man who had been stabbed. Father Josemaría immediately went to his bedside. In his notes he says, 'He was a Gypsy who had been stabbed repeatedly in a fight. Right away he agreed to make his Confession. He did not want to let go of my hand and, not being able to do this himself, he asked me to put it up to his mouth so that he could kiss it. He was in a pitiful condition – blood and other matter were oozing out of his mouth ... He asked for a crucifix. I didn't have one, so I gave him a Rosary. I wrapped it round his wrist and he kissed it, saying words of profound sorrow for having offended Our Lord.'[182]

In his journal a day or two later he wrote, 'A young man, a St Philip Brother, came to tell me that the Gypsy had died in a most edifying way, saying, among other things, as he kissed the crucifix of the Rosary, "My lips are rotten, not worthy of kissing you." And he called out for his daughters to look at him and to know that their father was good. That, no doubt, was why he had said to me, "Put the Rosary on me so it can be seen, so it can be seen." Jesus, I've already offered that soul to you, but now I do it again. Right now I'm going to pray for him the prayer for the dead.'[183]

Father Josemaría never forgot the words of the dying, Gypsy: 'Don't you think it's a most beautiful way of showing one's contrition?' he would say. And he would add, 'Since then there have been many times when I too have said the same, alone, without crying out loud: "with this rotten mouth of mine, I cannot kiss You, Lord." I learned from a dying Gypsy how to make an act of contrition.'

Father Josemaría was also during this time struggling tirelessly to become a more and more docile instrument for the mission God had entrusted to him. He never stopped working on his own character and training himself in the practice of the virtues. Every night before going to bed, through a detailed, in-depth and thoroughly honest examination of conscience he kept discovering new areas in which he could improve. He set himself demanding goals for following through on the inspirations he received from God and his main tactic was to struggle in the little things. 'Great holiness,' he would say, 'consists in carrying out the little duties of each moment.'[184]

Some notes of his from 1932 provide a record of these interior struggles:
- I mustn't ask questions merely out of curiosity.
- I mustn't complain about anything to anyone, except to seek direction.
- I mustn't flatter or criticise.

And although his character was so open and affable he must have thought there was room for improvement for he also noted down this resolution: 'Be sociable at home and make a point of talking with the others.'[185]

In his personal notes at this time is a fascinating reference to 'My Lady of the Kisses' the statue of Our Lady holding the child Jesus in her arms, which he always used to kiss before leaving the house and on his return. The note is especially interesting given the fact that he burned many of his spiritual notebooks because they contained accounts of what could have been supernatural experiences.

And Bishop Alvaro del Portillo, who succeeded him, said, 'It is very probable that there were many other experiences which he never revealed and which are known only to God. He wanted at all costs to make sure no one would get the idea from reading his notebooks that he was a saint.'

The entry is dated: Octave of the patronal feast of St Joseph, 20 April, 1932. Then next to it is written:

> Later on, if I have time, I'll catch up on some other notes I need to write up. For now I just want to jot down something that – once again! – makes clear the goodness of my Immaculate Mother, and my own wretchedness. Later yesterday, as usual, I humbled myself: I put my forehead on the floor, before going to bed, and asked my father and lord St Joseph, and the souls in purgatory, to wake me up at the right time ... As always happens when I humbly beg for this (no matter what time I've gone to bed) I came out of a deep sleep, just as if someone was calling out to me, certain that it was the right time to get up ... So I did get up and, filled with humble gratitude, I prostrated myself on the ground ... and began my meditation. Well, sometime between six-thirty and a quarter to seven, I saw for quite some time that the face of My Lady of the Kisses was bright with happiness, with joy. I looked very carefully. I thought she was smiling because it had this effect on me, even though her lips never moved. I was very calm and I spoke many affectionate words to my Mother. This same thing has happened to me on other occasions too – this which I have just related in such detail. I've tried not to give it any importance, almost not daring to believe it. I even came to the point of improvising a little test to see if it was just my imagination because I don't easily believe in extraordinary events. It didn't work. When I positively wished that she would smile, trying to make it happen by my own imagination, the face of My Lady of the Kisses kept the hieratic seriousness which the poor little statue possesses. In other words, my Lady, Holy Mary, on the octave of St Joseph has given a little caress to her child. Blessed be her most pure heart!

Then, 'Feast of St Mark, 25 April, 1932: This morning I was with my Father Sánchez. I decided to tell him what happened on the twentieth, though I felt a kind of reluctance or shame. It was difficult, but I told him.'[186]

CHAPTER 22

Prisoners of the Cárcel Modelo

To his constantly increasing labours Father Josemaría now added another corporal work of mercy: visiting the imprisoned. Some Catholic students in the early hours of 10 August 1932 had been involved in an armed uprising and had tried to take over the Madrid Post Office building. The government, having had information about the proposed attack for some weeks, were ready and waiting. As a result the uprising was quickly put down and the students arrested. Father Josemaría writes on the day it happened,

> Feast of Saint Lawrence ... At 5.00 this morning, I was awakened by shots, real volleys, and the rattle of machine guns. I went to Santa Isabel dressed as a layman. Our Adolfo is in prison [Adolpho Gómez was a young student who had joined Opus Dei in May the previous year. He had been among those students who had stood guard at night over churches and convents to stop them being attacked and burned down]. He is a great soul who understands the idea [of Opus Dei] and knows how to make sacrifices for it. May the Lord preserve him for us.[187]

Another arrested student was José Manuel Doménech who on Sundays used to go with Father Josemaría to the General Hospital to look after the patients. Most of the arrested students were sent to the Cárcel Modelo, or

'Model Prison', in Madrid. And they were put in the same prison yard as anarchists who had been involved in atrocities and in the burning of churches. On each side there were those who would have welcomed violent confrontation which could have ended in some of them slitting each others' throats.

As soon as he heard of the students' arrest Father Josemaría went to the Modelo but he was not permitted to see any of them. Several days passed before he was allowed into the prison. He went dressed in his cassock, which made him stick out like a sore thumb. And by wearing a cassock he was certainly risking being persecuted himself. This was the view of another student prisoner, José Palacios, who remembers that from then on Father Josemaría visited the prison frequently, even though his visits to detainees dressed as a priest made him in his words, 'a marked man'.

Visitors were only allowed to talk to the prisoners on the other side of the bars in the prison long gallery. And Father Josemaría would go to the long gallery and speak to them through the prison bars, either individually or in a group.

He told all who would listen to him that they must always remember they were sons of God. 'Abandon yourself to Him and you will have no worries,' he said. He also advised them to say the Our Father many times a day, meditating on the first two words, 'Our Father!' He encouraged the prisoners to have great devotion to Our Lady and urged them to receive the Sacraments frequently. Then he would tell them to use their time well while they were in prison by working and studying and adding a supernatural motive to all they did.

José Palacios took note of some of the things Father Josemaría was telling them and says, 'to make good use of the time, I set about giving a class and reviewing my French.' One day he asked Father Josemaría how they should deal with men like the anarchists so opposed to God and religion.

Father Josemaría replied that their imprisonment was a splendid opportunity to treat the anarchists with affection and to try to make them see their errors. 'You must realise,' he said, 'that they probably did not have Christian parents as you had, nor were they brought up in an environment like yours. What would you and I be like if we had been in their situation?'

The Catholic prisoners were very impressed by what Father Josemaría said to them. He also urged them to give witness to their faith by living and playing sports with the anarchists as if they were the best of friends. They should try to love those men as themselves, he said. Then he gave them a very practical piece of advice. 'Mix the teams so that there are anarchists and Catholics on both sides.' They did what Father Josemaría advised and played football with the anarchists. José Palacios remembers how he played as a goalkeeper and had two anarchists as full backs. 'I have never played such a gentlemanly and non-violent game of football,' he later recalled. 'Traditionalists and anarchists together! What a combination!'[188]

And, at this time, as Father Josemaría carried out his ever-increasing tasks, he was constantly assailed by gently persuasive, temptations such as: Would it not be better for him to live a more simple, quiet, holy life far away from his present non-stop activity, which was so demanding an existence. In his notes he writes. 'The temptation returns, whispering in my ears about a life of peace and virtue; not that of Father X or Brother So-and-so, but that of a simple little priest in the most remote rural parish, with no great struggles or great ideals calling for immediate action . . .'[189]

He would dismiss these temptations and continue with his demanding work and daily struggles. But he realized he needed a break. Earlier that year he had written, 'I need solitude. I am yearning for a long retreat, to speak with God, far from everything. If he wants this, he will give me an opportunity. There I will be able to settle so many things that are churning within me. And Jesus, surely, will impress on my mind some important details about his Work.'[190]

At the beginning of the month of October 1932 Father Josemaría was able to take himself off to the Carmelite monastery near Segovia to spend a week speaking to God, something he so much wanted to do. In the chapel of the monastery is the tomb of St John of the Cross where the saint's remains lie. He spent long hours in prayer in this chapel. And it was while he was kneeling before St John's tomb that he received the inspiration to place the apostolic work of Opus Dei under the protection of the Archangels, Saints Michael, Gabriel and Raphael and the Apostles, Saints Peter, Paul and John.

During the last days of the retreat he meditated on Our Lord's Passion, Death and Resurrection. The Devil, 'Old Scratch' gave him a bad time, raging around him and trying his best to disturb him.

Father Josemaría in one of the notes he made on this retreat writes,

> Last night, the devil was at large in my cell and again stirred up things from my past. He gave me a hard time. This morning, too. I offer it up to you, my God, as expiation. But I am weak. I can't do anything, I'm not worth anything – don't leave me. Grieved by all this, I had a talk with my father John of the Cross: 'This is the way you treat me in your house? How can you allow Old Scratch to torment your guests? I thought you were more hospitable ...'[191]

After returning to Madrid there was another setback in store for him. A few weeks later Luis Gordon, who had seemed so healthy and full of life, was suddenly taken seriously ill and died just before daybreak on 5 November 1932. The obituary notice Father Josemaría wrote the same day sets out Luis' virtues: 'A good model: obedient, most discreet, charitable to the point of extravagance, humble, mortified and penitent ... a man of the Eucharist and of prayer, most devoted to the Blessed Virgin ... a father to the workmen in his factory. They cried when they heard of his death.'[192]

Again God's ways seemed so illogical to him. Here was another young man in the prime of his life, who had been so faithful and so helpful. What great work he could have done. Father Josemaría felt he really could have accomplished so much with Luis' help. Many young men recently had only gone along with him until the moment he had asked for their commitment. Then they had left him. There seemed so many setbacks and so many failures. Now, two young men he could have relied on, Father Somoano and Luis Gordon, had both been taken from him. He seemed to be getting nowhere . . .

Then there came a great consolation. He was convinced his two helpers were in heaven. And from heaven, he told himself, they would be able help him far more than they ever could have done on earth!

It was around this time that he found a dirty, discarded picture of Our Lady. The picture lay on the ground near the entrance to one of the schools run by the Damas Apostólicas in the dangerous Los Pinos district. He was in the habit of picking up religious pictures that had been thrown out into the street and taking them home and burning them. But with this picture, which had been torn out of a catechism, he felt it had been rejected as a deliberate, offensive gesture. He wrote in his journal, 'For this reason I will not burn the poor picture, though it is badly done and the paper is cheap and torn. I will save it and put it in a nice frame when I have the money . . . and who's to tell me that there won't someday be a devotion, of love and reparation, to 'Our Lady of the Catechism.'[193]

At the end of 1932 Father Josemaría moved his family once again. This time it was to an apartment at 4, Martinez Campos. It was an apartment which was big enough for him to invite there the students who were going to him for spiritual direction. His mother soon became accustomed to having groups of young men in her living room. Even though he had not yet told her or any other members of the family about the Work God had entrusted to him, his mother and his sister Carmen gave him all the help and support they could. His mother treated the young men who came like sons. She made afternoon tea and loved to provide special treats for them so that they were like one big happy family.

One of the things Father Josemaría would say to young men who came was, 'I'll tell you a secret, an open secret. These world crises are crises of saints. God wants a handful of men "of his own" in every human activity. Then

... "pax Christi in regno Christi" – "the peace of Christ in the kingdom of Christ".'[194]

Father Josemaría also used to say he was not looking for Holy Joes. He wanted men of character, men with sufficient toughness and moral fibre to enable them to stand up to the sufferings, the hardships and the dangers that he realized would inevitably soon confront them.

One member of the Escrivá family who wasn't so enthusiastic about these get-togethers with the students was his brother, Santiago. He would arrive home and complain to his mother, 'Josemaría's lads have scoffed all the food again!'

Father Josemaría was demanding a great deal from those who wanted to join him, nothing less than apostolic celibacy and a lifelong commitment. He would say it was a personal and individual calling, a vocation, the most important decision in any individual's life. Each young man began by trying to sanctify his work and studies. Then Father Josemaría would help him discover the great spiritual adventure of being with Christ and of bringing other souls closer to him as they moved 'along the paths of prayer and love'.

Through Father Josemaría's intense prayer and mortifications, vocations slowly began to take shape, one by one.

As the year 1932 drew to a close there were three young men wondering whether they should devote their life to helping him in his Work of God.

There was Juan Jiménez Vargas, the medical student who had met Father Josemaría at the beginning of the year but had then preferred being actively involved in the day-to-day political struggle and the university debates. He had kept in touch and had gone with Father Josemaría to the hospitals.

Over the Christmas holidays he had a long talk with Father Josemaría. Then he decided that over the next nine days he would pray to the Holy Spirit to give him light and counsel.

Then there was Jenaro Lázaro, the sculptor, who was one of the Philippian Brothers. With Father Josemaría he had helped look after the sick in the General Hospital of

Madrid. It was after these hospital visits that Father Josemaría would talk to him about finding Christ as he sculpted and being an apostle in the modern world. And then there was José María González, a young man Father Josemaría had been praying for two years would have a vocation. In 1931 José was a chemistry student living with his parents near to the Church of the Foundation for the Sick where Father Josemaría was then chaplain. In those days José remembers that his family called Father Josemaría 'the boy priest'. That was because of his youthful appearance, his contagious cheerfulness – and also because they didn't know his name at the time. One day Father Josemaría asked him to pray for an intention of his and José agreed to do so.

The day was 25 March 1931 for it was on that day Father Josemaría wrote in his journal:

> Today, the 25th, the feast of the Annunciation of Our Lady, with my apostolic audacity (daring!) I went up to a young man who, with great piety and recollection, receives Communion every day in my church. He, in fact, had just received Our Lord when I said to him, 'Listen, would you be so good as to pray a little for a special intention that's for the glory of God?' 'Yes, Father,' he answered – and he even thanked me! The intention was that he, being so devout, be chosen by God to be an apostle in his Work. On other occasions, when I have seen him from my confessional, I have made the same request of his Guardian Angel.[195]

After gaining a degree in chemistry José María González left Madrid to take a teaching post at a grammar school in Jaén. Father Josemaría continued praying for him, convinced he would see him again. In December of 1932 the young science teacher returned to Madrid to spend Christmas with his family. Just before Christmas Day he was walking down Gran Via when he saw Father Josemaría coming towards him. His first reaction was to avoid being seen because he had already been talked into enrolling in several Catholic associations, which had turned out, in his view, to have been a waste of time. Father Josemaría, however, had already spotted him. He greeted him warmly and said he would like to have an opportunity of talking at greater length with him. They met again that evening and José then felt that what Father Josemaría was describing to him was just what he was looking for. He had been growing increasingly worried about the aggressively Godless attitude of some of the scientists he was coming in contact with. He wanted to continue with his scientific studies and be able to demonstrate the harmony that existed between science and Faith as a way of doing apostolate in his profession. This, he discovered to his delight in the course of the conversation, was exactly what Father Josemaría was proposing to him. He had one reservation. 'There's a monk I know. I've been to Confession with him several times. Do you think I could consult him before I commit myself?'

Father Josemaría told him, 'You're absolutely free to consult anybody you wish.' So José then went to talk to the monk and seek his advice before making a decision. After his nine days of prayer to the Holy Spirit, Juan Jiménez Vargas, returned to see Father Josemaría on 3 January 1933. His answer was, 'Yes! I want to join you in this Work.'

Then Jenaro Lázaro, the sculptor, said he too wanted to join.

The monk José María González went to consult gave him this advice: 'If this Work you speak about is in its beginnings, wouldn't it be better to go for a more fully developed institution? After all, it's better to work in a library that's well organised, than in one that's in the process of being put together.'

José's reaction was that it didn't matter whether the Work was just beginning or not. That wasn't the point. What he wanted to know was whether it was an ideal to which it was worth devoting his life. He decided it was.

He returned to see Father Josemaría on 11 February, the Feast of Our Lady of Lourdes. 'Yes,' José María González said. 'I will join you in this Work!'

'Another lunatic for the asylum,'[196] Father Josemaría would joke when anyone joined him. Now there were three wonderful, new lunatics, Juan Jiménez Vargas, a medical student, Jenaro Lázaro, a sculptor and José María González, a scientist. And the year 1933 had only just begun!

CHAPTER 23

The Class of Three

Father Josemaría was convinced at this time that the great social miseries were rooted in religious ignorance and coldness of heart towards God and our fellow man. 'One could well say,' he remarked about this time, 'that the chief enemy of God – since one comes to love God after getting to know him – is ignorance, which is the origin of so many evils and a great obstacle for the salvation of souls.'

And he wrote: 'Giving doctrine is our great mission. Herein lies the great apostolate ... to show to the multitude who await us the path that leads straight to Our Lord.'[197]

Just seventeen days after Juan Jiménez Vargas had joined him in his Work, on 21 January 1933, Father Josemaría went with him to the Porta Coeli, a home for orphans and delinquents. Father Josemaría used to go there to teach catechism and hear their confessions. And the nuns who ran the orphanage had agreed to let him have regular use of the visitors' room to give classes in Christian formation to university students. For the first class of formation, only three students turned up – Juan Jiménez Vargas and two of his friends, all medical students.

Father Josemaría also took with him to the orphanage the small picture of Our Lady he had found in the Los Pinos district that had been torn from a catechism. As a form of reparation, he had had it framed and backed with gold cloth so that it looked very beautiful and attractive. He placed the picture in the room where he was giving the talk so that it seemed to preside over the proceedings.

At the end of the class Father Josemaría took the three students to the orphanage chapel for Benediction. Juan was impressed by 'the way Father Josemaría prayed as he opened the Tabernacle and genuflected, and above all by the way he held the Monstrance in his hands when he gave the blessing.'

What Juan didn't know was that, as Father Josemaría was giving them the blessing, God was allowing him a glimpse into the future. It was not until fifty years later that Father Josemaría would describe what happened in the orphanage chapel:

> I placed Our Lord in the Monstrance and gave Benediction to those three. It seemed to me that the Lord Jesus, Our God, was blessing three hundred, three hundred thousand, thirty million ... white, black, yellow, of all the colours, all the combinations that human love can produce. And I have fallen short, because after half a century it is a reality. I have fallen short, because Our Lord has been generous beyond my wildest dreams.[198]

More and more students came to the Christian doctrine classes. Through these classes and their conversations afterwards with Father Josemaría they began to discover the wonder and depth of the Christian vocation lived in the middle of their daily occupations. The students also soon learned that they were studying Christian doctrine, not only for their own benefit but also so that they in their turn would be able to teach others. And two weeks after the first class at the Porta Coeli orphanage the students themselves were going out giving catechism classes to children in the deprived Los Pinos area, where the picture of Our Lady had been found. There the nuns of the College of the Divine Redeemer had agreed to let Father Josemaría use the college for the classes. One of the girls who attended the college and became Sister Pilar of the Missionaries of Christian Doctrine remembers how wretched and poor the Pinos district was at that time. People, she said, lived in huts made from old tin cans. The college was in a hollow and when it rained the water ran down the slopes forming a small brook. Hence the people of the neighbourhood nicknamed it 'Brook College'. Los Pinos was a very difficult place to get to. There was no way to it by car because there were no roads going into it and the last stop on the Metro was miles away. And for a priest to walk through the Los Pinos district dressed as a priest was indeed an act of heroism.

A few days before the classes began Father Josemaría and Father Lino Vea-Murgia, who was now a very good friend and helping in every way he could, went to the college to make the final arrangements. There had been a heavy fall of snow, which was very unusual for Madrid, and they had to trudge through it. One of the nuns who helped run the college at that time later recalled, 'One morning, which I remember very well, because there had been a very heavy fall of snow and everything was covered in white, we saw, from the community recreation room, which was on the upper floor, two priests in cassocks and cloaks approaching the college. It was early because everything was still white and clean. Later it became like a mudbath. It was Father Josemaría and Father Lino who had come to ask us to allow catechism classes at the college.'

Eleven o'clock on Sunday mornings was the time agreed for the classes. Father Josemaría and Father Lino together with the students, would arrive on the dot, despite all the difficulties they had had getting to Los Pinos.

It soon became quite clear that the ones who were benefiting most from the classes were the students who were giving them. As well as increasing their own knowledge of the faith they were also becoming more generous in their desire to perform good works and do apostolate. Father Josemaría encouraged them to invite their friends to the catechism study classes and within a year the number of students had increased immensely. Soon Father Josemaría was looking for other deprived areas to give catechism classes.

In February of 1933, Angel Herrera, publisher of the newspaper *El Debate*, was made president of Catholic

Action in Spain. Don Herrera then gave up the prestigious job as publisher to take up the new post. He later became a priest, then Bishop of Málaga and a cardinal. Soon after his Catholic Action appointment, on 11 February 1933, he asked for a meeting with Father Josemaría. At this meeting he informed Father Josemaría of his new post, which at that point had not then been officially announced. Then he told Father Josemaría he wanted to offer him an important job. Together with the papal nuncio Don Herrera had been instrumental in setting up a special centre of formation for priests who would assist Catholic Action at various levels. The job he wanted Father Josemaría to take was the post of director of this centre. But Father Josemaría refused to accept, much to the surprise of Don Herrera, who tried hard to persuade Father Josemaría to change his mind. He pointed out that what he was being offered was a key position and one of great responsibility since all the best priests in Spain would go to the centre. Father Josemaría replied that it was precisely for that reason he could not take the job – it was too important. 'Besides,' he added, 'there are many others who would do it better than me.' This was not just a polite excuse. He was fully convinced that other priests would be more capable of handling that important assignment than he would have been. But above all he believed that he himself could only be effective in the specific task that God had shown him he wanted him to do – and for which God had given him a special and particular grace.[199]

The following month, on 23 March, Father Josemaría learned that the ecclesiastical jurisdictions for the military and the royal courts were going to be abolished and be brought under the authority of the bishops. This meant that the Santa Isabel Foundation would come under the jurisdiction of the Bishop of Madrid and so would Father Josemaría who would need his permission to remain in the diocese. But he was no longer concerned about what the outcome might be. He noted in his journal:

> The Palace jurisdiction is going to disappear. This morning I was with Father Pedro Poveda [Founder of the Teresians] and he told me that he will speak with

Monsignor Morán [the Vicar General of Madrid and the Bishop of Madrid's right hand man] and that I will be able to continue on at Santa Isabel, the same as now. Well, it's all the same to me. I am a child of God. He takes care of me. Maybe I've already completed my mission in this place.[200]

Monsignor Francis Morán, the Vicar General, knew all about the work Father Josemaría was doing and had a very high regard for him. He in fact publicly expressed how highly he esteemed him at a meeting on 29 April, 1933. The following day Father Josemaría wrote in his notes:

> I went to see Father Poveda, who is so good, always so much a brother to me. He told me that yesterday there was a meeting of the rectors of all the foundations that have been transferred to the jurisdiction of the diocese. And it happened, as they were discussing their personnel, the Vicar General of Madrid (Monsignor Morán), who was presiding, gave this poor donkey a eulogy that delighted Father Poveda. When I left the Teresian Institute and caught the 48, what embarrassment...[201]

Two months later Father Josemaría met Ricardo Fernández, who was studying at the School of Architecture in Madrid. Ricardo was a very hard-up student and to help pay for his studies was giving private tuition to children in their homes. He was teaching at the home of the Romero family this particular day when Father Josemaría arrived. Ricardo was only able to have a short chat with him. Brief though the meeting was Ricardo was very impressed. That same night, 14 May 1933, he wrote in his diary, 'Today I met a priest, very young and enthusiastic. I don't know why, but I think he will have a great influence on my life.'

A little more than two weeks later they met again, this time at Father Josemaría's home. Father Josemaría gave Ricardo a book from his bookcase, the *History of the Sacred Passion* by La Palma. On the first page he wrote these words as a dedication, 'Madrid 29 V. 33. May you seek Christ. May you find Christ. May you love Christ.' It was this incident that he would later write about in his book, *The Way*: 'When I made you a present of that Life of Jesus, I wrote in it this inscription: "May you seek Christ. May you find Christ. May you love Christ." These are three very distinct steps. Have you at least tried to live the first one?'[202]

But shortly after receiving the book, Ricardo suffered a crippling attack of rheumatism which left him incapacitated for more than three months and it was not until November that he was able to move around again.

Father Josemaría would often talk to the first members about the need to 'materialise their spiritual life.'

> I wanted to keep them from the temptation, so common then and now, of living a kind of double life. On the one hand an interior life, a life of relation to God; and on the other a separate and distinct professional, social and family life, full of small earthly realities.
>
> No. We cannot lead a double life. We cannot be like schizophrenics, if we want to be Christians. There is just one life made of flesh and spirit. And it is this life which has to become, in both soul and body, holy and filled with God. We discover the invisible God in the most visible and material things.
>
> There is no other way. Either we learn to find Our Lord in ordinary, everyday life, or else we shall never find him.[203]

And it was around this time that he was given a very practical demonstration of someone who made a habit of finding God in his everyday life. Early in the morning as he was sitting in the confessional at the church of Santa Isabel he often heard a loud rattling noise. The noise always seemed to interrupt the early morning silence around the same time. This particular morning Father Josemaría decided to find out what was going on.

The noisemaker, he discovered, was John the milkman. Each day, John used to take his milk in churns on a hand cart around the city. But before doing so he would carry his churns, filled with the milk he was about to deliver, up the church steps and through the door at the top of the steps. This, Father Josemaría now realized, was the noise which had been disturbing the early morning silence.

Father Josemaría watched the milkman take his milk churns into the church and then he heard him say, 'Jesus, here's John the milkman.' Then John, after this short conversation with Jesus in the Blessed Sacrament, picked up his milk churns and took them back down the steps to his cart. And off he went on his milk round.

Father Josemaría was so moved by John's way of praying that he spent the rest of the day repeating: 'Lord, here is this wretch, this wretched priest who doesn't know how to love You like John the milkman.'[204]

From that day on he liked to tell people the story of John the milkman and how he each day took his milk churns to Jesus in the Blessed Sacrament and chatted to Him. He wanted to teach people to approach Our Lord in prayer with the same naturalness and trust as John the milkman with his milk churns.

CHAPTER 24

Tortured by Doubt

The vocations were slowly coming in. But Father Josemaría felt that the Work God had given him to do needed to grow more quickly. He began thinking about how he could meet and get to know many more people. From 8–16 June 1933, he went on a retreat at the Redemptorists' house in Madrid. It was on this retreat that he made the resolution to start some form of academy or college. The problem was that setting up an academy or college cost money. And he hadn't any money. There were only two members who were wage earners, Isidoro Zorzano, the railway engineer and José María González, the chemistry teacher, but their salaries would go nowhere near meeting the expenditure they would face.

Father Josemaría prayed about it and asked his members and many other people to pray for this attention.

A few days after the retreat, on 22 June 1933, he experienced what he describes as a 'cruel test'. He records what happened in a hand-written note:

> Last Thursday, the vigil of the feast of the Sacred Heart, for the first and only time since I have come to know the will of God, I experienced that cruel test which Father Postius warned me about some time ago. (When the Society of Jesus was dissolved by the present ungovernment, I lost contact with Father Sánchez for a while and Father Postius looked after me.) I was alone, in a side

chapel in the Church of Our Lady of Perpetual Help, and I was trying to pray before Jesus in the Blessed Sacrament, who was exposed on the altar in a monstrance. Suddenly, for an instant and without any reason being given which could explain it – there was none – this most bitter thought came into my mind: 'And what if all of this is a lie, an illusion of yours, and you are wasting your time ... and, still worse, you are wasting it for all these others, too?' This only lasted a few seconds, but how I suffered! Then I spoke to Jesus and said to him, 'Lord,' (the words aren't exact) 'if the Work is not Yours, demolish it; right now, at this moment, in such a way that I may know it.' Immediately I not only felt confirmed as to the truth of His will with regard to the Work, but also saw with clarity a point about the organisation of it, which had been baffling me. Until that time I hadn't had the slightest idea how to solve this problem.[205]

Father Josemaría had returned to Madrid after his retreat just when the students at the university had finished their exams and were preparing to go off for their summer vacations. He was able to have a get-together with them before they left and afterwards felt very much alone. On 12 August he writes, 'How lonely I feel sometimes. But it's still necessary to open the Academy, in spite of everyone and everything.'[206]

His plans for the Academy had to be put on hold, however, when he learned of the serious illness of his uncle, Father Teodoro Escrivá, his father's brother. Father Josemaría with his mother, sister and brother made two journeys to Fonz to see him before he died in the third week of September.

On his return to Madrid he was concerned that so little had been done about setting up the Academy. He writes in his notes: 'Oct 1, 1933: Tomorrow, five years since I saw the Work. My God, what an account you're going to ask of me! What a lack of responsiveness to grace!' And five days later, on 6 October, he writes, 'I don't lose peace, but there are times when it feels like my head is going to explode with all the ideas I have bubbling inside me for glorifying God with this Work of his. It hurts me to see that they haven't yet begun to be crystallised into something tangible.'[207] November came and they still hadn't found premises that would be suitable for the proposed Academy. He writes at this time, 'We're running around looking for a place. So many stairs to climb, and so much impatience! God forgive me!'[208]

Ricardo Fernández, the architectural student who had been crippled with rheumatism, reappeared on 4 November. Father Josemaría then spoke to him about the Work God had given him to do. Ricardo remembers him telling him that God wanted his plan from heaven to be realized on earth, that it was something for the whole world and for all times and that it could only be carried out by people who loved Christ and who would sanctify their work in the midst of the world and be nailed to His Cross. Ricardo's response was immediate. He said, 'I told him simply that I wanted to be that.' He used the word 'that' because at that time he didn't know the name of the Work that Father Josemaría had been talking to him about.

Yet another lunatic for the asylum! And another helper for the setting up the Academy.

Shortly afterwards they found an apartment, number 33, Luchana Street, which they thought would be suitable for the Academy. Then, in December, they managed to scrape up enough money to pay the first instalment on the rent. Father Josemaría's mother provided most of the furniture and the basic essentials to equip it. (Over the years many pieces of Escrivá family furniture would end up in centres of the Work).

'Each day when I was leaving my mother's house,' Father Josemaría would later confess, 'my brother Santiago would come up and put his hands in my pockets and ask, "What are you taking today to your nest?"'[209]

Ricardo Fernández, the architectural student, was given the job of getting the rest of the furniture. On the shoestring budget that was available, Ricardo found one way of doing it was going to the Rastro, the Madrid flea market, searching among the junk for good quality pieces at bargain prices.

The Academy came into being in the first months of

1934. Father Josemaría decided they would call it the DYA Academy, which were the initials of his apostolic motto, 'Dios y Audacia!' ('God and Daring!'). It could also stand for two of the Academy's courses, 'Derecho y Arquitectura' (Law and Architecture). Father Josemaría also drew the design for an impressive metal name plaque for the front door which Isidoro Zorzano arranged to be cast in a workshop in Málaga.

'The apartment,' Ricardo recalls, 'was relatively small. It had a visitors' room, two small classrooms, a study room, a small living room, a kitchen and an office for Father Josemaría.' But small though the academy was it was able to offer, as well as the law and architecture courses, classes in mathematics, physics, chemistry, and languages.

Pedro Rocamora, who used to serve Father Josemaría's Mass at the chapel of the Patronato, remembers that Father Josemaría had talked to him about the motto God and Daring as early as 1928. 'What Father Josemaría intended,' Pedro says, 'was that each young man should place his trust in God and, seeking to make himself Our Lord's ally and friend, set out to do good throughout the world with apostolic daring ... daring to be an apostle, daring to help the suffering, those in pain and the needy, daring to give advice even if unwelcome and to wrest a friend from the clutches of sin. This was the daring that Father Josemaría preached.'

Father Josemaría heard the young men's confessions in his office. When his room was needed for some class, which was often the case, he moved into the kitchen, which also served as the chemistry lab. He used to joke that he felt he was in a cathedral because so many were going to confession. Father Josemaría also gave classes in Christian formation and spiritual guidance to any students who might be interested.

The students paid only modest tuition fees, which didn't bring in sufficient money to keep the Academy going. It was always a struggle to pay the bills. At one point they had to have a whip-round among the students to pay the overdue rent.

The students were encouraged to study and work very hard. They were also urged to think about the way they treated their parents and other members of the family and how they could improve in this respect. The next step was getting them to think of how they themselves could contribute to making their homes brighter and more cheerful places.

The Academy itself was a very happy place. Students brought their friends and they in their turn brought their friends. Soon the Academy was full to capacity. But Father Josemaría and those running it still found themselves deep in debt and always desperately short of money.

It therefore came as something of a shock to them when Father Josemaría called them together and outlined his ideas for the future. 'The Father suggested to us, to his small group of sons gathered around him,' Ricardo recalls, 'that by the beginning of the 1934–1935 school year, in October 1934, we ought to have a larger place with a residence. Some of us could live there and thus make it possible to have an oratory with Our Lord present in the tabernacle.'[210]

Some of Father Josemaría's fellow priests thought he was mad to try to run any sort of Academy. One very worried and anxious priest specially went to see him to urge him to close it down because it was clearly a failure. And the idea of trying to set up a bigger and better Academy with a residence included was pure insanity. 'It is like jumping out of a plane without a parachute!' he was told.

But Father Josemaría decided it was going to be 'God and Daring' all the way. He felt it was Jesus himself who was spurring him on. The Lord seemed to be encouraging the enterprise. On one occasion Father Josemaría went to see the Countess of Humanes who had recently presented the Academy with a much-needed clock with the request 'not to eat it.' For she had learned that previous clock funds had been used to buy food. The Countess was a very good, devout woman who had never married and had been blind for many years. Father Josemaría told her of his plans for an Academy and residence and asked if she could help. Immediately the countess saw the wisdom in what Father Josemaría was telling her and she agreed to give him something. Although she was very wealthy, and never let anyone who worked for her go without, the countess herself lived in the strictest poverty and did not keep much cash on hand. She got up, went to her safe, took out all her jewels and gave them to Father Josemaría. It is this act of generosity that Father Josemaría refers to in *The Way*:

> What holy resources poverty has! Do you remember? It was a time of financial stress in your apostolic undertaking. You had given without stint down to the last penny. Then that priest of God said to you: 'I, too, will give you all I have.' You knelt and you heard, 'May the blessing of Almighty God, the Father, the Son, and the Holy Spirit, descend upon you and remain with you forever!'
> You are still convinced you were well paid.[211]

This was the decisive contribution. Father Josemaría now felt he had sufficient money for the new Academy and residence.

CHAPTER 25

'The Ravings of a Madman'

Father Josemaría and his family were still desperately hard up and every day they were struggling financially to make ends meet. He decided at this time that one way to help them would be to get rid of the expense of renting the Martinez Campos apartment and move into the house provided for the chaplain of Santa Isabel. He consulted Monsignor Morán, the Vicar General, who gave him permission to apply to the Ministry of the Interior, the Government department that had taken control of the Foundation. Father Josemaría also hoped that this would be a step towards officially being appointed as chaplain and what he thought of as 'stabilising' his position as a priest from an outside diocese working in Madrid. In his application, made on 26 January, 1934 and supported by Sister Maria del Sagrario, the prioress of the convent, Father Josemaría explained that he was carrying out the office of chaplain with no official recompense. He was simply asking to occupy the house provided by the convent for whoever served in that capacity. The reply came a few days later on 31 January, informing him that 'regarding your petition requesting that you be granted residence in the house: because you are temporarily serving as chaplain to the Augustinian Recollect Sisters of the Convent of Santa Isabel, and because of the favourable references given you by said community, this board has decided to grant your request ...' But there was no mention of the possibility of an official appointment. Soon afterwards Father Josemaría learned that Father Huertas, who was still officially the Rector of Santa Isabel was against the idea of him moving into the house and so decided not to do so for the time being. Then, no doubt after much prayer, he found more important reasons for not moving in. These he lists in his journal at this time:

1) My family couldn't live there without me living there too.
2) It wouldn't be good for me to live at the convent because I would be more tied to my family when I am trying to become freer.
3) Jesus wants, for the next school year, a student residence – and I have to live in it.[212]

For about eight years, ever since 1926 or 1927, Father Josemaría had lived an intense devotion to the Holy Spirit, the Third Person of the Blessed Trinity. Because he felt the Holy Spirit, was the least invoked of the Trinity he developed a special devotion to Him. and in April of 1934 he composed this prayer to the Holy Spirit:

Come, O Holy Spirit! Enlighten my understanding in order to know Your commands; strengthen my heart against the snares of the enemy; enkindle my will ... I have heard Your voice, and I do not want to harden my heart and resist, saying, 'Later ... tomorrow.' Nunc coepi! Right now! Lest there be no tomorrow for me. O Spirit of truth and of wisdom, spirit of understanding and of counsel, Spirit of joy and of peace! I want whatever You want; I want because You want; I want as You want: I want whenever You want.[213]

He gave this prayer in manuscript form to Ricardo Fernández, the director of the first Opus Dei residence. And years later Father Josemaría would offer this advice to a priest who was about to give a retreat:

Take with you a treatise of De Deo Trino (a manual on the theology of the Trinity) and pour into their hearts love of the Holy Spirit, and, thereby, love for the Father and for the Son. It's all connected because, from all eternity, the Son is begotten from the Father, and from the love of the Father and the Son proceeds the Holy Spirit. We will never understand this fully, but it doesn't cost me any effort to believe it. Every day I seek to go more deeply into the mystery of the Blessed Trinity.[214] And every year he made the Ten Days' Devotion to the Holy Spirit using the book written by Francisca Javiera del Valle.

In March of 1934 he began giving monthly Days of Recollection for men in a chapel the Redemptorists allowed him to use in Manuel Silvela Street. These Days of Recollection were held on a Sunday from morning to mid afternoon and about twenty to thirty young men attended. They consisted of three or four meditations given by Father Josemaría, the Stations of the Cross, the Rosary, some spiritual reading, a visit to the Blessed Sacrament and an examination of conscience.

Father Josemaría's working day was more crammed-full than ever. And more and more people were coming to him for spiritual direction. For all of them he tried to discover where the Holy Spirit was leading them. Some young men went to him for spiritual direction for years and he never once asked them to consider joining the Work. Others he guided into the priesthood or the religious life. Huego Quesada became a Carthusian monk and entered the Charterhouse of Miraflores after receiving weekly spiritual direction from him. He says that Father Josemaría helped him little by little to have presence of God, to see prayer as a simple and friendly dialogue with God, and to be mortified not only in special circumstances, but as part and parcel of his ordinary life. Father Josemaría's final words to him before he entered the Charterhouse were, 'Off you go, the Holy Spirit is leading you that way.'[215] Many other people Father Josemaría guided towards marriage, helping them to see that marriage was a Christian vocation and that God was calling them to the married state. About the matrimonial vocation, he would tell them:

Christian tradition has often seen in Christ's presence at the wedding feast in Cana a proof of the value God places on marriage, 'Our Saviour went to the wedding feast,' writes Cyril of Alexandria, 'to make holy the origins of human life.'
Marriage is a sacrament that makes one flesh of two bodies. Theology expresses this fact in a striking way when it teaches us that the matter of the sacrament is the bodies of husband and wife. Our Lord sanctifies and blesses the mutual love of husband and wife. He foresees not only a union of souls but a union of bodies as well. God has placed in our body the power to generate, which is a participation in His own creative power. He wants us to use love to bring new human beings into the world and to increase the body of the Church. Thus, sex is not a shameful thing. It is a divine gift, ordained to life, to love, to fruitfulness.[216]

To the end of his life he would tell married couples that what pleased God was that they should 'love one another very much'. He would say, 'The love of Christian spouses ... is like good wine. It improves with time, and appreciates in value ... Well, your love is far more important than the best wine in the world. It is a splendid treasure that Our Lord has wished to grant you. Keep it carefully.'[217]

Father Josemaría was devoting himself more and more to teaching people how to find God in their everyday lives. He did this in a variety of ways. He spoke to people individually. He gave classes. He gave Days of Recollection. He preached at every opportunity. He wrote letters to people. He heard confessions. He helped individuals with spiritual direction. And he continued visiting the hospitals looking after the sick and the dying. While fulfilling all these tasks he still had to find time to study for his law doctorate. Every day he got through an amazing amount of work and apostolate. What surprised people close to him was that he did it without ever seeming to be in a hurry.

Those who knew him in those days were convinced that his secret was prayer, his direct conversation with his Father God. This prayer Father Josemaría considered indispensable when it came to living his contemplative life throughout his whole day of tireless work. Even when he was outside in the street, walking to the various parts of the city, visiting the sick in their homes and in the hospitals, he was always praying, strewing his way with Rosary Hail Marys as he went along. Every day he managed to say all fifteen decades of the Rosary.

A note he wrote in this year of 1934 about his prayer and his dialogue with God reads:

> Prayer – even if I do not give it to You, ... You make me feel it outside the fixed times [these fixed times were half an hour in the morning and half an hour in the afternoon or evening]. Sometimes when I'm reading the paper I have to say to You, 'Let me read!' How good my Jesus is! And I, on the other hand ...[218]

There was, however, in some clerical circles, fierce disapproval of what Father Josemaría was doing. His teaching that marriage was a vocation brought criticism from certain sections in the Church because the word vocation was then used to refer only to a calling to the priesthood or religious life. It was argued that Father Josemaría, by telling people they had a vocation to marriage, was devaluing the 'true vocation' which was the vocation to the priesthood or the religious life. Vocation meant only that, for these critics, and nothing else. And some complained it was idiotic to tell ordinary men and women that they could become saints, and should try to become saints, in their daily work and their everyday ordinary lives. In their view it was just nonsense. More extremists viewed his teachings as the ravings of a madman and, even worse, they considered them heretical. Distorted and fabricated accounts of what was going on at the DYA Academy and what Father Josemaría was teaching then began to circulate.

On Monday, 28 May 1934, Father Josemaría received a note from the Chancery office requesting him to report to the Vicar General, Monsignor Morán. Father Josemaría had regularly kept the Vicar General informed of all he was doing and had always asked his permission for anything he took on, such as giving catechism classes in deprived areas of the city. But it now looked as if a serious complaint or complaints against him had been made to the Vicar General. Father Josemaría went the next day to see him and afterwards recorded what happened in his journal: The Vicar General welcomed me very warmly. He had me sit down (those who frequent the vicariate know well what a distinction this detail implies!), and he said to me, 'Tell me about the DYA Academy.' I told him absolutely everything. Monsignor Morán, with eyes half closed, listened and often nodded in approval.

Basically I told him

1) That I was very happy that he was asking me about this; that in my letters (I write him often) I purposely told him things so that he could ask me whatever he wanted about them.
2) The whole external history of the Work from October 2, 1928, to the present.
3) That we had gone to Luchana knowing that a great friend of his was living there; that we had done this because we had nothing to hide; and
4) About my priest sons; I praised especially the ones I knew, as any father would do.

He in turn,
1) Told me not to stop giving those Days of Recollection during the summer.
2) Let me know that I now had his permission to publish *Holy Rosary* and
3) Here comes the good part – asked me (as if there were no theologians or theological associations at hand in Madrid) to work up a plan of religious studies for university students.[219]

Father Josemaría couldn't have been happier at the outcome of the meeting to which he had been so summarily summoned. It was clear the Vicar General not only approved of what he was doing, but by asking him to work out a plan of religious studies for university students, was in fact giving him his blessing and encouraging him to do much more.

CHAPTER 26

'Josemaría, I've fooled you again!'

One of the reasons Father Josemaría managed to get through so much work was the way he lived order and kept to a plan of life, his daily timetable. Even though he was a very orderly person, he struggled daily to put more and more order into his life and make use of every available minute. He would advise his members, 'If you don't have a plan of life, you'll never have order.'

And he also wrote, 'You told me that to tie yourself to a plan of life, to a timetable, would be so monotonous! And I answered, "It is monotonous because you lack Love."' He believed in doing everything punctually for the love of God. 'If you don't get up at a fixed time you'll never have order,' he would say. 'With order your time will be multiplied, and you will be able to give more glory to God by doing more work in His service.'[220]

To those with disorderly jobs, such as doctors and journalists who had to deal with unforeseen events which could crop up at any time of the day or night, he would say, 'Each one of you has to learn how to construct his own order upon that apparent disorder.'[221]

Ricardo Fernández remembers how tired Father Josemaría used to look when he arrived at the Luchana flat and DYA Academy in those days. 'It hurt me to see him so exhausted. But somehow ... he would pull himself together and begin to see people. And he always did it with an attractive smile overflowing with good humour.

He made life so pleasant for those at his side,' Ricardo recalls.

About those years Father Josemaría would later confide, 'Do you know what I used to do – years ago, I was around thirty at the time – when I was so tired that I could hardly sleep? Well, when I got up in the morning I would say to myself: "You can have a little sleep before lunch." Then when I got out into the street, I would add, seeing all the work that awaited me that day: "Josemaría, I've fooled you again!"'[222]

At the beginning of July 1934 the nuns of Santa Isabel learned that Father Huertas, the priest who was still officially Rector of their Foundation, was about to resign. The nuns thought that this was the opportune time to get their chaplain, Father Josemaría, officially appointed Rector. But when they mentioned this to him he refused to apply for the post because he said Father Huertas had not yet resigned and so the position was not yet vacant.

The prioress, Sister María del Sagrario, thought otherwise. After consulting the rest of her community and the Vicar General, Monsignor Morán, she wrote on 4 July to the Director General of Social Services:

> I am sending you this letter before the Rector proffers his resignation because everyone knows he is leaving, and I am sure there will be priests applying for the position. Although I believe you will not take the step of offering it to any of them, knowing that there is someone already here who deserves the appointment, I am nonetheless taking the liberty of calling him to your attention once more, asking your forgiveness if I offend your delicate sensibilities. Trustfully and affectionately yours, Sister María del Sagrario, Prioress.

Soon afterwards Father Huertas left Madrid but did not formally resign as Rector until 1 October.

Father Josemaría had to inform the Vicar General what had happened, and that the prioress had requested that the civil authority should appoint him Rector of Santa Isabel. 'I myself have not submitted an application,' he says in his letter, 'nor do I intend to do so. I am totally open to whatever God wants and ready to carry out whatever orders you give.'[223]

In the meantime, in the first few days of August, the hottest part of the Spanish summer, Father Josemaría with his sons and his friends searched baking Madrid for a house or apartments that would be suitable for their new combined Academy and residence. They eventually found accommodation spacious enough for the Academy and residence in a block of flats at 50 Ferraz Street, near the Parque del Oeste. These were three large apartments, one on the top fourth floor and two on the floor below. They worked it out that they could have the Academy on the top floor and the residence in the two apartments on the floor below.

But the costs were spiralling. Before the landlord would agree to letting them the apartments he said he wanted a down payment of 25,000 pesetas. Then, they realized a lot of work would have to be done on the apartments to convert them into an Academy and residence. They would have to be redecorated and furnished. Showers would have to be installed for the residents, and beds and linen would have to be bought. They got together the 25,000 pesetas down payment and moved in. After taking over the apartments they had just over three weeks to get the Academy and residence ready for the start of the new academic year. Ricardo Fernández, who was finishing his architectural studies, was appointed director of the Academy and residence. One of his first jobs was to get permission for the residence from the authorities. With the government hostile to anything connected with Christianity, especially people wanting to start up new projects advocating Christian lifestyles and values, this must not have been an easy task. But Ricardo got the required permission. On 30 August Father Josemaría went to the shrine of El Cerro de los Angeles, not far from Madrid, to say Mass. He wrote in his notes:

> After Mass, during my thanksgiving, without having thought of this beforehand, I was suddenly moved to dedicate the Work to the Blessed Virgin. I believe that

this impulse came from God ... I think that today –as simply as that – a new stage began for this Work of God.[224]

A great deal of work still had to done before the Academy-residence could open. All kinds of people came to the rescue offering to lend a hand. University lecturers worked on the floors, engineers painted walls and lawyers and medical students worked as carpenters. The money again ran out. Some of the students responded by offering their savings and Josemaría and his followers went around asking all their friends and acquaintances for donations.

In a letter dated 6 September 1934, Father Josemaría wrote to his friend, Father Eliodoro Gil:

> We are worried. We have rented a new property at 50 Ferraz Street. We have wonderful projects in mind that are perfectly viable and could become realities right away, except that when we put all our money together, we found ourselves 15,000 pesetas short, and we don't know where we're going to get that money. Please earnestly keep this intention in your Masses and in your private prayers.[225]

And in another letter at this time he wrote:

> We are worried about this wretched money ... I can't lie: humanly speaking, I see no possible solution. Yet there must be a solution. We can't turn back now. Prayer, prayer and more prayer.[226]

There is no hint of the financial problems, however, in his letter to Monsignor Morán, the Vicar General, also dated 6 September:

> My dear most venerable Vicar General: Once again I must take up some of your valuable time to inform you, in the first place, of the new address of the DYA Academy. It is now at 50 Ferraz Street. We are renting three apartments there, one for the Academy and the other two as a residence. The house looks really good.

The move will be made about the middle of the month.[227]

With this letter to the Vicar General he had committed himself. There was now no turning back. Like the Conquistador Cortés, he had burned his boats. He decided the only thing left for him to do was to turn to his family for help. With the death of his uncle, Father Teodoro, the family had recently inherited the small estate at Fonz, where his mother and family were now staying. After being so poor ever since the family business failed, they were now comfortably off for the first time in twenty years. But Father Josemaría, after much prayer and penance, had decided to ask them to sell their inheritance. He left Madrid by train on 16 September and shared a compartment with a family that had a monkey with them. As the train rattled along Father Josemaría ignored the antics of the monkey and the noise of the family. He prayed by looking out of the train window and trying to spot churches where Our Lord would be present in the Blessed Sacrament. He wrote in his notes, 'From the moment we left Madrid I kept myself occupied with a heavenly game. I kept scanning the horizon so that I could say something to Jesus every time we passed a tabernacle.'[228]

He spent the night in Monzón and arrived in Fonz the following afternoon. He immediately took all of the family into his confidence, his mother, his sister Carmen and his brother Santiago. He explained to them for the first time about what had happened on 2 October 1928 and the Work God had given him to do: to open up a new way of holiness so that ordinary men and women could become saints in the middle of the world. He then told them that he wanted to ask a special sacrifice of them. Would they sell their small estate at Fonz. And would they let him have the money for the new academy and residence he wanted to open in time for the new academic year which would then be in about two weeks' time.

He was certainly asking a great sacrifice of them. The estate at Fonz was the only thing of value they possessed or were ever likely to possess in the future. But the whole family immediately agreed to sell their recently inherited estate and let him have the money. He suggested they should not make up their minds immediately but take time to think about it. But they told him they didn't want time to think about it. They all said that their minds were made up and they were not going to change them. Afterwards he wrote this letter to his sons in Madrid:

> Fonz, September 7, 1934. May Jesus keep you safe. I arrived this afternoon, at five. I have spoken with Mama and with my sister and brother – I have earnestly commended the matter to Saint Raphael ... and he heard us. My mother will write to you a few lines. Tomorrow I'm going to Barbastro with my sister, Carmen, to set the whole business in motion.[229]

The estate, which included a large farm at Pilau, was then put up for sale and soon found a buyer. The sale, in fact, caused quite a stir in the village. The people in the area thought it very strange that the Escrivás should be dispensing with what they considered to be such a good property.

There is a letter, which Father Josemaría wrote three days after seeing his family and is dated 20 September, 1934. In it he relates exactly what happened and how each member of the family responded to his request. His letter says:

> Fifteen minutes after my arrival in this village (I'm writing from Fonz, though I will be mailing this letter tomorrow from Barbastro), I spoke about the Work, in general terms, to my family. How much I had pestered our friends in heaven, in anticipation of this moment! Jesus caused everything to go very well. I will tell you word for word what their responses were.
> My mother, 'Fine, my son – but don't beat yourself and don't wear a long face.'
> My sister: 'That's what I thought! I even said so to Mama.' [His mother and sister, in spite of his precautions, were well aware of the growing intensity of his mortifications – a clear sign that something important had come into his life.]
> And, the little one [his brother Santiago]: 'If you have sons ... they'll have to treat me with a lot of respect, because I am ... their uncle!'

And right away, all three of them saw it as entirely natural that their money should be used for the Work. Glory be to God, their generosity is so great that if they had millions, they would give that money just as freely.[230]

His mother up to this time had always been a sure source of support for her son but from then on she collaborated with him in an even more effective way. She seconded all he wanted to do and even knew by intuition the things he left unsaid. She subordinated all her plans, for herself and for her family, to those of God and she placed at her son's disposal all the resources she had.

After moving into the Ferraz Street apartments, one of the first things that Father Josemaría and his followers did was to decide which was the best room. This would be made into a small chapel or oratory. For some years Father Josemaría had dreamed of having an oratory where he could say Mass and have the Blessed Sacrament in the tabernacle. Now this dream was about to become true.

Almost immediately more difficulties arose. The political situation suddenly started to worsen. It began to look as if they couldn't have chosen a worse time to open a students' residence. In October 1934, at the beginning of the academic year, the Communists tried to foment revolutionary uprisings throughout Spain so they could take control of the government. This communist inspired revolt, known as the Red-October campaign, eventually failed. There were outbreaks of violence in many parts of the country and a general strike in Madrid but the only part of Spain where the Communists' plan produced anything resembling a revolution was in the Asturian region. Here the uprising turned into a fierce onslaught on the Catholic Church and before the army could regain control of the area fifty-eight churches were destroyed and thirty-four priests murdered.

As a result of the nationwide unrest students from the provinces did not return to the capital and the university postponed the start of its school year.

A minimum of twenty students were needed to make

the residence a viable proposition but even adverts in newspapers failed to produce a single application. Eventually they opened with just one student, a law student.

At the beginning of December the Ministry of Labour, Health and Welfare came to a decision about who would be the Rector of the Santa Isabel Foundation. They chose Father Josemaría. The decree was signed by none other than the president of the Republic, Niceto Alcalá-Zamora y Torres. It read:

> As proposed by the Secretary of, and in accordance with the rules laid down in the Decree of February 17, 1934, I hereby appoint to the position of Rector of the Santa Isabel Foundation Don José María Escrivá Albás [The name was incorrect. It should have been Escrivá de Balaguer], Licentiate in Civil Law. Approved in Madrid on the eleventh day of December in the year nineteen hundred and thirty-four. Signed by Niceto Alcalá-Zamora Y Torres and also by the Secretary of Labour, Health and Welfare, Oriol Anguera de Sojo.

When Father Josemaría went to the Ministry of the Interior to pick up his official letter of appointment he found some official had already drawn up the document confirming his acceptance of the post, giving 19 December as the date of commencement. This created an immediate problem for Father Josemaría. No priest could accept any ecclesiastical position offered by the civil authority without first being authorized to do so by the bishop. He hastened immediately to the Vicar General, Monsignor Morán and told him what had happened. Monsignor Morán's response was to congratulate him and to promise him he would sort out the problem with the bishop. Then, on learning that Father Josemaría's ministerial permits were about to expire, he immediately renewed them until June 1936.

But reaction to Father Josemaría's appointment in certain clerical circles in Saragossa was very different. He learned that some of his fellow priests were very critical of him. They considered that it was a bad thing for a priest to have any dealings whatsoever with the Republic since in their view this suggested an agreement with its anti-religious policies.

The nuns of Santa Isabel, however, had got what they wanted. Their good chaplain, Father Josemaría, was now Rector of their Foundation. And they were delighted. It was in this month of December that Father Josemaría and his Academy-Residence again ran into serious financial trouble. Father Josemaría, optimistic as always, kept saying he was sure they were coming to the end of their difficulties. He turned for help in their financial difficulties to Saint Nicholas. He liked to tell a particular story about St Nicholas. One day, the story went, the saintly Bishop Nicholas heard of the plight of three young women. No young men would marry them because they were not only very plain but, even worse, they didn't have a dowry, a great drawback in those days. St Nicholas's solution was simple. He left a goodly sum of money on their window sill for their dowries. And all three ladies soon afterwards found husbands and ended up happily married.

It is from St Nicholas, pronounced Sancte Nicolaus we get our Santa Claus. So when faced with pressing financial problems, which was so often the case, Father Josemaría would turn to St Nicholas, who was, he would joke, 'the saint for financial difficulties and for marrying the unmarriable.[231]

On Saint Nicholas's feast day, 6 December, with the current difficult financial crisis involving the Ferraz Street Academy-Residence in mind, Father Josemaría appointed St Nicholas as Intercessor. As he was about to say Mass, he promised the saint, 'If you get me out of this one, I will appoint you Intercessor!' But just before going up to the altar he repented and added, 'And even if you don't, I'll appoint you just the same.'[232]

Gradually, the tense political situation throughout Spain began to improve and at the beginning of the new year of 1935 students started to return to the capital. In January the number of their residents had crept up to eight. This was twelve short of the break-even number and produced insufficient income to the pay the rent on both apartments. The only solution, Father Josemaría decided, was to give up the top fourth floor where they had the DYA Academy and move it down to the two apartments on the third floor which was the residence and where there was plenty of room.

Not wanting his young followers to be discouraged he decided to break the news to them in the oratory where he felt he could better help them to look at it from a supernatural point of view. This he did on 21 February. He told them that in life you had to know how to get round difficulties and sometimes you had to take a step back in order to jump further forward.

> Let obstacles only make you bigger. The grace of Our Lord will not be lacking: inter medium montium pertransibunt aquae! – 'through the very midst of the mountains the waters will pass.' You will pass through mountains!
>
> What does it matter that you have to curtail your activity for the moment, if later, like a spring which has been compressed, you'll advance much farther than you ever dreamed?[233]

Afterwards everyone was very happy and full of confidence. The young men prayed harder and redoubled their efforts to bring their friends to the academy. The new Academy-Residence's financial crisis gradually lessened and many other money problems were solved over the years, thanks to what he was convinced was the intercession of St Nicholas.

It was about this time that Father Josemaría moved with his family out of the Martinez Campos apartment and into the chaplain's house at Santa Isabel. He now had to devote most of his time to the Academy-Residence. Though there was no longer a grave financial crisis they were still continually plagued by money problems. At the end of the month there usually was not enough money to pay the rent or the grocery bills and Father Josemaría had often to go to see their landlord and beg him to be patient. It was sometimes very late at night when he left the residence and set off for Santa Isabel. On dark winter nights the streets and alleyways of Madrid held many dangers for priests and his family would wait anxiously for his return. They used to keep looking out for him from one of the windows of the chaplain's house until they saw his cloaked figure emerge from a side street, when they would breathe a sigh of relief. His mother was always anxious until he arrived home.

Father Josemaría was finding that the more he mortified himself the better things progressed. So he increased his mortifications. Ricardo Fernández's bedroom was next door to the bathroom where Father Josemaría used the discipline at the Ferraz Street residence. Ricardo could hear the strokes of the lash through the adjoining wall. He says:

> The Father – I don't know how often – would shut himself up in the bathroom and start hitting himself with the discipline. One time I noticed, because the Father got careless for a moment, that his discipline ... had bits of metal attached. I can't recall if they were nails or steel nuts or what exactly, but I am sure they were pieces of metal. The Father didn't know that I could hear the sound of the lashes, but they used to bother me a lot. I would plug up my ears for a long time, but still the sound of the lashes would go on, whack, whack, whack ... I thought it would never stop. I never dared say anything to the Father, but when he had left, if I went into the bathroom, I could see that the discipline had drawn blood. Despite his careful attempts to clean up, I would find a stretch of the tiled wall spotted with blood ... I would have given anything not to have seen or heard these proofs of his penances.

CHAPTER 27

Enter Alvaro and Pedro

Father Josemaría's prayers, harsh penances and endless apostolic activities continued to bear more fruit. It was at this time, early in 1935, that an engineering student, Alvaro del Portillo, made his appearance. Alvaro, who was destined to play a vital role in Father Josemaría's life, was a brilliant student and a great bullfighting fan. So keen was he on bullfighting that he and some friends occasionally rented a small bullring to practise their matador skills against young bulls. Alvaro was also a devout Catholic. He went to daily Mass and Holy Communion and was a very dedicated member of St Vincent de Paul Society. To help the poor he used to venture into the most deprived and dangerous areas of the city. One such slum area was San Ramón where people struggled to survive in sub-human conditions and were very hostile to the Church and religion. Many lived in shacks made of cardboard and tin cans. The St Vincent de Paul Society provided various kinds of help to these poor people, including money, food and medical care. The student members of St Vincent de Paul also taught catechism in these areas. About a year earlier Alvaro had been badly beaten up as he was on his way to teach catechism with a group of other student members of St Vincent de Paul. It happened on a Sunday, in February 1934. A gang of about fifteen people were lying in wait for the students as they approached San Ramón. The attack had clearly been planned well in advance because the people living there were leaning over their balconies 'waiting for the fun to begin'. In the attack Alvaro was hit with a monkey wrench and received a nasty wound on the back of the head, which poured blood. Another of his companions almost had his ear torn off. Luckily for them they happened to be near a subway. They fled into it and escaped by jumping on the first train that came in. Alvaro arrived home covered in blood and had to be taken to hospital for treatment. His wound then became infected and he went down with a high fever and had to be treated by the doctor every day for quite some time. But this incident didn't put him off helping the poor families in the deprived areas. And it was through his efforts to help the poor that he came to hear of Father Josemaría. One day in 1935 Alvaro was walking through a field of wheat and barley on his way to the Arroyo del Abronigal district when he noticed that three or four of his friends were in deep conversation. So he asked them what they were talking about. They replied, 'Father Josemaría Escrivá and the apostolic work he's doing.' One of the students, Manuel Pérez, then told him some more interesting things about Father Josemaría and afterwards Alvaro said he would like to meet him.[234]

His first conversation with Father Josemaría left a deep impression on him. Alvaro recalls, 'He asked me right away, "What's your name? Are you that nephew of Carmen del Portillo?"'

Carmen del Portillo was indeed his aunt. She was one of his father's sisters and was Alvaro's godmother when he was baptized. Carmen lived with her sister Pilar. Both sisters were single and did a great deal of charitable work. They helped in particular the sisters of Damas Apostólicas and their Foundation for the Sick. And it was during their visits to the Damas at their Foundation that Carmen and Pilar met Father Josemaría after he had become their chaplain. On one occasion when Carmen was speaking to Father Josemaría she told him about her nephew Alvaro. She thought very highly of Alvaro and said that he was a very good young man. 'So, Father Josemaría had remembered me,' says Alvaro, 'and even something else she had told him about me. When I was little she said I liked bananas but couldn't say the word quite right. I would say palátanos instead of the correct word plátanos, the equivalent in English of saying bamamas. So Father Josemaría had added, "Then you're the fellow who likes bamamas so much."'

Though the conversation couldn't have lasted more than five minutes Alvaro sensed Father Josemaría had a great affection for him. Then Father Josemaría suggested they should get together for a longer conversation and they made an appointment for four or five days later. But when Alvaro turned up for the meeting Father Josemaría wasn't there. 'It seems he had suddenly been called to someone who was dying and he couldn't reach me because I hadn't given him my phone number.' Alvaro recalls.[235] So the crucial meeting between the man who founded Opus Dei and the man who was to be his right-hand man and successor was delayed for a few months.

It is about this time that another architectural student, Pedro Casciaro, also entered the story. Pedro, a meticulous observer and note-taker, was, it must be said, quite a character. He was the great grandson of an English gentleman called Peter Casciaro who specialized in mineralogy and accountancy. He moved to Spain to build a railway and then made a fortune working mines, some as far afield as the Russian Urals. He ended up with estates in Spain and Algeria and built a typical Englishman's folly. This was his Los Hoyos estate overlooking the Mediterranean on the outskirts of the village of Torrevieja. The estate is surrounded with walls and is like a fortified castle, with ramparts, sentry boxes and gun emplacements. The locals called it 'The Stockade.' Pedro's father, Peter Casciaro's grandson, was a professor of history and geography. He was also a leading left-wing intellectual and a republican at a time when the word republican was synonymous in many people's minds with 'anti-clerical' and 'anti-Catholic.'

Pedro himself says:

I had picked up a certain distrustful anti-clericalism from my father and was aware of having a strong prejudice against priests and religious, almost like an allergy ... So it was when, in 1935, three years after my arrival in Madrid, that a lifelong friend, Agustín Tomás Moreno spoke to me very highly of Josemaría Escrivá, a priest he had recently met and offered to introduce him to me.

Pedro's first response was to make a sarcastic remark. And when Agustin mentioned the priest again Pedro once more put him off. But Agustin persisted and Pedro finally agreed to meet Father Josemaría.
What made him change his mind?

> I must confess that it was out of curiosity, pure and simple. I was curious by nature. I liked dealing with older people and becoming conversant with new situations, taking everything in, right down to the last detail. Of course, I went along to meet the priest with the resolute intention of not discussing personal matters with him. I was going along to see, to observe, to analyse. No more. Agustin and I arranged to meet one afternoon towards the end of January 1935. He took me to 50 Ferraz Street.

Pedro was in the habit of going around Madrid making sketches of buildings and writing numerous notes about the things he observed. As a result, he provides us with a wonderful description of the new residence and of his first meeting with Father Josemaría:

> We went up to the first floor. As always I was taking notes of everything. Beside the door there was a gleaming plaque which read Academia DYA. We went in. The entrance hall made a good first impression on me. It was not as I had thought it would be. I had imagined a large and rambling place without any warmth. Instead I found myself in the hall of a modest, middle-class family home, tastefully decorated and, above all, extremely clean. The atmosphere was cordial and relaxed. It was a good start. I liked it. We were shown into a little sitting room where we waited for a few minutes.
> Soon a young, smiling priest of thirty of so, came in.

He stopped for an instant, looking amiably at me over the top of his round horn-rimmed glasses, leaning forward very slightly. 'Father, this is my friend Pedro Casciaro,' Agustin said. Then the young priest asked Agustin to excuse us for a few minutes so that we could be alone together. He made me feel as if I were somebody important. We sat down to talk and that conversation was enough to put aside all my reservations at one stroke, for the Father (as we all called him according to the way of addressing priests prevalent at that time) was certainly completely unlike any idea I had formed of him. I had expected an other-worldly character or something equally strange, in accord with the caricature my prejudices had painted. I found instead a young thirty-three-year-old priest who was energetic, cordial and kind, very spontaneous, and natural. Right from the start he infused into me both great confidence and, at the same time, a respect for him far beyond what I owed simply to his years. I was particularly struck by his goodness, his infectious joy, his good humour ... and I poured out my heart to him as I had never done with anybody else in my whole life. I could not say how long we talked. It was probably not more than three-quarters of an hour. I only remember telling him as I said goodbye: 'Father, I would like you to be my spiritual director.'

Pedro didn't have much idea of what a spiritual director or spiritual direction was. All he knew of the subject was that a good friend of his, a fellow architectural student, went to some priest for spiritual direction and he had also seen in newspaper obituaries among the list of mourners the name of priests described as 'his spiritual director'.

That day Father Josemaría also showed Pedro the Oratory or the chapel. Pedro recalls:

I remember it perfectly. It was a quite little chapel in a room off the hall which led to a spacious, peaceful patio. Reverent, simple, and pleasing, it had obviously been done with love. On the front wall above the altar, there was a painting of the disciples at Emmaus talking to the Lord. Soon afterwards, it was replaced by a carved wooden statue of Our Lady of Pilar against a background of olive green damask. As I say, I did like the oratory but as proof of my scanty religious formation, I had not noticed that it had no tabernacle.

Pedro was impressed and, before leaving, arranged to see Father Josemaría on a regular basis.

CHAPTER 28

The Man with a Beard

It was only after meeting Father Josemaría again that Pedro realized that the initial impact he had had on him was not just a passing impression.

> The more I talked to the Father, divulging my innermost self to him, the more I discovered just how fine his spirituality was, and above all, I discovered his tremendous capacity to love and his great understanding. That was not something only I experienced. Many other friends and classmates of mine came to know him too. Like me, they immediately felt understood by the Father. It was clear to see that he really loved us and took us very seriously.[236]

Pedro also came to understand that Father Josemaría took upon himself all their concerns and did not confine himself only to purely spiritual matters:

> I always tried to raise some doubt or query by way of additional material outside my normal confession, so he could answer it for me. However one of the first effects of his spiritual guidance was to uncomplicate in a surprising way my involved mode of being; thus it became more difficult to raise queries because, one after the other, all my doubts were being cleared up.

At one point, for lack of a more satisfactory problem, Pedro decided to ask for advice about a family matter. Pedro's father, who was now the director of the Institute at Albacete, was a little concerned about his son's choice of career. Time and time again his father had said to him, 'An architect! And what if one day there is a crisis in the construction industry? Or if you can't build up a good clientele ...? What you ought to do is carry on and get a Science degree as you have already done the first two years of it. That way if you have problems with architecture in the future, you'll still have another string to your bow.'

His father's suggestion was not at all to Pedro's liking. 'I was willing to do the first two years of the Science degree because it was a sine qua non for getting into Architecture. But Maths/Physics, as we called it, was for me just that: an entry requirement, and that was all.'

When Pedro mentioned his father's suggestion to the Father Josemaría, contrary to Pedro's hopes, Father Josemaría thought the advice extremely well-founded:

> Even though he understood that it would mean a great effort for me, he explained what a good idea it was from a spiritual point of view to have a demanding timetable. He said that this way I would avoid the pitfall of a too laid-back or 'bourgeois' life-style, so common then among students who had succeeded in getting into a specialised school. He talked to me about the apostolate I could do among my fellow students in the science faculty. 'If you can manage it, it would please your father. But think it over.' Those words were a kind of challenge and fired me up enough to enrol the following year for third year in Maths/Physics.

Pedro also managed to persuade one of his classmates at the school of Architecture, Paco Botella, to sign up with him for the additional course. That way Pedro felt 'it would be less boring.'

Paco Botella was a tall, thin young man with a high forehead, who wore thick glasses. Like Pedro he was full of life but very precise in what he said. Initially, their friendship had got off to a very bad start as Pedro recalls:

> During a water-colour painting class I said, in typical student banter, that his drawing of Moses was coming out very well. He was in fact painting Venus. My barbed witticism evidently did not please him too much. My attitude towards him changed when I saw him going to Communion one day in the parish church of the Immaculate Conception which was very near my lodgings. I realised that he might perhaps appreciate the apostolate going on at the Residence. Everything favoured our friendship. We were the same age. He was from Valencia and, though I was born in Murcia, I had roots in Alicante. We were studying for the same subjects . . . and we lived almost next door to each other.

It would be a most eventful year for them both. Pedro and Paco were beginning what would turn into a life-long friendship. They would both be greatly influenced by Father Josemaría and both end up joining Opus Dei.

In those first months of 1935 it was obvious to all those around Father Josemaría how eagerly he was looking forward to having the Blessed Sacrament in the chapel of that first residence. He had hoped to inaugurate the oratory on 19 March, the Feast of St Joseph. Every penny had been spent on providing things for the oratory and no effort had been spared. They had managed to obtain beautiful vestments, a ciborium, a chalice and the oratory furnishings. Mother Muratori, a Reparation nun who had been very supportive, had loaned them a wooden tabernacle. But there were still some other essential items they needed such as the cruets for the water and wine, a paten, a sanctus bell and a tabernacle lamp. And, as they were once again experiencing grave financial difficulties, it seemed impossible they would be able to raise the money to buy them. On the eve of the feast of St Joseph, Father Josemaría made a list of all the things they still needed, and then he put the list away and entrusted the matter to St Joseph.

'In the depths of my soul I was devoted to St Joseph,' he says. 'I began to ask St Joseph to grant us the first tabernacle.'[237]

The very same day the porter of the apartments came up carrying a package that he said a man had left with him. The man, who had given no name, had specifically asked him to take the parcel to Father Josemaría. When Father Josemaría opened the package he found it contained every one of the items he had listed. They had everything required for the oratory. It was never discovered who the mysterious donor was. The only description the porter could give of him was: 'He was a man with a beard.'

Father Josemaría was overjoyed with the mysterious donation. He was convinced that his prayers had been answered by St Joseph himself. As a sign of gratitude he decided to attach to the key of the tabernacle a medallion engraved with the words, 'Ite ad Joseph' ('Go to Joseph') the phrase from the Old Testament used by Pharaoh to tell the Egyptians how they could obtain food during the famine by going to his Chief Minister. From that time on, all tabernacle keys in Opus Dei centres throughout the world have this medallion.

Father Josemaría was at last in a position to ask the Bishop of Madrid for permission to have the Blessed Sacrament in the oratory. On 29 March he received a verbal message from the Vicar General, Monsignor Morán, that he had the Bishop of Madrid's permission to say his first Mass in the oratory on Sunday 31 March. And afterwards he could have the Blessed Sacrament in the oratory tabernacle.

It must have been shortly after receiving this permission that Pedro Casciaro went to have his regular chat with Father Josemaría and found him particularly happy.

> Normally when we met I would do the talking first. The Father would listen very attentively until I had finished, without interrupting at all. He would ask me about my interior life, my studies, my parents, and so on. Then he would give me his advice. Not so that day. It was he who started talking, explaining how the Bishop of Madrid had granted him the permission which they needed to reserve the Blessed Sacrament in the chapel of the hall of residence ...
>
> As I listened to him I was wondering to myself how it

could be. For if there were a single institution in Madrid where the faith was really lived out in a wonderful way – I thought – it was in that residence, and if there were an exceptionally holy and intelligent priest, he was the one in front of me at that moment. So, in my ignorance I concluded that the bishop really should have given his permission sooner!

Father Josemaría spoke at length about the Eucharist in words which revealed his deep and sincere devotion to Jesus in the Blessed Sacrament. 'Our Lord must never feel lonely or forgotten here, even if He sometimes is in some churches. Here, in this house, where so many students live and so many young people come, He will be happy in the midst of all our devotion. You help me keep Him company.' I was moved by his ardent love for the Eucharist. Since I passed fairly near the hall of residence on my way to the School of Architecture, I enthusiastically decided to pop into the oratory as often as I could to pray for a while in front of the tabernacle. It must have been then that he dictated to me the words of the spiritual communion, 'I wish Lord, to receive you with the purity, humility and devotion with which Your Holy Mother received You, with the spirit and fervour of the saints.'[238]

The first Mass in the oratory, on 31 March 1935, the last day of the month, was dedicated to St Joseph and was a very special occasion. The oratory was packed. The altar was adorned with flowers and rows of candles of graded size sloped upwards toward the Crucifix above the tabernacle. Father Josemaría before giving communion said a few words of thanks to their new 'Resident' – Jesus.

Afterwards he encouraged all the students and their friends to pay a visit to Him, present in the Blessed Sacrament of the new chapel. He told them that they should go often and speak to Jesus in the tabernacle. 'Our Lord has been waiting for you there for twenty centuries,' he would say.[239]

With the Blessed Sacrament in the tabernacle the atmosphere in the residence became even more happy and homely. The students would contribute to collections for the destitute and poor in the deprived areas. And they would also help people they called 'Our Lady's poor'. These were people who had come down in the world but were trying to hide their hunger and poverty because they felt very ashamed. The students would visit them and take them a special treat or perhaps a book they wanted to read but couldn't afford to buy. The number of Sunday catechism classes also multiplied at this time and soon Father Josemaría was giving a second Day of Recollection together with a class of formation for workers in Carabanchel.

'Since we have had Jesus in the tabernacle of this house,' Father Josemaría would write about this time, 'it's been phenomenally noticeable: He came, and our work increased in both range and intensity.'[240]

In April there were six more residents. This brought the total to fourteen, six less than the number needed to break even, which meant they were still losing money every week. Father Josemaría was also finding that he was having another unexpected cross to bear. This was the criticism of some of the priests he had been gathering around him since 1931 to collaborate with him in the Work God had given him to do. Some of them told him that the Academy-Residence was a failure, a disaster in fact. They insisted that he had made a serious error of judgement and should close it down. Father Josemaría consulted with his spiritual director, Father Sánchez and with his good friend Father Poveda as to whether they thought he had committed a serious error or judgment. Both encouraged him to continue. What was happening, they said, was undoubtedly a trial from the Lord.

Some of the priests began so vigorously opposing what he was doing that instead of helping him, they became a hindrance and an added burden.

Both Father Sánchez and Father Poveda advised him to have nothing further to do with some of them. But in his notes at this time he writes:

> Rather than follow the advice of Father Sánchez and Father Poveda (implicit in the case of the former and

very clearly stated by the latter) to throw out those priests ... I chose instead – because I saw the virtuousness of all of them, and their undeniable good faith – the middle course of putting up with them, keeping them outside the activities specific to the Work but always, when need be, making use of their priestly ministry.[241]

Despite their continued opposition he retained a special affection for those diocesan priests, several of whom would die as martyrs because of their priesthood in a little over a year's time.

What became clear to him, as a result of this conflict with his fellow priests, was that in future the priests needed for the expansion of the Work would have to come from the ranks of laymen formed in the spirit of Opus Dei.

As the months of 1935 went by, more students were attracted to the residence by the warmth and cheerfulness they found there, especially after having negotiated Madrid's politically venemous and treacherous streets.

The residence was for them like a safe haven. And for many it seemed more like a home from home. The students and their friends in fact treated it as if it were their home. Like members of one big, happy family they joined in helping with the work that needed doing around the place. They knocked nails into the walls to hang pictures, they moved furniture around and helped rearrange the rooms or did any other odd jobs. Every day more and more new faces appeared, until the residence regularly overflowed with young people

At about this time, Pedro Casciaro gives us this fascinating glimpse of how Father Josemaría was bringing him closer to God, through weekly spiritual guidance. This was being done, Pedro explains:

> not all of a sudden, but little by little, patiently, with an intensity which increased with time, without rushing things but without slackening off either. He was teaching me how to pray for a little while every day; how to

converse with the Lord and keep up a continuous awareness of being in His presence throughout my day as a normal ordinary student.

With regard to this last practice, one day I brought up the difficulty I had over it. 'You see, Father, when I really get down to something I put all I've got into it and completely forget everything else.' That was true. When I was studying, I would get so engrossed in my books that the hours flew by without a single reference to the Lord. Even while drawing I was so wrapped up with the problems of descriptive geometry that it seemed to me there was no room in my mind for anything else. In reply the Father presented me with a Crucifix, which I still have, for me to carry around in my pocket and place on my desk or on the drawing board. 'Glance at the Crucifix now and again, or say a few aspirations, and you will be able to turn your work into prayer'. What about remembering that I was in the Lord's presence as I walked through the streets?' That was not too easy either. I loved walking around Madrid gazing at the facades of buildings, studying the structure, or analysing the architectural hits and misses which I found along the way. The Father was asking me to do all this and be absorbed in God all at the same time! But how? 'Let's see,' he said, 'Tell me exactly which streets you go along from Castello Street where you live to the School of Architecture or the University.' I started to recall them ... He then listed the images of the Blessed Virgin which I could locate on my way. 'On Goya Street there is a pastry shop, just round the corner from Castello Street, which has a figure of the Immaculate Conception in a niche. When you reach the statue of Christopher Columbus, as you cross the Castellana, you will find in one of the bas-reliefs round the pedestal of the statue a scene of the Catholic King and Queen, where there is an image of Our Lady of Pilar; and as you go up the Boulevards ...' I was amazed. I, who observed everything so carefully, had not even noticed the existence of those images which could help me to remember God's presence on my daily round. Then I realised that this was not simply the result of the Father's keen powers of observation. Only a soul in love with Our Lady could have detected them. From that day on I tried to put into practice what he told me. Little by little, my working hours acquired a new supernatural meaning, and my walks through the streets of Madrid, new contemplative perspectives, totally unsuspected until then.[242]

It was at this time, May 1935, that Father Josemaría began putting down on paper the future role that married men and women would play in the Work. They would, he envisaged, carry the light of Christ into the very heart of human activities, in their professional, family and social lives.

CHAPTER 29

Alvaro's Decision

Pedro Casciaro, because he was taking both architecture and maths/physics courses, was having to study very hard for the innumerable exams he now had to take. But he still managed to continue with his regular spiritual direction with Father Josemaría. Pedro says that in the midst of all his hard work the Father was helping him

> To live an increasingly devout life without ever diminishing or submerging any of my legitimate human aspirations. On the contrary, he made it more possible for me to achieve them. I knew the essentials about Opus Dei. I knew Opus Dei was a way towards holiness in the midst of the world for ordinary Christians through sanctifying their everyday work. The Father explained it to us in these or similar words: The divine paths of the earth have been opened up. What did we have to do to become saints? The Father had told us in many different ways, but it can be summed up admirably in this one phrase of his: 'Get to know Jesus Christ; make him known, take him into every place.'
> Although I did not belong to the Work, in a way I felt part of it; not just one person in a small group owing its existence to particular local conditions of the moment, but part of an incipient apostolic undertaking that would last for all time. The Father shared with us his universal longing for apostolate. He had got us to pray

for the future expansion of the Work. We knew that learning languages such as German and Russian, which he also insisted on, had a compelling apostolic raison d'être. Opus Dei had to spread to all four corners of the earth.

At the end of June 1935, with the exams over and the academic year ended, Pedro left Madrid and headed for his holidays on the family's Los Hoyos estate at Torrevieja. There in the relaxed and easygoing atmosphere he became aware of the absence of the spiritual striving and great ideals which the Father was passing on to them. Then something happened. 'Caught up by this holy impatience for Jesus to be loved, I too desired to make Him known and to take Him to thousand of souls,' he says. His feelings he found reflected in a point in *The Way*: 'So it is, so it has to be, with the horizon of your apostolate; the world has to be crossed. But there are no paths made for you. You yourselves will make the way through the mountains with the impact of your feet.'

The phrase 'Through the mountains ...' repeated itself in his mind. He realized that he had not queried till then exactly how this future growth of Opus Dei was to happen:

> Nevertheless I was certain the Work would spread to all five continents one day. How I had no idea. But I was convinced that one day it would be so. Of that I had no doubt. It was part of the faith I had in the Father's words. When would it happen? I thought then that its expansion would occur many years later, and I suspected I would hardly witness it in my own lifetime. As can be seen, I had understood the basics about Opus Dei. But little did I appreciate what the Father meant when he said to us: Dream and your dreams will fall short. Yet despite my lack of vision, I did want to help the Work grow insofar as I was able. Deep down, I felt an increasing desire to make Our Lord known. Indeed, I too wanted to take Jesus everywhere! But I did not know how to. And I wondered how in the future I would be able to make the demands of family and

profession compatible with the burgeoning desire to participate somehow in the work of apostolate. I experienced a strange yearning; it was the same old itch for adventure, except that now it was for a much higher and more noble ideal than when I had gazed out across the blue sea at the steamships laden with salt, sailing out from the Torrevieja Port for unknown lands.[243]

The academic year had also ended for Alvaro del Portillo, the engineering student who had first met Father Josemaría about six months earlier but had missed him on their next appointment because Father Josemaría had been called to someone who was dying. Just before going off on vacation, on Saturday, 6 July 1935, Alvaro decided he would once more look up Father Josemaría. On this occasion he was able to have a nice leisurely talk with him about many things. Afterwards Father Josemaría said to him, 'Tomorrow we'll be having a Day of Recollection, so why don't you stay around and make the Day of Recollection with us before leaving for your vocation?'

Alvaro somehow felt that he didn't dare say no. 'But,' as he said later, 'I wasn't very enthusiastic about it, since I didn't know what it was all about.'

The next day, Sunday, 7 July, Alvaro duly turned up at the Ferraz Street residence for the monthly Day of Recollection. Father Josemaría gave three meditations in the morning and two in the afternoon. Alvaro remembered that one of Father Josemaría's meditations in the morning was 'about love for God and love for Our Lady which left me aglow.'

He was so moved by Father Josemaría's preaching that Sunday morning that there and then he decided to commit his life to Opus Dei. He went to tell Father Josemaría of his decision thinking it would surprise him. But it was Father Josemaría who surprised him. He told Alvaro again how four years earlier his aunt Carmen had spoken to him about her nephew, Alvaro. 'I've been praying for you ever since,' he said.

Father Josemaría then advised Alvaro that he would have to write a few lines to ask for admission to Opus Dei. 'I wrote four lines in true engineer style,' Alvaro recalls. 'I started off by saying, "I know the spirit of the Work and want to ask for admission" – something like that.'[244]

Alvaro at the time was just twenty-one years old. And he would in later years say it was then that he began his 'true existence'. For forty years he would live at the side of the founder of Opus Dei and be his great helper and close companion. Alvaro was one of the first three members of Opus Dei who were ordained priests and from that time on was Father Josemaría's confessor. Alvaro was a man, Father Josemaría always believed, who had been sent by God to be at his side. After Father Josemaría's death in 1975 it was Father Alvaro who was unanimously elected to succeed him as President General of Opus Dei. And when Pope John Paul II established Opus Dei as a Personal Prelature, on 28 November 1982, Alvaro became its first Prelate.

Despite his exhausting schedule in that year of 1935, Father Josemaría put together a course of formation specially for Alvaro. For his part Alvaro would never forget how Father Josemaría's affection for sons was shown in the way he spent himself, giving them formation and never allowing tiredness to get the better of him. 'When I asked to join the Work,' Alvaro says, 'the Father, exhausted as he was by the amount of work he already had to do, did not hesitate to start a series of classes of formation just for me. It was just one more burden that he added to the numerous demands that already filled his days.'

Regarding his early formation given him by Father Josemaría, Alvaro recalls, 'He encouraged me to say many aspirations, to make many spiritual communions, and to offer up many small mortifications during the day.' It was from what Father Josemaría told him at this time about making aspirations, or very short prayers, that Alvaro, many years later, was able to solve the mystery of the pebbles which Father Josemaría used to pick up and put in his pocket when he was a young priest in his first parish of Perdiguera.

It was after Alvaro had succeeded him and was then Bishop Alvaro del Portillo, that he was told about the pebbles. He then remembered that during his early courses of formation Father Josemaría had told him:

> There are spiritual authors who recommend counting the aspirations said over the course of the day, using beans, peas or something similar. They suggest putting them in one pocket and moving them to the other whenever you raise your heart to God with one of these prayers. In this way you can see exactly how many prayers you have said, and whether or not progress has been made that day. But I don't recommend this to you, because there is also the danger of vanity or pride. It is better to let your Guardian Angel do the counting.

'Obviously while he was in Perdiguera,' Alvaro concluded, 'he was using this little device to see how well he was living the presence of God. But he afterwards abandoned this practice, presumably for the very reason he gave me.'[245]

One of the first things Alvaro noticed about Father Josemaría was his closeness to God.

> I can testify that his union with God grew year by year, in a marvellous crescendo, until the very end of his life. As far back as 1935, when I barely knew him, it was obvious to me that he thought only of Our Lord and his service. He gave to every task he carried out his full attention, but at the same time was completely immersed in God. He truly lived the counsel he gave to others: 'Keep your feet on the ground and your head in heaven.' By both word and example he taught us how to put all our faculties at the service of our daily tasks – in professional work, in the priestly ministry, in whatever area – but always with our thoughts turned to the Lord ... This union with God was nourished by specific periods of time devoted to mental prayer: as a rule, half an hour in the morning and half an hour during the afternoon. He established this practice as a norm also for all his sons and daughters.

And Father Josemaría would later comment:

> It is not enough to spend the whole day in prayer, as, with the help of God's grace, all of us strive to do, seeking to live in Our Lord's presence at every moment. It's not enough, just as it would not be enough to have radiators in every room of the house – one also needs a furnace. For us, the furnace is those two half hours of mental prayer.[246]

From the first day that Alvaro met Father Josemaría he noticed something else. That not only during his personal prayer, but also whenever he preached a meditation or gave a class, and all the time he spent working at his desk, he kept before him a crucifix. And Alvaro noted it was always the same one:

> It was of a fairly good size, four or five inches in length, which (until about 1950) he constantly carried it around in his pocket. His brother Santiago, struck by the size of it, would remark – using a term used to described pistols by the military – that it was a 'regulation' crucifix. You might say that the Crucifix was in fact the weapon of the Father.

He was also impressed by the way Father Josemaría lived the virtue of poverty.

> I noticed that he often referred to the virtue of poverty with an expression that was full of meaning for him: 'Poverty, my great lady.' That's what he called it from the time he was thirty-one or thirty-two years old to the end of his life. What he was talking about was not privation for its own sake, but rather a true treasure which leads to a real personal union with Christ, in the nakedness of Bethlehem and of Calvary: a prerequisite of the effectiveness of an apostolate. And that's why none of us was surprised at the insistence with which he encouraged us to live a life of poverty. He was always illustrating this with concrete, compelling examples: 'Don't hold on to anything as if it were your own' ... 'Have nothing superfluous' ... 'Don't complain when you lack something necessary' ... 'When the choice is up to you, take the

poorest thing, whatever is least desirable' ... 'Don't mistreat the objects you use' ... 'Make good use of time.'

And Alvaro also records what Father Josemaría said to him about the death of one the first members, Luis Gordon, who was a wealthy businessman.

> The death of Luis was providential, because it meant that Opus Dei had to continue to grow in the greatest poverty. If he hadn't died, we would have had material means, temporal means, which might have been harmful to us. It was necessary that this Work of God should have been born in poverty, just as Jesus was.

And Alvaro also recalls a time during the Spanish Civil War when Father Josemaría was in Burgos and learned of the death of José Isasa, another member of the Work who had been studying architecture.

> The news was given to him by José's parents, very good people who were, of course fully aware of the vocation of their son. Not long before he died, the young man had expressed the wish that everything that he had be given to the Work. But Father Josemaría decided not to ask for anything, even though there were serious financial problems and the relatives of the dead young man were very favourably disposed. He chose this course of action out of a conviction that the Lord would be better pleased with our perseverance in poverty.[247]

Alvaro also witnessed, then and later, what he calls 'the heroism with which Father Josemaría mortified his sight.'

> He imposed on himself concrete renunciations, even in matters of legitimate curiosity. He did not gaze into shop windows, and when travelling by car he often decided not to look out of the car window, thus giving up the pleasure of enjoying the scenery. He would often explain that 'seeing' and 'looking' are two very different things; that seeing is a neutral physiological fact, while

looking involves the application of the will in observing with attention, to weigh the details. The Father did not 'look'.

In those early days Father Josemaría set Alvaro a special task. 'From the beginning of my vocation, in 1935, the Father encouraged me to study Japanese,' Alvaro says 'which I did, though not with very encouraging results!'

Having postponed his vacation until August, Alvaro then went to stay with his family who were holidaying at La Granja. While there he spent much of his time doing apostolate with his friends, one or two of whom, because of his efforts, very soon became interested in Opus Dei.

CHAPTER 30

Dangerous Journeys

Pedro Casciaro's vocation, compared with Alvaro's, was a little more protracted and a little more complicated. In September Pedro was back at his books in Madrid and reunited with his fellow students. One of them was Miguel Fisac who had stayed in the capital all summer long and had continued assiduously going to the Ferrez Residence.
Pedro recalls:

> He seemed rather restive and, as we knew each other very well, I asked him what the matter was,' He explained that he was considering the possibility of becoming a member of Opus Dei. Being a member of Opus Dei! That was something new to me. Then I understood there was a small group of students and professional men who had given their lives to God. Here was the way to make those apostolic ideas I had dreamed of in Torrevieja a reality. My friend was in the throes of a vocational crisis, asking himself if this was really what God wanted of him. I tried to soothe him. But, trying to calm him down, I came to feel troubled myself. I began to wonder, 'And what if God should call me to take that path? What if . . . ?' I thought the best way of settling my growing anxiety was to ask the Father about it. For, I repeat, the Father had never made the slightest suggestion along those lines. Nor had he given me any specific advice or directives. Even though it was

he who had sown in my soul a profound desire to seek sanctity at all costs and the urge to know and love God's will and to respond as generously as I could to the Lord, he had always left me completely free. He had never spoken directly about the possibility of my giving my life to God in Opus Dei. I felt completely at sea.

But Pedro began to wonder if Our Lord really was asking him for something. And if that were the case, what was the 'something' He was asking for?

I went to see the Father and related my unease. He suggested leaving all my worries in the Lord's hands since He is God of peace. Restored to a relative degree of tranquillity I continued visiting the Residence where some changes had taken place. The house was now full of students lodging there, many of them from Bilbao. So many university students were coming to various types of spiritual formation which the Father offered that the Circles (the name given to these meetings for spiritual formation) took place wherever there was a free room, because there were times when we could hardly fit in the house. Meanwhile I went on talking to the Father, who was helping me overcome the spiritual decline which often results from summer holidays. He encouraged me to live in God's grace and not forsake a short plan of life, which as yet did not include daily Communion, but just on Sundays and sometimes Saturdays. I started to struggle with those aspects of my Christian life with renewed effort; but I found that as I grew closer to the Lord my uneasiness about a possible self-giving to God in Opus Dei welled up once more in my soul. Then perhaps to counteract that spiritual agitation, I tried to enjoy myself for the next few weeks. Perhaps I went too far. I went to the cinema often with friends who did not go to Ferraz Street. We spent more money than usual.

It reached the point where his friend Paco Botella received a letter from his father saying that his friend of his, Pedro Casciaro, might well be a great chap as he said, but that since becoming friends with him he was becoming a complete spendthrift!

Father Josemaría had taken to the new Ferraz Street residence his small statue of Our Lady 'My Lady of the Kisses'. And he never went in or out of the residence without first kissing the statue.

'I don't think I ever did it mechanically,' he says. 'It was a human kiss, the kiss of a son who is afraid ... It was the kiss of a son who was worried that he was too young and who went to seek in Our Lady all the tenderness of her affection. I went to seek all the fortitude I needed in God through the Blessed Virgin.'[248]

And every day he became more and more convinced that the Work was born and was developing 'under the mantle of Our Lady'.

CHAPTER 31

'Woman is Stronger than Man'

Pedro Rocamora was a young man who used to serve Mass for Father Josemaría at Santa Isabel. Pedro was greatly impressed by the way Father Josemaría said this daily Mass. This is how he describes it: 'Each word he said had a profound meaning. He savoured the concepts. Father Josemaría seemed to be detached from human surroundings and was, as it were, tied to the divinity by invisible bonds.'

It was at Santa Isabel that Father Josemaría was able to hear the confessions of the first women members. These women had started going to him for confession and spiritual guidance because they, like Pedro Rocamora, were so impressed by the way he said Mass.

Working with women, however, was proving to be much more difficult than with men. With men, he could give them spiritual direction anywhere, in the street or in a cafe or in a flat. But to give spiritual direction to women he needed the fixed grille of a confessional in a public church, as Canon law laid down in those days. One of the things he used to say to them was that they had to try to become saints. 'Woman is stronger than man,' he would tell them, 'and more faithful at the hour of trial: Mary Magdalene and Mary Cleophas and Salome. With a group of valiant women like these, closely united to our sorrowful Mother, what work for souls could be done in the world!'[249]

Father Josemaría wanted his followers, men and women, to be like the early Christians described in a letter written in the second century to Diognetus:

> They do not live in towns reserved for them alone, nor do they use a dialect of their own. Their manners have nothing unusual in them. They live in Greek or barbarian cities as chance dictates. They conform to the local customs in matters of food and clothing. While at the same time they manifest the strange and paradoxical laws of their way of life. The Christians are in the world the way the soul is in the body.

And Father Josemaría would write:

> You want to be a martyr. I'll place martyrdom within your reach: to be an apostle and not call yourself an apostle, to be a missionary – with a mission – and not call yourself a missionary, to be a man of God and to seem a man of the world: to pass unnoticed.[250]

On 15 September 1935 he went on retreat at the Redemptorists' house in Madrid, spending the whole week in silence and prayer. As soon as he returned from his retreat he started to make fresh plans for expansion. The following year in 1936, he said he wanted the Work to spread to another city in Spain and to another country. The next city in Spain would be Valencia and the next country would be France. And they would take the Work to the very heart of France, to Paris.

At the time Father Josemaría was making these plans, Pedro Casciaro and Paco Botella were drawing ever close to the Work. They had such a packed timetable for their lectures and classes that they didn't seem to have so much as a free minute. 'Paco and I were always in a rush; from the house to the university, from there to the School of architecture and back again to the university,' Pedro recalls.

Then one day in October, a few weeks after Father Josemaría had returned from his retreat, Paco happened to mention to Pedro that he noticed that on some evenings after classes had finished Pedro, instead of heading towards the boulevards, went off somewhere else with a group of friends. Pedro told him that he and his friends went to the Ferraz Street residence and he then explained the work of apostolate which Father Josemaría was doing. Paco replied that he would like to meet this priest and asked Pedro to arrange a time.

Pedro precisely notes what happened next: 'The Father met him two days later on October 13 at 5pm'. Paco then started going to the Circles on Saturdays and their friendship deepened ...

> We used to go everywhere together, the Ferraz Residence included. Both of us also went with other classmates from the School to spend three days in Toledo. Before going I took leave of the Father. He advised me to make the most of those days, to do as much good as I could to my friends. He also said I should try to go to Mass. It was a wonderful three days. We did a lot of sketching in the city, with its ochre-coloured buildings clustered around the cathedral and almost entirely surrounded by the riverbed of the Tagus. I thought it was splendid, as though time had stood still there. I loved the cathedral, the Alcazar, the synagogues, the famous country houses on the banks of the Tagus; so much so that at the end of the trip Paco and I decided to stay two days longer. During this time we talked a lot about the Father and the vocation to Opus Dei as we wandered up and down the steep winding city streets or drank coffees in Zocodover Square. Paco's restlessness brought mine from a few weeks earlier to the surface again. Paco had been turning over the question of a vocation for years. In fact he had come to Madrid with the inner certainty that it would be there that God would make him see his vocation. My spiritual disquiet was equally intense, though much more recent. Anyway, we were both facing the possibility in all it radicalness of giving ourselves completely to God.
> On our return to Madrid I decided to attend a monthly Day of Recollection ... Paco came too.

Paco gives us these details of the recollection:

> The Father spoke in the oratory on a single central theme in all the meditations and talks. That topic was vocation. He talked about the rich young man who refused to respond to the Lord's call and went away sad; the Father encouraged us to be generous with God. Pasco notes that the love of God, which shone through the Father's words, 'took us with a force which was supernatural'.

And Pedro says,

> As with Paco that Day of Recollection was decisive for me. In the first meditation on the rich young man I saw quite clearly that I could not do what the young man in the Gospel did – go away sad. At the end of the recollection I sought out the Father and asked him to let me be a member of Opus Dei. Again the Father advised me to be at peace. He said it was better for me to wait a little and in the meantime to intensify my spiritual plan of life.
> For how long? At first he spoke in terms of one month. A whole month! It seemed so long. I asked him to make it shorter. Could it not be in weeks? 'Father,' I explained to him, 'since I began wondering about a vocation I've had no peace. I can't concentrate on my studies, and these days I have a lot of study to do!' I insisted so much that I achieved a shortening of the term to nine days. He advised me to make a novena before coming to a decision. Nine days? At that moment nine days seemed an eternity to me. Couldn't it be fewer? 'Do a triduum,' (three days) he conceded finally. 'Commend yourself to the Holy Spirit and act in full freedom, because where the Spirit of the Lord is, there is freedom.' He spoke a lot about freedom and advised me to ask God, as I received Holy Communion over the next three days, for the necessary graces so as to make my decision freely. 'In libertate vocati estis.'
> I cannot think of a single person who got to know the Father reasonably well without being captivated by his

cheerfulness, his constant good humour, his extraordinary way with people, and his love of freedom. Concerning this last point, I should like to observe that I was very independent. My self-reliance was due both to my character and to the way in which I had been brought up. Perhaps that was why the Father's teaching on valuing people's freedom of conscience was so dear to me. He was always reminding us that love of freedom consists above all in defending other people's freedom. He said: 'We have been called in freedom as Scripture teaches.'

I started the triduum to the Holy Spirit on Monday November 18. When I finished it, my decision to give myself to God in Opus Dei was reaffirmed. I decided to make a formal request to the Father for admission to the Work. The Father had already told me that the way to ask for admission was by a handwritten letter addressed to him. Naturally, people who were asking to join gave him their letters by hand. I do not know why, but I thought I had to send my letter through the mail and wait for a reply. Which is what I did. I wrote the letter, posted it . . . I calculated that the Father would get it the next day. So, I thought, that when I went to Ferraz Street again to talk to the Father five days later, he would have had enough time to consider his answer. During those uncertain and expectant days I talked things over with Paco. On the day I was to talk to the Father, Paco and I were studying together before lunch in his hall of residence. I seem to recall that we were working on some cosmography experiments. Paco did the calculations on a blackboard and I looked up the corresponding logarithms. But I was unable to concentrate. I was thinking about my vocation the whole time, constantly losing the thread and making mistakes. I could not keep my finger on the right line in the log tables, the result being that Paco ended up losing his temper with me. I apologised, telling him my mind was elsewhere. When he heard that he became worried and asked me over and over again what was the matter.

It was then Pedro told Paco he had decided to join the

Work and that he was going to see the Father that same afternoon. Paco's response was to want to know what the Work was and Pedro gave this explanation to him. It was, he said, to give oneself to the Lord totally, while continuing in the world as before, more committed to it than ever, yet carrying the Lord in one's heart at every moment of the day, while at work, and while doing apostolate. It was, he added, like the life of the early Christians.

Pedro recalls:

> As soon as I had explained the Work to Paco, I asked him what he thought of my decision. As he had much more religious formation that I had, I realise now that his answer would have had a lot of influence on me, for better or for worse. But he refused to comment. He only listened to me with great interest and asked various questions. I kept on insisting: 'But, Paco, what do you think? Tell me clearly.' He was not to be drawn. That surprised me. When we said good-bye he became very thoughtful. After lunch we met again in a Maths lecture. We left before it ended and continued talking about my vocation as we went along the boulevards in the direction of Ferraz Street. It was then that Paco told me that he too was going to ask for admission to the Work. 'You as well?' I felt great surprise and a great joy. But first of all he had to talk to the Father, and Paco wanted me to tell him. When we got to 50 Ferraz Street he kept insisting, 'Tell the Father that I want to join the Work. Tell him Pedro, tell him!' That night I telephoned Paco to let him know that the Father would see him at 6pm, three days later. And so it was, three days later, that he talked to the Father, who let him ask for admission to Opus Dei immediately. The speed of it was quite a surprise for me. Later I understood that it was perfectly fair, taking into account Paco's deep religious formation and his long desire to give himself fully. And so, thanks to this chain of circumstances we both ended up asking for admission to Opus Dei at practically the same time.

Two more for the lunatic asylum. Father Josemaría was delighted.

Though something was troubling Father Josemaría at this time. He was unhappy about not being able to have a better tabernacle in the chapel of the Ferraz Street residence. The one they had been loaned was a very poor one made of wood. And it also saddened him to have to give solemn Benediction with a monstrance of little value, one made of iron; only the lunette which held the consecrated host was of silver.

Alvaro says,

> Since that time I heard him say that he wanted to use only precious objects for the worship of Our Lord, even if he had to go hungry to do it. Again and again, and particularly in the last years of his life, I heard him say this: 'People today are so stingy towards Our Lord. And I just don't understand it. Even if there were a man alive who would give to the woman of his dreams a piece of iron or concrete as a present, not even then, would I give to my Lord a bit of iron or concrete, but always the very best that I could.' Throughout his life he sought to give to the service of the Lord the very best that he had. I know that shortly after 1928 he wanted to commission the making of a chalice that would have a precious stone encased in its base in such a way that nobody could see it. It was to be a hidden sacrifice, something for Our Lord's eyes only. Many years later after he had moved to Rome he was finally able to realise this dream of his when a lady gave him a very large emerald.

Pedro Casciaro and Paco Botella went off to spend the Christmas of 1935 with their families. It was the last Christmas before the Civil War. Before setting off they raised with Father Josemaría the possibility of living in the Ferraz residence after the holidays, which he thought was a good idea.

During the Christmas holidays Paco received an apostolic assignment. Father Josemaría asked him to inform the auxiliary Bishop of Valencia, Monsignor Javier Lauzurica, of his wish to begin work in Valencia.

A General Election, the Government then announced, would be held on 16 February 1936. Towards the end of

1935 left-wing politicians again began attacking religious beliefs and practices and once more tensions mounted.

Manuel Azaña was the leader of the Left and one of the key figures behind these attacks. He was not a Communist but he was anti-clerical and committed to a policy aimed at destroying religion. He liked to boast, 'Spain has ceased to be a Catholic country.'

Father Josemaría at this point decided it would be too dangerous for him and his family to remain at the Santa Isabel chaplain's house. There wasn't time to search for another apartment so as a temporary measure he quickly moved his family into a boarding house. And he asked Pedro Casciaro if he could lend a hand and help his family move out of the Rector's house.

Pedro says, 'Perhaps because of a certain flair I had for moving furniture around, the Father asked me if, classes permitting, I could lend a hand with the removal.'

Pedro remembers that it was one Saturday that he and Paco went to meet Father Josemaría's mother. And it is from Pedro that we learn that because of the great love and affection the members of Opus Dei had for Father Josemaría's mother they had begun calling her 'Grandmother'.

Pedro leaves us this description of her:

> Although she was about sixty and had prematurely white hair, her face was still young. She radiated dignity, serenity and gentleness, and at the same time there were traces of interior suffering. I was under the impression that her eyes were tearful.

Paco, who was also helping with the removal, thought the cause of her tears was the fact that the Father wanted a bed to be left in the Rector's house. As their chaplain in such dangerous times he didn't want to abandon the nuns. Pedro also says,

> I was very shy at my first meeting with Grandmother ... I did not know how to address her. I settled for Señora. She was very much a lady in all her expressions and gestures and in her way of speaking. She had a gentle,

very quiet voice. After that first day when Paco and I helped her with the move, we had many opportunities to meet her. From then on she would always refer to the two of us together – 'Pedro and Paco' or 'Paco and Pedro'. All the others of whom she was so fond, each had their names to themselves: Alvaro, Ricardo, Isidoro. Our names on the other hand always formed an inseparable duo as far as she was concerned.

After moving his family to the safety of the boarding house, Father Josemaría took the opportunity to do something he had wanted to do for a long time – move into the Ferraz residence with his sons. In his journal he writes at this time, 'January 31, 1946: It is almost midnight ... Jesus has been so kind to arrange things so that I get to spend a month here with my sons. My mother, sister and brother, meanwhile, will stay in a boarding house on Calle Mayor.'[251]

CHAPTER 32

Terror Outside, Tea and 'Cakes' Within

Historians have noted how the political situation in Spain at the beginning of 1936 closely resembled that of Germany during the rise of Hitler. Moderate opinion in both countries was crushed as extremists gained control of the political parties of Right and Left. The governments in both cases proved to be incapable of controlling private armies and of preventing terror and violence. In Spain the General Election on 16 February 1936 resulted in a narrow victory for the Popular Front, an alliance of the Left wing parties. The Popular Front received 4.7 million votes compared with the Right's 3.9 million.

Manuel Azaña became president and the religious persecution immediately intensified. Priests and now even ordinary Catholics were assassinated in the street. Churches were again burned and looted. The assassination gangs roamed freely and unchecked.
  To reach the residence students had to walk through streets in the city where confrontations, political demonstrations and street fighting were daily occurrences. The students would often experience chilling face-to-face encounters with fanatical youths wearing red kerchiefs, with clenched fists raised in proletarian salute and their eyes filled with indoctrinated hatred. The old order was crumbling and the fires of hatred were deliberately and systematically being fanned.

With President Azaña allowing so much religious hatred Father Josemaría realized it would now be impossible for him and his family to return to the Rector's house at Santa Isabel.

His daily trek across Madrid from the Academy-residence to Santa Isabel to say Mass for the nuns was becoming more perilous with every passing day. In March even more politically orchestrated attacks on religion were launched. Churches were again set ablaze and priests beaten up and killed.

On 11 March 1936 Father Josemaría records in his journal:

> Fires continue to rage, both in the provinces and in Madrid ... This morning, while I was celebrating Holy Mass at Santa Isabel, the government ordered that the guards be disarmed [The people voluntarily guarding churches and convents] ... I, with the consent of the nuns, took a ciborium that was almost full of consecrated hosts and consumed them all. I don't know if anything will happen. Lord: enough of these sacrileges![252]

Two days later what he feared would happen, did.

> On the thirteenth they started to attack Santa Isabel. They broke down some doors. Providentially, though, the mob had run out of petrol and could only set on fire the outer door of the church before they were chased away by a couple of guards ... The people around here are very pessimistic ... At Santa Isabel there is nothing but trouble. I can't understand why the nuns haven't all had heart attacks! Today [March 25, 1936], when I heard everyone talking about priests and nuns being assassinated and about fires and assaults and all kinds of horrors ... I shuddered and – this is how contagious terror is – for a moment I was afraid. We must serve God with joy and without fear! I won't stand for having pessimists at my side.[253]

He still continued going to say Mass at Santa Isabel every

day and walking the streets of Madrid dressed as a priest. He wore his conspicuous priestly attire for two reasons because of the holy pride he had in his priesthood and because he wanted at all times to be a servant of God and of souls, available to anyone in spiritual need. Even though he realized this was increasing the odds of him being killed, he didn't want to do anything that might hide his priesthood from anyone who might be in need of a priest and of the Sacraments.

He would walk along the streets immersed in saying his Rosaries. If he found himself in difficult or dangerous situations he would make entreaties to Our Lady such as, 'Most sweet Heart of Mary. Mother, my mother! Don't abandon me!'

And throughout the whole day he would send heavenwards a battery of short prayers or aspirations.

Usually he drew these aspirations from Scripture or from the treasury of Christian Tradition and he always put his whole heart in to them, all the devotion and intensity of which he was capable: 'Sweet Heat of Jesus be my love!' 'Sweet Heart of Mary be my salvation' In times of great difficulty he would use this prayer to reinforce his hope. 'Montes, sicut cera, fluxerunt a facie Domini.' 'The mountains dissolve like wax before the face of the Lord.' (Ps. 97:5)

He would also pray, 'Domine, fac cum servo tuo secundum magnam misericordiam tuam' ('Lord, deal with Your servant according to Your great mercy') 'Lord, I abandon myself to You, I trust in You, I rest in You.' 'I believe in God the Father, I believe in God the Son, I believe in God the Holy Spirit. I hope in God the Father, I hope in God the Son, I hope in God the Holy Spirit. I love God the Father, I love God the Son, I love God the Holy Spirit.' He would also pray, 'Omnia in bonum!' 'All for the good!' This prayer he had printed on thousands of cards as a way of encouraging people to accept always the will of God and to live with Christian hope. And always he would ask the help of the Guardian Angels, 'Sancti angeli custodes nostri, defendite nos.' 'Our holy Guardian Angels, defend us.'

Amid all the hardships and terror, on 19 March 1936,

the feast of St Joseph, he was able to celebrate a happy occasion – the replacing of the wooden tabernacle with a new, more dignified tabernacle which had been specially made by the sculptor Jenaro Lázaro. This made him very happy.

His love for the Eucharist was apparent in so many particulars, even in the way he would go about setting the flowers beside the tabernacle. He would say, 'When you place a flower near the tabernacle give it a kiss and say to the Lord that you would like that kiss to be consumed along with the flower, to be used up just like the candle of the sanctuary lamp gets used up as it shows people with its flame that God is here.'[254]

At this time he asked everyone to offer their daily Mass and some small sacrifices for his intentions. The first intention, he told them, was that they would find an even larger building which could become a permanent students' residence. The present Academy-residence was now full to capacity. The apartments they were renting at 50 Ferraz Street had once again become too small for their needs so they had to move part of the academy next door to number 48.

The second was that they would broaden their horizons so they could go to other cities and to other countries.

Amid all the tension and increasing persecution he was continuing to make plans for the expansion as if nothing unusual was happening and was living an intense 'today, now'.

Pedro Casciaro, who with Paco Botella was greatly enjoying living in the Ferraz Street residence has left us an unforgettable picture of the first members and the happiness and serenity that existed inside the residence while political insanity and violence raged outside. He says:

> There were only a few of us around the Father, very few indeed. Just a handful of young men, mainly undergraduates, and one or two who had recently graduated ... I remember Alvaro del Portillo, who was then just a young twenty-one year old civil engineering student. The director of the Residence was Ricardo Fernández, a twenty-five year old architect. Then there was Juan

Jiménez Vargas, a medical student. He was twenty-two, active, resolute, a man of few words. There was José María Hernández, an engineering student whom we called Chiqui. He was twenty-one, almost my own age. José María González was a chemistry teacher and a little older. He was twenty-nine and doing a doctorate. At that time I also heard them talk a lot about Isidoro Zorzano, a young engineer the same age as the father who had been in the same class as him at secondary school.

These first six months of 1936 were a particularly intense time for Pedro Casciaro:

> I was launching out in my vocation and experiencing the joy of living in a centre of Opus Dei for the first time. I was following a spiritual plan of life proper to a member of the Work. As I was studying two degree courses simultaneously, the Maths/Physics course and Architecture, the number of classes I had to attend had multiplied. These included three hours of water-colour painting under Antonio Flores Urdapilleta. I did not get out of the School of Architecture before 6 or 6.30pm, and I still had lots of jobs and hours of study left to do. In the midst of all that hard work there were some especially heart-warming moments every week, when we particularly experienced the Father's loving care and the family warmth ... These moments came on Sunday afternoons when Paco and I would be alone with the Father. We would sit around his worktable and he would talk to us about Opus Dei. Meanwhile other members of the Work would begin to appear and then we would have a get-together. Alvaro del Portillo was often the first to arrive. I can still see the room in my mind's eye. There was a desk, a bookshelf with some tomes on it, a book cupboard, a sofa-bed, two Spanish-style armchairs, and one or two chairs in the same style. That was the office where the Father used to work. At times Ricardo used it as the Residence Director's office. The Father kept some handwritten notebooks which reflected the spirit and rules of the Work in the bottom of the book cupboard.

What did Father Josemaría talk to them about? Pedro tells us:

> In his energetic way he opened our eyes to the richness of Christian life as children of God in Opus Dei. If I had to summarise it I would use his own words with which he repeatedly exhorted us 'personal holiness, personal holiness. I have no other recipe,' he used to say. 'We are here to become saints, for vocation demands holiness.' He reminded us that 'God expected heroic sanctity: this is a demand in the call we have received. We have to be really, properly, saints; and if we are not, we have failed. If anyone is not fully determined to be a saint, let him leave.'[255]

Pedro goes on to say,

> The Sunday afternoon get-togethers were very supernatural and dynamic, and at the same time enjoyable and entertaining. The Father would talk of the future expansion of the Work as well as of more immediate plans. Valencia and then in Paris ... And then, the whole world would follow ...!
>
> Since these get-togethers used to happen around tea-time, I remember introducing the English custom of taking afternoon tea (which we used to have in my own family). And as the British sense of social nicety stipulated that little cakes or biscuits should be consumed with the tea, we had the brainwave of toasting the bits of bread left over from lunchtime and spreading a little syrup of them. Hey presto! Cakes! As can be seen, we had no money but we made up for it by ingenuity and good humour. Our cosy little tea-room, lit by a lamp over the desk which left the rest of the room in shadow, had other uses apart from serving as Ricardo's office. It was there that the Father attended to the spiritual needs of the people who came to see him. I remember another small but significant detail. When he was alone, he always left the door ajar so that anybody who wished to would find it easy to go in and have a chat.

A regular visitor to the residence was Father Blas Romero Cano from La Mancha. Father Blas was about fifty and taught them Gregorian chant. The Father wanted them to care with the utmost attention to detail for everything related to Our Lord, especially when connected with the liturgy which is why he arranged for them to have special singing classes with Father Blas. Pedro gives us a memorable picture of him. He says,

> I shall never forget those classes in the early afternoon with Father Blas. He came on Saturdays before the Residence began to fill up with students. Before he arrived we would get a cap and a good dose of sodium bicarbonate ready for him. Those two elements were much more important to the singing lessons than might appear at the first glance. No cap, no lesson: for Father Blas said he would get a cold without his cap on. As for the sodium bicarbonate, he could not sing without it. He often asked us for it; we would give it to him and between hymns he would take it, first sprinkling some onto his hand and then popping it down his throat, continuing all the while to conduct the choir vigorously, as we began our rending of the second psalm: Quare fremuerunt gentes. (Why this turmoil among the peoples.) Quare fremuerunt gentes. Father Blas did his level best to combine and harmonise our voices; but despite his efforts and ours, only very rarely did he achieve the desired rendition. And when the class came to an end, we would still be repeating for the umpteenth time ... Quare fremuerunt gentes.

Though there were very few members at that time Pedro Cascario tells us that they did not form a close circle because Father Josemaría continually encouraged them to open out like a fan and not to isolate themselves from their friends and fellow students.

> One day, at the beginning of 1936, I asked the Father how many of us there were altogether, and in consequence what rank I held. Detecting the lack of humility which my question implied, the Father replied with an

answer which impressed rather than disconcerted me. This was what he conveyed to me: 'I have met, I have come to know deeply, and I have guided many souls of gravely and terminally ill people on my rounds in the hospitals of Madrid. Among them are some men and women who have understood perfectly what the Work of God is attempting to do. Some of them have offered up their pains and their death for the Work to go forward. Others have offered up not just their suffering but their very selves, that last bit of earthly life which still remained to them, and I accepted them into the Work. Then the Father spoke to him about Luis Gordon the industrial engineer who had died in 1932. He said it could be that Our Lord wanted to take him so that the Work could be born really poor, without any financial assets of its own, as it never would have. He said Luis had already come into a lot of money which he wanted to leave to the Work; but heeding an inner inspiration, the Father said he dissuaded him from doing so.

Pedro Casciaro and his friend Paco twice went with Father Josemaría to visit Chamartin de la Rosa, an old cemetery, which now no longer exists, where some of the first members of the Work were buried. 'First we prayed a response for the dead at the grave of Father José Maria Somoano, a young priest who had died on July 16, 1932, the feast day of Our Lady of Carmel,' Pedro says. 'The Father mentioned that it was widely held that Father Somoano had been poisoned simply because he was a priest.'

Then they went to pray at the grave of María Ignacia García, one of the first women members of Opus Dei, who died with tuberculosis offering up all her pain for the Work. 'At that time the Father only told us that María had been very good and very faithful to the Work. There was a simple iron cross and a little railing round the grave to mark the spot,' Pedro records.

CHAPTER 33

The Special Guest

It was about this time when Spain was only a matter of weeks away from Civil War that Father Josemaría had a memorable meeting with his very good friend Father Pedro Poveda, who often went to him for spiritual help. Concerned about the assassination of priests all over the country and the imminent danger that a greater bloodbath might soon engulf them, the two priests discussed the possibility that one or both of them might have to face martyrdom on account of their priesthood. They then both arrived at the same firm conclusion. Death would not interrupt their friendship. If one of them were killed, in heaven he would be an even greater friend of the other. More and more students were now turning up at the residence for spiritual guidance from Father Josemaría. Other older people came too, such as José Maria Albareda, a professor at the Madrid Institute and Eugenio Sellés, a lecturer at the National Institute of Toxicology, both of whom would later risk their lives helping Father Josemaría when he was a hunted priest. Another regular visitor was Alejandro Guzman who gave them a piano which was put in the room they used for lunch when they had visitors. This room had a homely round table, a small bookcase, a violin for purely decorative purposes and the recently donated piano.

Once again at this time they were in financial difficulties and Alvaro del Portillo describes the upkeep of the

Academy and Residence as 'a daily miracle'. Pedro Casciaro one day asked the Father directly how the residence kept going and he told him that he was continually having to appeal to his mother, Doña Dolores, whose small capital it was they were spending. This was the money that had come from selling the estate at Fonz. Alejandro Guzman also helped financially and a lady called Doña Concepcion Ruiz was in Father Josemaría's words a 'very generous woman.' There was also the Countess of Humanes, the blind lady who had given Father Josemaría her jewels. The Countess lived in an old house which had a private chapel where the Father would sometimes go to say Mass and renew the Blessed Sacrament. He would ask Pedro Casciaro to go with him on some of his visits as he knew he loved antiques. The countess had a collection of pictures and objects of great value in her house, which testified to the ancient lineage of her family. 'On occasions, after thanksgiving after Mass,' Pedro says, 'we went into the dining room to have breakfast. I still recall gratefully the York Ham and special preserves with which Doña Maria regaled us before the usual milky coffee and sponge cakes. After breakfast she would show us round the elegant rooms of her house, pointing out very accurately each picture and each object saying, "Do you see this picture? It is of one of my ancestors, painted by Vicente Lopez." And so she would continue, without ever making a mistake, in spite of her blindness.'

By the staircase there was also a dark, calamine statue which Pedro asked her about. 'Ah, you mean the calamine gentleman?' the Countess asked and then began to talk about the statue as if it were an old family friend.

Father Josemaría would afterwards pull Pedro's leg about it. 'Perico, do you remember the calamine gentleman?' he would joke.

The good lady died a few months later during the Civil War. Immediately after her death, a band of armed militia invaded her home and looted everything in it, right down to the floorboards.

With the residence running at a deficit and their desperate shortage of funds Father Josemaría would sometimes surprise them by what they thought was a certain extravagance. Every Wednesday he used to invite to lunch Father Norberto, the priest who had been his assistant chaplain at the Foundation for the Sick and would also go to the expense of transporting him there and back by taxi.

As Father Josemaría normally only used trams or the underground, spending money on taxies for this particular priest seemed rather extraordinary. Father Josemaría liked to provide food for Father Norberto which was better than the normal fare and to offer him some little extra. Pedro Casciaro who sometimes had lunch with them, was always moved by the consideration the Father showed towards that priest. 'For instance,' Pedro says, 'before he arrived he would suggest topics of conversation which might interest the priest so that he would enjoy himself. It was not an easy task. I found that particular guest rather hard work.'

As Pedro felt these invitations demanded a considerable sacrifice to Father Josemaría, not only financially but also in time and patience, he suggested that the Father should stop them or at least space them out. In reply the Father told him that the good priest was in poor health and had very few friends and that they should show understanding to priests who were lonely.

'I did not fully understand his answer,' Pedro says, 'until years later when the Father remarked to me that we had to teach people who came to the Work to live in God's presence, giving them a new light every day ... For example, on Wednesdays in honour of St Joseph, he said it was a good idea to really exert ourselves in charity and patience with someone whom we found particularly difficult or had made us suffer.'

Alvaro del Portillo remembers Father Norberto as being a very lonely man because of an unusually difficult personality. And he says, 'The Father told me that he tried to treat this friend, to honour him, as though he were Saint Joseph.'

Alvaro also recalls another of Father Josemaría's difficult guests. He was a doctor considered by some to be a genius. But he was so odd that he didn't have a single friend, apart from Father Josemaría who went to see him quite often and would sometimes invite him for lunch. The doctor was also a person who could not tolerate any opinion that differed from his. Father Josemaría would never contradict him and he would always afterwards say to Alvaro, 'Well, you know, nobody likes this fellow, everyone shuns him, so let him get some affection from us.'[256]

During their financial difficulties Father Josemaría taught them to live what he called 'a bashful poverty', a kind of poverty which hid itself from the view of other people. Pedro noticed several ways in which the Father lived this poverty. Immaculately dressed as he usually was, he always wore the same cassock. And Pedro, says, 'I also discovered that a gesture he used to make frequently, putting his pocket watch to his ear, was not simply a habit as I had thought. That old watch of his would stop every second day and every first day as well, and he had no money to get it repaired.' Later Pedro discovered that he called his Guardian Angel, whom he kept asking to keep it going 'my watch-mender'.

And when the Father said Mass wearing a big gothic-style chasuble Pedro noticed 'that he used to genuflect in such a way that his right foot was always hidden under his cassock and alb. Similarly when he knelt at the foot of the altar to say the prayers after Mass, he ensured that the alb would cover the soles of his shoes. Later I discovered why. Those shoes, for all that they were spotlessly clean, urgently needed resoling or, better still, entirely replacing with a new pair.'

And Pedro adds, 'It was not surprising that he wore his shoes out, for he used to walk miles from one end of Madrid to the other, from Santa Isabel Street to Ferraz and from the Salamanca district to Vallecas.'

The staff of the residence at this time consisted of an elderly lady, who worked for a few hours a day and did the cooking and a boy who served the food in the dining room and kept the place tidy. Some nuns, the Handmaids of Merciful Love, whose convent was also in Ferraz Street, took care of the laundry and ironing. Their founder, Mother Esperanza, whose Cause of canonization is now under way, was suffering at that time what is called 'the incomprehension of good people'.

Pedro says:

> The Father used to go to the convent to visit Mother Esperanza from time to time, I accompanied him on a few occasions and came away with the impression that he went there to give her encouragement. He told me that she was a very holy religious and that the Lord was allowing her to go through some very difficult trials. One of those religious remembers how the Father said to them. 'The Cross can be very heavy, but on you go! The Lord managed, His Saints do not turn back. Saints reach the end of the course. On you go! A day without the Cross is a day without God.'[257]

It was about this time that Pedro Casciaro and Paco Botella discovered something else that Father Josemaría got up to while they were usually attending lectures at the university or at the School of Architecture. The pair normally left the Residence first thing in the morning in a great hurry to be in time for their 8 a.m. lectures but one morning they stayed behind for some reason and found Father Josemaría going round making the students' beds, sweeping the floors, cleaning bathrooms, tidying up and doing the general housework. They realized the Father must have been doing this for some time.

Alvaro del Portillo says the reason Father Josemaría did this work was that the domestic staff was so small, just the woman cook and the young boy. 'It therefore fell to him to clean the rooms and make the beds for the nearly twenty students who lived there,' he says. 'Some of us would help him in this – most often the architect Ricardo Fernández, who at that time was the director of the residence. The Father did these domestic chores while the residents were at the university. He was very happy to perform this service.'

Pedro and Paco could not help him every day because of their classes. But they decided to take turns attending lectures so that one of them could make notes for the one who stayed behind helping with the housework. 'It was no small task,' says Pedro, 'for there were twenty odd beds and some twelve rooms.'

The domestic chores did not finish there. There were jobs to be done in the evenings after the cook had left and that was when they went into the kitchen to do the washing up. Paco recalls,

> The Father would come in and don a white overall. Pedro and I had our overalls on too, and we would all set to, each to his own specific job. That was our routine day after day and we enjoyed being there with the Father. And at the appointed time everything was shipshape.

The last thing they did in the kitchen in the evening was to leave breakfast laid out ready for the next day. Pedro remembers that;

> For milk, we used Nestles powdered milk. Paco or I saw to that very necessary duty, alternating by the week. I at that time weighed almost 80 kilos, while Paco was all skin and bone as he always was. The Father used to refer jokingly to 'the fat cows and the lean cows' as he shared these tasks with us. I have memories of him in the kitchen with Ricardo, washing plates, polishing apples with a cloth and doing other humble tasks. Naturally the residents who were not members of Opus Dei had not the slightest inkling of who it was who did those jobs.

CHAPTER 34

The 'Poisoned Sweets' Rumour

Soon after the victory of the Popular Front the most extreme of the political sects began to emerge as the dominating force following a political power struggle. Hatred of religion began to be even more fanatically promulgated. Those churches and convents that escaped being burned down were now taken over by Marxist and other extreme groups.

One of the most dangerous areas of the city was around the Santa Isabel Foundation where Father Josemaría was still going every day to say Mass. The Church of Santa Isabel was close to the Saint Carlos Faculty of Medicine where students regularly took to the streets to demonstrate. It was also near the railway station in Atocha where there were numerous sweatshops. This was one of the districts of Madrid most affected by street riots, which by this time had become a regular feature of life in the city. To get from the Ferraz Street Residence to Santa Isabel's Father Josemaría had to travel miles, either on foot or by tram. This together with all the other journeys he made to the various areas of the city as part of his priestly work added to the disturbing daily nightmare.

In April Prime Minister Alcalá Zamora was dismissed. This caused an internal rift in the army.

Among all the increasing unrest Father Josemaría was able to instill serenity into all those around him and into the many people who came in contact with him. Pedro Casciaro says:

His reflective, balanced attitude was in total contrast to the polarisation all around us. He never discussed political matters. His judgements of events were always exclusively priestly ones. His feet were firmly on the ground. But at the same time he had an unshakable faith in the fact that the Work would become a reality, even though the circumstances did not appear to favour the apostolic expansion for which he had us pray so much. He suffered a lot, for the Church and for the situation in his country, which he loved greatly. He respected any opinion relating to public life which a Christian could legitimately hold. Among the members of the Work and the undergraduates his apostolate reached, there were, of course, very diverse political views.

Emiliano Amann, one of the residents at the time, remembers how the Father continued to propel the Work forward despite the critical state of affairs. In a letter to his parents he wrote at the time he said: 'More and more people come to the Academy for lessons in architecture, medicine, law and science. By next year I am sure there will be preparatory classes for the School of Agronomy.'

At the end of Holy Week 1936, from 10 to 13 April, Father Josemaría gave a retreat in the residence. A rather plump young man wearing baggy trousers attended and said he wanted to join the Work. He did so shortly afterwards on 12 April. His name was Vincente Rodriguez but everyone preferred to call him Vincenton, the name which stuck. One thing they all noticed about Vincenton was that he always appeared to be in a cheerful and in a festive mood.

Immediately after Easter Father Josemaría and Ricardo Fernández went to Valencia to look for premises for the new residence they proposed to start in that city. They stayed three days talking to people and seeking help.

When they returned to Madrid they found the hate campaign was swiftly heading towards a climax. As a result of the political unrest many families were getting out of Madrid as quickly as possible. Many large houses were up for sale and going cheap. After searching most of Madrid for suitable premises for a new students' residence they finally found the ideal building in the very street they were already in. It was number 16 Ferraz Street, which was a splendid, spacious building owned by the Count Real and facing the Montaña Army Barracks.

At the beginning of May false stories began to be spread to bring religion into disrepute. One absurd story that travelled like wildfire through Madrid was that priests and nuns were going around giving poisoned sweets to workers' children. As a result of the poisoned sweets propaganda mobs again went on the rampage, burning and pillaging churches and religious houses. Priests, monks and nuns again fled for their lives, many of them taking refuge in people's homes. This latest outbreak of violence brought the total number of religious buildings destroyed in the first few months of 1936 to one hundred and sixty.

At the Santa Isabel Foundation the nuns were living in daily fear of being burned out but with great tenacity and courage they stayed in their convent. Then came another setback for them. Father Josemaría, as Rector, was officially notified that the church and convent of Santa Isabel had been confiscated by the state. The nuns were ordered to move out immediately. They left on 17 May 1936. Some moved into a private house in Angel Square, where they wore ordinary clothes. Others went to live with their families. Father Josemaría would visit them at the house and Pedro or Paco would go with him. Occasionally they both went. Pedro says, 'We saw how in such difficult circumstances the Father comforted them and gave them spiritual encouragement.'[258]

The religious persecution at this stage was taking its toll of him, mentally and physically. He began complaining in his intimate notes that his Communions were cold, that he couldn't 'even pray properly one Hail Mary' that it seemed to him 'as if Jesus has gone out for a walk'. It was as if God was leaving him all alone. He was very unhappy with himself. He felt he had 'no desire for anything'. He complained he was unable to organize his ideas and felt 'somewhat lame and arthritic, despite the heat'. He had no energy for mortifications. He yearned for 'a few days of peace'.[259] At the beginning of May he wrote to the Vicar General, Monsignor Morán, 'I feel I must be very straightforward with you, Father. I'm fat and flabby and very tired.'[260] The diagnosis was obvious and matter-of-fact. He was completely worn out and mentally and physically exhausted.

Two days later he went to see his good friend Father Poveda who had once suffered from the same symptoms. Father Poveda gave him the same advice as the Vicar General, Monsignor Morán, had given him. He would have to have a complete rest, preferably in bed. He accepted this advice and a little later writes in his notes, 'I went to my mother's house and spent the whole day in bed, without speaking to or even seeing anyone, and for a while I felt a little better. It's physical exhaustion.' He then worked out that over the past eight months he had given about 340 talks and meditations most of them at least half an hour long. And on top of that he was directing individual souls and visiting many, many people in need of priestly care. He concludes, 'That explains why I have these terrible moments when I am sick of everything, even of what I love most. And the devil sees to it that my times of physical weakness coincide with a thousand little vexations.'[261]

'I'm weak, weak in every way, in body and in soul,' he writes in another note, 'despite the great front I put on. This is making me act strangely. I don't want to be this way. Help me, dearest Mother.' And there is even a note of complaint, 'Lord, will you let me complain just a tiny little bit? There are times (because of my wretchedness, mea culpa) when I feel I can do no more. Now I've made my complaint. Forgive me.'[262]

By the end of that month of May the depressing dark clouds that seemed to have enveloped him looked as if they might be dispersing and allowing him a glimpse of the sun. He writes, 'May 30, 1936: Last night I slept very well. I did not wake up until a quarter past six. It has been a long time since I got that much sleep all at one stretch. I also feel an inner joy and peace that I wouldn't trade for anything. God is here the best thing I can do is to tell Him my troubles, because then they cease to be troubles.'[263]

He was recovering. But it was a hard and difficult recovery. He was faced with so much to do and living in a tense political situation about to erupt into civil war.

The Falangists and Communists, the two extreme political parties of the right and left, were now both putting the final touches to their plans to overthrow the left wing coalition regime. The Falangists were planning a national uprising to save, as they saw it, the Spanish nation and the Catholic Church from Marxist socialism and eventual Soviet domination.

The Communists, who from the very beginning had been determined to establish a dictatorship of the proletariat, were planning a revolution which would end with total power in their hands.

The Communists had finalized their plans by the beginning of June. On 6 June the Spanish Communist Party circulated to all key officials precise orders for the start of the struggle. These orders laid down the armaments and the actions of special raiding parties, as well as the co-operation that would take place with secret Red cells working within the military and in the towns that were to be taken under their control. The detailed orders also named the government officials, civil governors, security personnel, party members and those of the bourgeoisie who were to be executed. The death list ended with the chilling words, 'incluso de sus familiares, sin exclusion de ninguno' (including all family members, without any exception).

Father Josemaría still carried on working as normal. Everyone who met him was struck by his infectious courage. He was concerned about starting the Work as soon as possible in Valencia where they were still looking for suitable premises. When these were found, he wanted Ricardo Fernández, the director of the Ferraz Street, Residence, to go to Valencia to set up the new residence. He also asked Isidoro Zorzano to get temporary leave of absence from the Andalusian Railways and come to Madrid to take over from Ricardo. He continued to pray that peace and common sense would prevail and asked everyone he knew to pray for this intention.

Each day droves of students and their friends continued to run the gauntlet of angry left-wing protesters to get to the residence, where inside its walls they found peace still reigned and people talked of love of neighbour and love of human freedom. This is a description of a meditation given by Father Josemaría just weeks before the outbreak of the Civil War.

> Before Mass, the Father gave a meditation. He sat beside the altar, at a small table with a dark green covering. A small lamp threw a circle of light on the tabletop. He took a small crucifix from the pocket of his cassock and placed it before him, along with his watch. Next to it was the Gospel and a medium-sized notebook with notes for the meditation ... Two candles were lit, one on either side of the tabernacle. He himself was half in shadow – only the Blessed Sacrament and his words commanded attention. He spoke about the sanctification of ordinary work and about love of neighbour and love of freedom. He often opened the Gospel for passages he had marked with strips of paper. He read them slowly, almost letter by letter. From there, from the holy Scripture, he elaborated on everything. From time to time, he looked at the tabernacle and spoke to Christ in glowing words – the meditation became prayer. Father Josemaría told them, 'We have to transform every part of our lives into the service of God: work and leisure, laughter and tears. In the fields, in the workshop, in the study room, in the political arena, faithfully persevering in our normal lives, we must make everything an instrument of sanctification ...'

And to sanctify all this, he said they had to see Christ in their neighbour and love freedom.

'Avoid,' he said, 'the abuse of freedom. This abuse is becoming more dangerous in our times. It is manifest throughout the world. It arises from the desire, contrary to the legitimate independence of men and women, to force them all into a single mass, so that they are forced to believe things that are really matters of opinion as though they were spiritual dogmas. And this perverted view is promoted through power and propaganda, in a scandalous way ... You are free! Listen to me well. You are very free!'[264]

And Father Josemaría would often repeat to the students the words of Jesus in St John's Gospel.

> I give you a new commandment:
> love one another; just as I have loved you,
> you also must love one another.
> By this love you have for one another
> everyone will know that you are My disciples. (John 13:34–35)

He also had the verse copied out in Latin on a piece of imitation parchment and framed.

> MANDATUM NOVUM DO VOBIS:
> UT DILIGATIS INVICEM, SICUT DILEXI
> VOS, UT ET VOS DILIGATIS INVICEM.
> IN HOC COGNOSCENT OMNES QUIA
> DISCIPULI MEI ESTIS, SI DILECTIONEM
> HABUERITIS AD INVICEM. (Joann XIII. 34, 35)

The framed quotation was put in one of the main rooms of residence for all to see. 'Look at it closely,' he would say. 'Twenty centuries have gone by and it is indeed still a new commandment because very few people have taken the trouble to practise it.'[265]

Father Josemaría was now very much aware that being a priest meant he could be killed or simply 'disappear' any day. Several times he took his handful of members aside and asked them, 'If I were to die now, would you carry on with the Work?'[266] And when they confirmed to him that they would he would tell them, 'Have a lot of faith in God, and a little faith in this poor sinner'.[267]

Then he would emphasize that the work was of divine origin. This, he would tell them, was the guarantee of its permanence not only in the years ahead, but in the centuries to come.

He also decided that it would now no longer be safe to

carry on giving classes of Christian formation in the Academy and residence for it could be raided at any time. He taught his members to trust above all in the Will of God. He told them that no matter how serious the situation became they must never forget that prayer and the supernatural means were more important than anything else.

The Communists had now mobilized 250,000 troops of revolutionary militias. These militias units took up positions in front of public buildings. Then they began raiding government offices, seizing documents and confiscating whatever land or property they wanted.

The government seemed to have little or no control over the militant left wing organisations such as CNT (Confederacion Nacional de Trabajo, National Federation of Labour and POUM (Partido Obrero de Unificacion Marxista, United Marxist Workers' Party). And day by day the agony intensified.

PART II

THE HUNTED PRIEST

CHAPTER 35

'A Crime Punishable by Death'

It was about this time that Pedro Casciaro had a short talk with Father Josemaría that would etch itself on his mind. One day, for some reason or another, he had not gone off to his usual lectures. About 11 a.m. he was coming out of the oratory when he saw Father Josemaría in the hall. He was saying his breviary, sitting on a bench under a wall-hanging worked with the motto *per aspera ad astra* (through the arduous to the stars). Pedro recalls:

> I said nothing so as not to disturb his concentration but as I was passing he forestalled me with a motion of his hand, his eyes never lifting from the book. He finished the psalm, marked his place in the breviary with one finger, and looking at me with love in his eyes he asked me something I did not expect in the slightest. 'Pedro, would you be willing to be a priest if you heard God's call?' I was dumbstruck. It was the last thing I expected to hear at that moment. But I answered him immediately, 'I think so Father.' I went back into the oratory. Shortly afterwards the Father came in. He knelt beside me and, pointing to the red carpet (which covered the plinth on which the altar stood), he said in a whisper. 'A priest has to be like that carpet. Over it the body of Our Lord is consecrated. It's at the altar, it's true, but it is there to be of use. Furthermore, it is there so that everyone else can have something soft to tread on and you

see how it does not complain, it does not protest ... Do you understand what the service of a priest is? You will see that, later on, in your life you will reflect on these things.' From that day on I often spent my time of prayer contemplating first the tabernacle and then the carpet. That was all the topic I needed ...[268]

Despite all the violence and political unrest, negotiations were concluded for purchase of Count Real's house, 16 Ferraz Street on 1 June. Father Josemaría then speeded up transferring the residence there. One of the reasons for doing this was that he didn't want to pay rent any longer than necessary on the old residence. Many people thought he was mad and wondered why he was still trying to carry on as normal when it looked as if everything would blow up in their faces at any moment. But for Father Josemaría, even in those terrible months leading up to the Civil War, there always seemed hope for the future.

Before they could move into the new residence there were alterations and renovations that needed to be done. As there was no money to pay workmen, students and lecturers and their friends once again joined in and lent a hand. Soon the new residence was taking shape.

Towards the end of June when the university examinations were over Father Josemaría told his young members that he wanted them to spend a few days in the mountains. On Saturday, 27 June 1936, they set off for Rascafria, led by Juan Jiménez Vargas who was an expert climber. The newest member Vincente Rodriguez (Vincenton), a former Boy Scout was very knowledgeable about camping and had managed to get hold of a large tent and all the necessary camping equipment. In those last days of June, as Spain plunged inevitably towards civil war, the young men were able to lose themselves in mountain adventures, hiking, climbing and swimming in the lakes and rivers. They returned physically and spiritually renewed to Madrid. The city now seemed to be like a gunpowder barrel with a fuse attached. A fuse that someone or something was about to ignite at any moment.

Isidoro Zorzano arrived from Málaga to join them at the

Ferraz residence at the beginning of July. On 2 July three lorries arrived to begin moving the furniture to the new residence. On the following day, 3 July, Pedro Casciaro and Paco Botella went off to stay with their families for a couple of weeks. Paco, whose parents lived in Valencia, would also be looking around the city for suitable premises for the new residence which they were hoping to open in time for the start of the next academic year. As soon as Paco had found somewhere the plan was that Ricardo Fernández would go out and join him immediately. Ricardo could then complete the legal formalities for purchasing the building and become the director of the new residence. Paco would stay on in Valencia to help him and would continue his studies there. Before joining his parents, Pedro Casciaro had been a little concerned about meeting his father. 'My Father had worked on the propaganda which had helped the Popular Front to victory in the last elections. As that coalition had adopted a mode of persecuting everything religious I feared a confrontation with him, something I wished to avoid at all costs.' But when Pedro mentioned this to Father Josemaría he immediately put him straight. He told Pedro he ought to go and see his family. He had to put his duty as a son first. And he recommended that Pedro should pray for his father and not get embroiled in politics with him.

Ten days after Pedro and Paco's departure, on 13 July, the press reported the assassination of José Calvo Sotelo, the right-wing leader. The Communists and the police were linked with the murder and the government banned the distribution of two leading newspapers because their reports revealed too many details about what had happened. Rumours spread like wildfire and after the assassination thousands of Falangists were arrested in police swoops.

The general feeling was, 'It's now only a matter of hours.' The fuse to the gunpowder barrel had been set alight and was burning furiously.

On 16 July, three days later, Paco Botella sent a telegram announcing that he had found a house that would be suitable for a residence. The next day, 17 July, Ricardo headed for Valencia after Father Josemaría had given him his blessing.

The following day, Saturday, 18 July, the news came through that the army in Spanish Morocco had revolted against the left-wing Madrid government and was calling for other army units to join them. The Civil War had begun.

The Madrid garrison joined the revolt and the Montaña Barracks, which faced the new Madrid residence and into which Father Josemaría and his sons had just moved, became the focal point of the rebellion. The Communists reacted swiftly and efficiently. A general strike was announced and Republican shock troops and the left-wing militias surrounded the barracks. The militias also erected barricades throughout Madrid and detained many people. Anyone they suspected might be an army officer or 'rich' or 'distinguished' was arrested and shot. All priests became wanted men. To prevent the Madrid army garrison breaking out from the Montaña barracks, the Communist militias gathered together civilians, including women and children, and herded them against the barrack gates. If the army tried to fight their way out the civilians would be shot. The army was trapped inside their barracks and could only wait.

On Sunday, 19 July, more militia units took up positions around the barracks in preparation for an attack. From their new residence, Father Josemaría and his sons could see all that was happening. It would be safer, Father Josemaría decided, for the young men whose families lived in Madrid to leave the residence and try to get home. He heard their confessions. Then, from about eight o'clock onwards that Sunday night they started to leave one by one. Father Josemaría gave each one his blessing and asked them all to phone him as soon as they were safely home. Isidoro Zorzano, who was the director of the residence and José María González, whose father was an army officer, stayed with him.

The attack on the Montaña army barracks began that night after the militia had brought up artillery and armoured vehicles. There was a five-hour bombardment of the barracks, including an air attack. The battle raged throughout the night. Bullets tore into the residence and embedded themselves in walls and ceilings.

Early in the morning of Monday, 20 July, Republican shock troops, which included the Guardia de Asalto, stormed the barracks and captured it.

The soldiers who surrendered were lined up. Those considered 'class enemies', according to the 6 June instructions issued by the Communist Party, were herded into the courtyard and executed by firing squads. The captured officers suffered a different fate. They were taken to the highest floor of the barracks and thrown to their deaths.

From the residence, Father Josemaría, Isidoro Zorzano and José María González witnessed the carnage. 'People seemed to have gone mad. They had slain so many right there in front of us,' Father Josemaría would later say.[269]

It was now clear to the three left in the residence that the militia could come at any moment to search the building.

They would have to get out. They prayed to Our Lady and the Guardian angels. They also realized that if Father Josemaría went out dressed as a priest he would be shot as soon as he stepped outside the door. Fortunately some overalls had been left behind by someone who had been working on the residence, and Father Josemaría agreed to wear them. 'I put them on and headed into the street,' Father Josemaría later recalled. It was now about one o'clock in the afternoon. He was the first to leave. Before stepping out into the street to try to mingle with the jubilant crowds he made the Sign of the Cross. He was alone and so vulnerable. The overalls fitted him very badly and, as he was going out bareheaded, he was also aware that his priestly tonsure was clearly visible.[270]

If anyone recognized his tonsure his end would be swift and brutal.

But no one in the rejoicing, revolutionary crowds noticed it. A man wearing a suit and tie would have been considered an enemy of the people and most likely shot. But a man in ill-fitting overalls was accepted as part and parcel of the revolution.

Father Josemaría made his way to his mother's apartment, which was nearby in Dr Cárceles Street. He spoke by telephone with Juan Jiménez Vargas and learned that all his sons who had left the residence had arrived safely back at their homes or were at the homes of their friends.

Father Josemaría then began to make short notes about what was happening. The staccato style of these notes with words often abbreviated conveys the breathless tension and anxiety of those times. They cover five days from 20 July to 25 July. Here are some extracts:

> Monday, 20th: Worried about everyone, especially Ricardo [Ricardo Fernández who had gone to Valencia to start the new students' residence] ... A bad night, hot ... All three parts of the Rosary ... Don't have my breviary ... Militias on the roof.
> Tuesday, 21: No Mass ... We consider going to live at Ferraz ... Juan (on the phone) says no. Juan comes over in the morning.[271]

Juan, who had qualified as a doctor, was able to move about freely. He had been to the city mortuary to find it was overflowing with corpses. And there were so many bodies arriving that they were piling them up outside. He confirmed the rumours that firing squads were carrying out mass executions all over Madrid.

That day Father Josemaría also rang the funeral parlour across from the church of Santa Isabel and learned that the church had been burned down. The convent too had not been spared.

> Wednesday, 22: Can't say Mass, and am worried about my people. I call Juan and he is not in (at 8) ... Not drinking water for everyone, especially our people [He was offering the sacrifice of not drinking water during those hot days and nights for everyone, especially his sons] ... I pray for the dead ... Have decided not to use the phone ... Rosary novena to Our Lady of Pillar ... We light candles in front of a picture of Merciful Love ... We heard, 'Don't fire back at the snipers. Wait for another chance. One bullet per target!' ... Thursday, 23: No Mass! ... It's awfully hot. Yesterday I thought I was getting used to it. Going to try to get hold of a breviary ... Didn't tell Juan to go to 16 [The residence at 16

Ferraz Street] and bring me mine because the boy is very reluctant to go there, even though he passes right by it. Says it's not prudent ... Juan comes over (at 8.30); hasn't been able to receive Communion, because the churches are either burned or confiscated ... He's going to Isidoro's place, and then to the Residence to get my ID card, etc. He's thinking of going to the post office, to see if there are any letters. Doesn't think it is possible to bring the prayer book ... I find a missal ...'[272]

Two days later, on Saturday, 25 July, the Feast of St James the patron saint of Spain, the Republican Government expropriated all buildings belonging to religious institutions and that same day ninety-five of the imprisoned Catholic clergy were executed. Shortly afterwards churches were ordered to close and the government decreed that anyone taking part in an act of religious worship would be guilty of a criminal offence. Hearing Mass would be 'a grave crime punishable by death'.

CHAPTER 36

The Wedding Ring

It was also on Saturday, 25 July, in the morning, that Juan Jiménez Vargas went to the Ferraz Street residence. It nearly cost him his life and proved all his fears about the dangers of returning to the residence were justified. Juan had only just entered the building when there was a violent pounding on the door. A militia patrol had come to search the building. These militias, armed units of the revolutionary parties and unions, socialists, Communists and anarchists, were imposing their own law and summary justice in the Republican controlled areas. They raided whatever houses they liked, arrested anyone they considered 'suspicious' and in many cases took them outside and shot them in the street. These militias were completely outside any government control and in Madrid they would kill at will and terrorize the population for more than nine months, until May of 1937 when they were finally brought under military discipline. The militia patrol that had raided the residence was of the FAI (Federación Anarquista Ibérica, Iberian Anarchist Federation). They made a thorough search and found Father Josemaría's cassock and his discipline which told them that a priest had been living there.

Juan answered their questions as best he could by giving them vague answers such as that some medical students lived there, that the owner of the house was a foreigner and that the chaplain did not come there very often.

The militia then declared the house was seized in the name of the CNT (Confederación Nacional de Trabajo, National Federation of Labour).

'Do you live here?' one of the militiamen asked Juan.

'No,' he said.

'Let's go to your house then,' they said.

Juan took them to his home. He was convinced he would either end up in prison or be shot. In his bedroom he had a box in which there were files containing the addresses of the students who went to the residence and blank ID cards signed by him when he was secretary of the Association of Traditionalist Students. These were students politically opposed to the left-wing revolutionary groups now in power. To be found with a Traditionalist Student ID card was a death sentence in itself. There was also the danger that the revolutionaries would connect the list of students at the residence with the Traditionalist Association and then all the students' lives would be in danger. The militiamen meticulously searched his room but, inexplicably, did not notice the box.

After finishing their search the militia were still not satisfied. They told Juan he would have to 'accompany' them, which was usually the militia's way of saying they were taking their prisoner 'for a walk' and shooting him. It was at this point that Juan's mother made a dramatic plea for his life and the militia patrol leader changed his mind about taking Juan with them, saying. 'We don't kill anyone. The ones who do the killing are the socialists.' And pointing to his pistol he said, 'We carry this only as a preventive measure.' Then he told the others, 'Let him stay!'[273]

The patrol disappeared, leaving Juan with his mother.

Juan quickly made himself scarce. Outside on the street he met Alvaro del Portillo and they discussed the official Republican Government communiqués which were maintaining that the Uprising was just a limited rebellion which would soon be put down. Juan and Alvaro both came to the conclusion that the government reports were not true and they could be facing a long war.

Juan then rejoined Father Josemaría at his mother's apartment. He found the priest deeply worried about what might be happening to his sons, especially those who were out of Madrid, the two who had gone to Valencia, Ricardo Fernández and Paco Botella, and also Pedro Casciaro who was with his family miles away in Torrevieja. Father Josemaría knew that all of his sons, apart from Isidoro Zorzano, who had Argentinian citizenship, were in danger of being arrested and shot for their Christian activities. One of them, José María Hernández, the engineering student they nicknamed Chiqui, was arrested soon afterwards and put in the notorious San Antón jail, a former school that had been turned into a prison.

Alvaro del Portillo also ended up as a prisoner in San Antón towards the end of that year, just because he came from a Catholic family. It was a jail where death could be dispensed at the whim of the guards at any moment. Alvaro has described two terrifying incidents. 'There was a chapel,' he said, 'in which about four hundred of us were incarcerated. One day a Communist soldier stomped up to the altar on which there was a picture of a saint and he put a cigarette butt on the saint's lips. One of the fellows with me went up and took the butt away. He was killed on the spot for doing that. There was an incredible hatred of religion.' Then Alvaro tells of another incident in which he nearly had his brains blown out. 'One day one of the guards came up to me – his name was Petrof, a Russian name [probably one of the many Russian secret police in Spain during the Civil War] – and he put a pistol to my temple and said, "You're wearing glasses – you must be a priest." He could have killed me at any moment. I think the only reason he didn't was because God thought I still had a lot of fighting to do against the devil, or because I was not worthy of heaven. It was terrifying.'[274] Father Josemaría fervently prayed for his sons and for their safety and offered many mortifications.

Pedro Casciaro was for the time being safe and living under his father's powerful protection. His father, a few days after the outbreak of the Civil War, had been elected Provincial President of the Popular Front. It was a post he had had to accept. It would have been too dangerous to refuse. One of his father's cousins who was a judge, was himself tried for refusing to pass an unjust death sentence.

The Wedding Ring

As with so many families, the Casciaros embraced varied political views. Some of Pedro's cousins were naval officers and were eliminated by the forces of the left. Some naval officers were shot but many were thrown overboard into the sea and drowned. One uncle was a radical socialist mayor while others were socialists, moderate Republicans or Monarchist councillors. Another cousin, who was in the Falange, was jailed in Alicante with José Antonio Primo de Rivera, the Falange founder. And yet another cousin was a volunteer in the International Brigade.

Pedro's father, despite his powerful position in the new political set-up, deplored the dramatic turn events had taken, especially Calvo Sotelo's assassination. Shortly after the war began he saved many people's lives, especially priests and religious. In his house he kept the Blessed Sacrament and in the room where it was hidden he had a lamp always burning. He had also recently appointed a librarian at the Institute at Albacete. Unknown to almost everyone the new librarian was a priest. Under Pedro's father's protection he was able to minister to the sick and the dying in the area.

Fr Josemaría stayed in his mother's apartment for about ten days. Then at the beginning of August, shortly after Juan had rejoined him, he received a warning from the caretaker of the apartments. Someone had informed the militia that 'wanted people' were hiding in the building. The militia might swoop at any moment to search the whole apartment block. Father Josemaría and Juan made plans for an immediate departure.

Just before Father Josemaría left, his mother came to him and gave him his father's wedding ring and asked him to wear it. People would then think he was married and she believed that wearing the ring would reduce the risk of him being arrested as a priest, and shot.[275]

Father Josemaría put on the ring and, together with Juan, left the apartment using the back staircase. Outside in the street, dressed as a layman, he walked aimlessly from one part of Madrid to the other, aware that he was now one of the most despised and hated of men – a priest. In that month of August 1936, the first month after the outbreak of the Civil War, the Communists and their supporters murdered 2,077 priests, nuns and other members of religious orders. This was an average of almost 70 killings a day. Father Josemaría was now trapped in Madrid, the city that was at the very centre of the bloodbath, the city where it seemed to him as if the very powers of hell had been unleashed.

CHAPTER 37

The Door the Militia Failed to Open

As a hunted priest, day and night on the run, he was always looking for somewhere to hide. The Spanish Civil War was a time of unbelievable terror for Catholics in the Communist controlled areas of Spain, especially in the capital, Madrid. Apart from the priests and nuns who lost their lives, there are many recorded instances of ordinary men and women, who were arrested and shot, simply because they were found to be wearing a religious medal or had a holy picture in their home. The young priest Father Josemaría, the founder of Opus Dei, was well known in Madrid for his priestly zeal, and as a result was pursued with great determination by the security police and certain militia units. Outside on the streets, every hour was filled with tension and fear. He was aware that at any moment the security police or the militia might spot him, or someone in the crowd might recognize him and denounce him. There was constant danger everywhere he went, every waking minute. And the danger extended to anyone who might be with him, such as Juan Jiménez Vargas or Alvaro del Portillo, who steadfastly remained at his side, helping him in every way they could.

Alvaro says of those days, 'We moved from place to place, sleeping where we could ... At times even friends didn't want to have us. Some took us in, but greatly feared they might be denounced. For to shelter a priest in your house at that time was like signing your own death warrant.'[276]

One day Father Josemaría learned of a terrible incident which caused him great distress. A man, who resembled him, had been arrested and summarily executed by the militia. The priest-hunters had undoubtedly thought they had caught the much-wanted priest. After killing the poor man they hanged him on a tree near to where Father Josemaría's mother lived for all to see. It troubled him very much to think that it was on his account that this man had lost his life. From the very moment he heard about it, he began to pray for the man who had been mistaken for him. And every day for the rest of his life he remembered him in his Mass.[277]

In those early days of the Civil War, when he was constantly on the run and unable to get hold of any altar breads or wine for saying Mass, he would celebrate what he called 'dry Masses'. He would say all the prayers of the Mass but omit the consecration. For those parts of the Mass which changed each day according to the season or the feast day he would say the prayers from the Mass for vocations, where there is a plea to Our Lord to send labourers into His harvest. The Gospel, which he knew by heart, was always the passage where Jesus calls Peter and Andrew as they cast a net into the sea, and then calls James and John, as they are in their boat with their father repairing their nets.

At the moment of Communion he would say the spiritual communion taught to him as a child by the Piarist priest. 'I wish, Lord, to receive you with the purity, humility and devotion with which your Holy Mother received you, with the spirit and fervour of the saints.'[278]

The first refuge Father Josemaría was able to find was a flat on the third floor of a huge apartment block in Sagasta Street. It was the home of Manuel Sainz, one of the young men who had got to know Father Josemaría through the DYA academy, and whose family had been dispersed by the terror. But even gaining access to the flat presented a problem. He had to enter the building without being seen by the doorman. Political committees were now in charge in all buildings. Porters had to inform them of all the residents' comings and goings and report all stranger. The committees in their turn would pass on anything suspicious to the security police or to the militia.[279]

About midday Father Josemaría succeeded in getting into the flat without the porter noticing him and Juan Jiménez Vargas joined him later in the afternoon.

Manuel, who was not afraid to go out on the streets, did the shopping. One day in the middle of August he made Father Josemaría very happy. He risked going to the Ferraz residence and returned with some letters he had got from the doorkeeper. One of them was from Pedro Casciaro in Torrevieja. Then a few days later a letter arrived from Ricardo Fernández who was trapped in Valencia. This letter, which had been sent to Isidoro, announced that he was alive and well.[280] What had been worrying Father Josemaría most was not having news of his sons.

On 28 August Manuel brought home with him his cousin, Juan Sainz.

As a precaution, Juan Sainz was kept in the dark about Father Josemaría's true identity. Two days later, on 30 August, when Manuel had gone out, they heard loud voices on the stairs.

'We realised that the militia had entered the building on one of their periodic searches,' Juan Sainz recalls.

True to form, the militia began their search in the basement and systematically worked their way through each floor, checking every apartment. 'Before they reached our floor, we climbed an inside staircase leading to an attic,' Juan Sainz says. 'Like all attics, it was dusty and full of discarded furniture. The ceiling was so low we couldn't stand up. The heat was stifling . . . it was August and very hot.'

The three of them – Father Josemaría, Juan Jiménez Vargas and Juan Sainz – sweated it out in the attic from lunchtime until late in the afternoon, and every minute the militia drew closer.

'Then, we heard them entering the attic room next to ours to search it,' Juan remembers. 'Father Josemaría turned to me and said: "I'm a priest. This looks bad. If you want, you can make an act of contrition and I will give you absolution."'

Juan Sainz thought the end had come. 'I'll never forget that incident with Father Josemaría. It took great courage to reveal that he was a priest. For, had the militia entered, I could have tried to save my own life by denouncing him. But he rose above the danger and the fear and exercised his priesthood by offering me the possibility of the Sacrament of Penance.'[281]

As the militia drew closer Father Josemaría prayed fervently to his Guardian Angel for help and asked his two companions to do the same. Then they heard a militiaman's footsteps approach the door of their attic. Father Josemaría made the Sign of the Cross over them and gave them both absolution. Juan Jiménez Vargas asked him in a whisper, 'Father, what will happen if they find us and kill us?'

'We'll go to heaven, my son,' Father Josemaría replied. And when he had said this his two companions relaxed and a great sense of peace came over them. Father Josemaría continued praying silently and intensely.[282]

The footsteps halted before the door. There was a pause. But the door didn't open. There was another pause. Then the footsteps began to recede.

'Astonishingly, after having searched the entire building the militia did not enter the room where we were hiding,' Juan Sainz recalls.[283]

Why their attic room wasn't searched is a complete mystery. For that day the militia had opened every door and searched every room on every floor of the vast apartment block. The door of their attic must have been the only one that day that the militia had failed to open.

The three stayed in the attic until about eight o'clock at night, which was the time the main doors were usually closed. Juan Jiménez Vargas then went down the stairs and knocked gently on a door of one of the flats. A young woman opened it and Juan asked if he could have a glass of water. The apartment turned out to be the home of the Countess of Leyvas who, on learning that Juan was hiding from the militia in the attic with two others, invited all of them for the night.[284]

It was then they found out that Manuel Sainz had returned home in the middle of the search and the militia had arrested him.

The following morning the militia swooped again. The raid was so swift and sudden that it caught everyone by surprise and the three hadn't time to get out of the Countess's flat. Militiamen were everywhere. They ordered the tenants to open the doors of their apartments and all their outside windows. The tenants were also commanded to put their lights on so they could be clearly seen from outside by militiamen.[285] Father Josemaría and his fellow fugitives crept into the dining room, the only room without an outside window. Militiamen roamed the corridors and occasionally yelled orders through the open doors of the flats. But they did not seem to be entering many of the flats. Father Josemaría tried to relieve the tension by telling jokes. The Countess then suggested saying the Rosary, which Father Josemaría led. Later, to their relief, they heard the militia departing once more.[286]

For two days they hid in the Countess's flat. The Countess wanted them to stay longer, even though she knew the militia were killing anyone caught giving refuge to priests, women included. Father Josemaría had to insist they move on.[287]

Before they left, however, the Countess gave them yet more help. She took it upon herself to make sure that the caretaker was fully occupied and giving her his full attention as they slipped out of the building.

CHAPTER 38

The Key Thrown Down the Drain

Before leaving the Countess's flat they had received an offer of help. It was from a widow with two children who said they could stay in her home. But Father Josemaría turned the offer down. One of the children was very young, and staying there would have been too risky for everyone concerned.[288]

Another flat was found in the Herradores Plaza. It was flat no 4. But hiding in the Herradores Flat soon seemed as if they had jumped out of the frying pan into the fire. One night the plaza was suddenly surrounded by police and militia. The porters in charge of the various flats were made to bring the keys and open the flat doors so the police and militia could round up all those inside. But a strange thing happened. The porter responsible for flat no 4 was not notified of what he had to do. And, perhaps even stranger still, the militia made no attempt to enter flat no 4.[289] When the search was over the fugitives once again fled the building.

Finding another hiding place proved very difficult indeed.

Everywhere they went they encountered the same response. People were too frightened to help a priest or anyone with him. At one stage Father Josemaría went to a house and pleaded: 'Just let me stay here a couple of hours.' But they wouldn't let him in the house. They were too terrified.[290]

The Key Thrown Down the Drain 247

He and his two companions continued walking the streets of Madrid. During the day they trekked from one end of the city to the other and at night they slept rough wherever they could lay their heads. This went on until Father Josemaría decided it would be safer if they separated. So they parted.

Alvaro found refuge in a house belonging to friends of his family. The house, in Serrano Street, was next door to what had become the headquarters of the Director General of Security, the dreaded security police. Being so close to the security police they might have felt gave them a certain immunity. After all it was one of the last places that anyone would expect fugitives to choose as a hiding place. An Argentinian banner was also displayed at the front of the house in the hope it might deter the militia from searching the building.

Alvaro, after a month not daring to venture out of doors and having lost touch with Father Josemaría, one day decided to risk walking as far as the state civil engineering offices, where he was working as an engineer when the civil war broke out. He was curious to see if there were any wages for him. When he got to the state civil engineering offices he boldly went inside, gave his name and asked about his wages. He found, somewhat to his surprise that he was still on the payroll and he was able to pick up pay for all the weeks since the start of the Civil War.

Alvaro left the civil engineering offices quite pleased with his achievement and decided to celebrate his windfall by having a glass of beer. He chose a busy cafe in Alonso Martinez square called La Mezquita. It was a very dangerous thing to do. The police and militia were in the habit of suddenly pouncing on people in cafes and demanding to see their papers. Alvaro had no papers. And, as he said later, 'I didn't even have the sense to go inside the cafe. Without a care in the world I sat down at a table near the pavement. It never crossed my mind that at any time I could have been asked for my papers, in which case I would have been jailed immediately. It must have been our Guardian Angels, Father Josemaría's and mine, that prompted me to do such a crazy thing. All of a sudden I saw José María González's father running towards me looking as nervous as could be.'

'Thank God you're here,' he said to Alvaro. 'Do you know who's at my house? The Father! He asked me to let him rest for a short time because he was so exhausted. He's so tired he can hardly stand up.' He also explained to Alvaro that there was a problem with the caretaker who was a militia spy. This meant that it would not be possible to hide Father Josemaría there for long.

'So without thinking twice,' Alvaro recalls, 'I said, "Then let him come with me!"' The house was very close by in Caracas Street so Alvaro immediately went there and got the exhausted Father Josemaría back to his comparatively 'safe' house next to the security police. There was one final difficulty. To get inside they had to elude the sentry outside the security police building. This they successfully managed to do and Juan Jiménez Vargas soon afterwards joined them there.[291]

Thanks to Father Josemaría their life in that house next to the security police soon became happy, prayerful and contented. 'The Father would preach the morning meditation and then help us keep busy all day long,' Alvaro said. 'Since without books we couldn't read or study he would invent things to entertain us or occupy what free time we had.' They were like a wonderful, happy family, very united and helping and caring for each another. And as the terror raged outside during those September days of 1936, they managed to enjoy weeks of blessed happiness.[292] It was too good to last. Their serenity was abruptly shattered on the first day of October. It was then that one of Alvaro's brothers, Ramón, came to warn them. The militia were searching other places belonging to the family that owned the house they were hiding in. And the militia had killed people they had discovered in these other properties.

'The Father,' Alvaro says, 'then asked Juan Jiménez Vargas to look for another refuge. He told my brother and me, who didn't know what to do, to stay in the house until the next day to await news about whether or not a new hiding place had been found. In the meantime the Father managed, after several phone calls, to speak to José María González, the chemistry teacher, who said he was sure he could find us another safe place. Father Josemaría then went out to meet him.'[293]

The place they had arranged to meet was the Paseo de la Castellana. As soon as he saw Father Josemaría, José María González greeted him with great joy and affection, and then took a small key out of his pocket and handed it to him together with an address. 'Go to this house and stay there,' he said. 'It belongs to a family I'm very friendly with – they're now out of Madrid. And you will be able to trust the porter.'

'But how can I stay in a stranger's house?' Father Josemaría asked. 'What if someone comes or calls? What could I say?'

'Don't worry,' was the reply. 'There's a maid there who is also totally trustworthy – she can give you whatever help you need.'

'But how old is she?' Father Josemaría asked.

'Oh, I'd say about 22 or 23.'

Father Josemaría then said, 'I can't – I wouldn't even want to – stay locked up day and night with a young woman. As a priest I have a commitment to God which is more important than anything else. I'd sooner die than take a chance of offending God and failing in this commitment.'

He then walked to the nearest drain and dropped the key down it.[294]

Father Josemaría later made his way back to the house next to the security police headquarters. Alvaro and his brother Ramón were there waiting for him.[295]

'He greeted me and started weeping,' Alvaro recalls. 'I asked him, "Father, why are you crying?" I was very moved by his obvious suffering. He was so extraordinarily human and loved his friends with all his heart.'

Father Josemaría then told Alvaro how, during the time he had just spent walking through the streets of Madrid, he had learned of the violent deaths at the hands of the militia of his two good friends, Father Lino Vea-Murguía and Father Pedro Poveda.[296]

Father Lino was a priest who helped him a great deal. It was he who had trudged through the snow with him to arrange the first catechism classes in the Los Pinos district.

Father Josemaría thought so highly of him that he had asked him to hear the confessions of the first members and their friends.

The militia had caught Father Lino in his flat. They had burst in on him just as he was finishing saying Mass. Ripping off his vestments, they took him outside and shot him.

Father Pedro Poveda, who was the founder of the Teresian Institute, had also been arrested at his home. He had been taken away by his captors and the following morning his body – with three bullets in it – was found at the entrance to the cemetery.[297]

At Father Pedro's request Father Josemaría used to give spiritual guidance to the Teresians and Father Pedro himself often went to him for spiritual advice. It was with Father Pedro that he had had a last never-to-be-forgotten conversation shortly before the outbreak of the Civil War. The two friends had discussed the possibility that one or both of them might undergo martyrdom on account of their priesthood and they asked themselves the question, 'If they kill us, what will become of our friendship when we meet again in heaven?' And both priests had come to the same conclusion: if one of them were killed, in heaven he would remain the friend of the other. And when they both met together in heaven they would have even greater affection for each other than ever they had on earth.[298] The Father, Alvaro says, 'maintained forever the conviction that death does not interrupt friendship'.[299] Father Pedro Poveda was canonized by Pope John Paul II on 4 May 2003.

The day of Father Josemaría's return to the house was the eve of the eighth anniversary of the founding of the Work. He told Alvaro that Our Lord often gave him a special favour on such anniversaries and he was convinced that something was going to happen this time. It did. And what happened was this. Father Josemaría suddenly became aware he was confronted with martyrdom. His knees began trembling with fear and all the strength drained out of him. It seemed as if his legs were going to collapse under him. Then the fear and tension suddenly lifted to be replaced with a wonderful peace. He later explained that this was God's gift for that anniversary. God was helping him to see that without his help he was a coward. As a result of this experience Father Josemaría understood he was being shown that, in the terrible days ahead, it was God's help he would always have to rely on, not on his own strength.[300]

There still remained the problem that the militia might raid the house at any moment. They decided to move out as quickly as possible. And right after they left a militia patrol arrived to search the house.

And so it was that three men on the run ended up on 3 October, discouraged and exhausted, sitting on the edge of the pavement at Cuatro Caminos. They were Father Josemaría, Alvaro del Portillo and José María González, a priest, an engineer and a teacher of chemistry, desperately wondering where they could find another place of refuge for a fugitive priest. It was then José María González remembered a young chemistry professor, Eugenio Sellés, who had met Father Josemaría at the Ferraz Street residence about a year earlier. He lived with his wife in Chamartín, which was at the end of the tram line and across an empty stretch of land where the militia brought groups of prisoners at night to be shot. There were also several checkpoints that would have to be avoided.

Juan Jiménez Vargas, who as a doctor had a certain freedom of movement, went to see him.[301] The professor would always remember the day when Juan asked him if Father Josemaría could stay in his home. It was a simple request but involved making a terrifying decision. The professor realized he was putting his life on the line but he agreed to take the risk of having a priest in his home. That same night Father Josemaría appeared at his door accompanied by Alvaro.

While staying in Professor Sellés' home Father Josemaría spent most of the day in the professor's study, afraid to leave it in case someone came into the house.

Professor Sellés remembers the remarkable atmosphere Father Josemaría created in his home. 'Despite the dangers, our meals were enlivened by his cheerful and interesting conversation. What struck me was his trust in God, his complete abandonment. He showed no sign of tension. It was if nothing untoward was happening.'[302]

Others who risked their lives to help him also remembered how Father Josemaría abandoned himself into the hands of God and ceaselessly repeated the brief aspiration, 'Fiat!' ('Be it done!') 'Fiat!' ('Be it done!') 'Fiat!' ('Be it done!'). And everyone who came in contact with him at this time felt the strength of his unshakable faith. But the tentacles of the religious persecution seemed to be stretching everywhere, touching everyone and transmitting a chilling fear. All Catholics were terrified about what might happen to them. Families removed all religious symbols and images from their homes. Everybody lived in fear of the security police or the militia arriving on their doorsteps to invade their privacy and search their homes. Finding a single religious picture or medallion was considered sufficient reason for arrest and imprisonment. And once in a prison cell accused of a crime connected with religion, execution was often literally only a short walk away in another part of the prison.

Professor Sellés and his wife, however, courageously continued to keep a picture of the Holy Family in their bedroom. 'What I remember best is the Rosary we prayed each evening,' the professor recalled. 'It was led by Father Josemaría and we knelt before the picture of the Holy Family.'

Father Josemaría also said Mass in the professor's home. The top of the piano was his altar and the crucifix on his Rosary served as the altar crucifix.

But with each passing day the dangers increased for fugitives hiding in people's homes. Neighbour often denounced neighbour if they had the slightest suspicion that there was a stranger next door, or if they saw or heard anything out of the ordinary. It was unsafe to stay in one place for more than one or two days.

At this point Father Josemaría decided the best way to avoid the secret police and the militia would be to go out again on the streets. This way, he wouldn't be putting anyone at risk. So he began once more walking the streets of Madrid, going from one end of the city to the other, back and forth, back and forth, forcing himself to keep on the move during the hours of daylight and at night sleeping rough in whatever place he could find to lay his head. Sometimes he was so exhausted he fell asleep standing on his feet.

CHAPTER 39

Refuge in an Asylum

Juan Jiménez Vargas together with fellow doctor Joaquin Herro continued the desperate search for another hiding place. Their quest led them to another doctor. He was Dr Angel Suils who ran a psychiatric clinic or mental asylum in the outskirts of Madrid and who had been one of Father Josemaría's classmates at Logroño Institute. Dr Suils was approached and asked if he would be willing to shelter Father Josemaría in his asylum until another safe place could be found. Dr Suils replied that he would be only too happy to 'admit' his old classmate. During the Civil War Dr Suils, a good and caring man, was to save many lives by allowing fugitives to be 'patients' in his psychiatric clinic.[303]

The only problem was how to get Father Josemaría to the mental asylum. Joaquin Herrero, who was a doctor at the emergency hospital in Madrid, came up with the ideal solution. He arranged for the official hospital car to collect Father Josemaría and take him as a mental patient to the asylum. The car provided the perfect cover. It had a Communist Red guard for a driver and boldly displayed a portrait of the Republican leader, President Azaña. It would have no difficulty getting through any check point. Early next morning, on 7 October, Father Josemaría was picked up at Juan's flat by the hospital car complete with Red guard driver. Joaquin Herro sat next to the driver and Father Josemaría was put on the back seat. Joaquin told the Red guardsman, 'The man is mentally ill. He isn't dangerous but he suffers from delusions of grandeur and I am taking him to the asylum for treatment.'

To help convince the driver this was so Father Josemaría began talking to himself and saying, 'I am doctor Gregory Maranon! (Maranon was a leading Liberal, author, biographer and medical scientist) I am a person too well known in the whole of Spain to be locked up.'

But the Red guard's immediate response was, 'Look, if he's so crazy, I think we'll be better just stopping the car and shooting him.' And he meant it. Joaquin had quickly to convince him that the treatment would be worthwhile. For the rest of the journey Father Josemaría remained silent.[304]

Dr Suils' clinic was a large converted house called Casa de Reposo and could accommodate up thirty people, including patients and nurses. It consisted of a semi-basement for the most seriously mentally ill and two other floors for 'patients under observation'. And it was surrounded by a garden. Its official title was the Psychiatric Sanatorium of Cuidad Lineal. Among the severely mentally ill in the semi-basement were some very sad cases. There was an old lady whose moods swung from apathy to raging anger. It was thought her madness had been caused by her son who, after committing a crime of passion, had killed himself. There also was a man who stalked the garden and the corridors threatening invisible persecutors and spitting at them. And there were individuals who had entered the clinic pretending to be mentally ill and had ended up truly insane. Most of the people 'under observation' on the other two floors were refugees feigning mental disorders. One exception was a six-year-old boy. His parents, who were landowners, had been murdered in Extremadura. The woman taking care of him had managed to get him to Madrid but the murderers of his parents were looking for him so they could kill the heir of the estate they had seized.[305]

The asylum was under the control of the UGT, the General Workers' Union, and had been approved by the Medical Association of Madrid with 'Comrade Angels', as its director and 'controlled by its personnel, completely subject to the socialist union.'[306]

Most of the nurses and staff were Communists or Communist sympathizers who looked for any signs that the patients might be feigning insanity. If they suspected anyone they informed the security police who would suddenly appear and take the person away to be shot.

It was at this time, in early October of 1936, that the Spanish Civil War gave the world a new word: fifth-column. It is now defined as an organized body sympathizing with or working for the enemy within a country at war. The word is accredited to the Nationalist leader General Mola. Believing Madrid would soon be captured, he announced that the capital would fall as a result of the four columns of General Varela, which were then advancing towards it, and of a fifth column already inside it: the supporters of the Nationalists.

This injudicious statement provoked a frenzied reaction from the Popular Front revolutionary parties. The various militia units and the security police began to raid and search houses all over the city and made thousands of arrests. Anyone who was not a member of a revolutionary party was considered a possible fifth-columnist, or potential traitor or spy.[307]

And in all districts of Madrid spread the dreaded tentacles of Communist 'checas' which were based on the Soviet CHEKAS, the name formed from the initial letters of the Pan-Russian Special Committee for the Supression of the Counter-revolution and of Sabotage, the forerunner of the NKVD and KGB. The Spanish checas, whose members were often self-appointed, condemned people to death on unverified accusations of informers and on the flimsiest of evidence. In Madrid alone there came to be more than 200 checa committees for the elimination of Fascism.[308]

Juan Jiménez Vargas, who was going about Madrid trying to keep in contact with everyone, was most at risk. On 15 October, he wrote in his diary: 'Last night the police went around Madrid asking for documentation in people's homes and arresting many people. The personal ID card is not enough. They demand evidence of being trusted by the Popular Front.' And further down he wrote: 'A little argument took place at Joaquín's [the home of his colleague Dr Joaquín Hererro who had made the arrangements to get the Father to the asylum in the hospital car]. His mother told me yesterday that she was praying a lot for me because I'm taking my life in my hands by walking around on the streets so much! I told her that I must have nine lives, like a cat, and still have plenty left, because with all the doctors I've been to and all the blows I have suffered in my years, I haven't managed to use up more than four or five.'[309]

At that point the diary ends for Juan later that same day was about to lose another of his 'lives'. As he later explained, 'Just as I was waiting for Isidoro to go with him to the insane asylum, a patrol showed up and I got arrested.'[310]

Father Josemaría, to his great sorrow, now had two sons in prison, 'Chiqui' (José María Hernández), and Juan Jiménez Vargas who had been his main link with the outside world. His immediate response was to intensify his prayers and penances for all his sons, especially those in prison.

Isidoro Zorzano had been born in Buenos Aires though his parents had returned to Spain shortly afterwards. This made him an Argentinian citizen, even though he did not have any documents to prove it such as an Argentine passport. He took over Juan's role. Wearing an armband displaying the Argentinian flag he was able to move around in relative safety.

Everyone lived in fear. One day the militia appeared in the asylum looking for Fascist traitors. They entered the administrator's office and said to him, 'Don't bother changing your clothes, comrade. We just need ten minutes of your time so you can make a statement at the station. You'll return in the same car.' He was never seen again.[311]

Dr Suils himself taught Father Josemaría how to imitate a mentally sick person. And Father Josemaría would feign mental illness whenever anyone was watching him or during checks by the security police. On another occasion the security police made a sudden swoop, most probably acting on information from one of the nurses, and seized a man who, it was later learned, was the Duke of Penaranda. The first Father Josemaría knew of it was after the Duke had been arrested and taken away. He was very upset that he had not been able to give him any spiritual help before he was taken to what was almost certain death. After the incident Father Josemaría went to Dr Suils and complained that he had not known about the arrest. He pointed out that he was, first and foremost, a priest and he didn't want anyone hiding in the clinic to be arrested without having a chance to prepare for death. 'From now on,' he said, 'no one is to be taken from here without my hearing his confession and giving him absolution.'[312]

A group of Communist security police armed with submachine guns also suddenly appeared and one day began making a very thorough investigation of everyone of the patients. The chances of surviving this check looked very bleak for any of the fugitives hiding there until a patient, who really was crazy, approached one of the security police. In an instant he had grabbed the policeman's submachine gun and snatched it away from him. Everyone moved back expecting a spray of bullets at any moment. 'Is this a string instrument or a wind instrument?' the crazy fellow wanted to know. The Communist police retrieved their gun but were clearly shaken by the incident, which brought an immediate end to their investigation.[313]

'These people all belong in straitjackets!' one security policeman angrily complained as they marched out of the building.[314]

Of the three nurses looking after the patients, Father Josemaría found that two were Communists or Communist sympathizers and bitterly anti-religious. These he knew wouldn't hesitate to denounce anyone who was a practising Catholic. As a priest he would have to be especially careful when they were around. But the third nurse, who was the head nurse, Father Josemaría found could be trusted. Her name was Maria Luisa Polanco.

María Luisa Polanco herself remembers what happened next. 'Father Josemaría after some time had passed told me he was a priest,' she said. 'Previously he had described himself as a lawyer' (which of course was quite true for he was also a qualified lawyer). By telling her he was a priest, Father Josemaría was literally putting his life in her hands.

He went to tell her that he intended to say Mass in his room. Which must have something of a bombshell to her. He then asked, 'María Luisa, do you want to guard where I am going to say Mass and see no one enters while I am saying it?' And a stunned María Luisa agreed to stand guard for him.

In the corridor between the room of one of the Communist nurses and Father Josemaría's room was a small couch. Father Josemaría suggest to Maria Luisa that she should sit on the couch while he was saying Mass and 'if anyone approaches, just knock or speak in a loud voice,' he said.[315]

María Luisa did as he asked. She sat on the couch apparently reading while acting as lookout for Father Josemaría.

Fully aware of the repression of religion in the Republican areas of Spain, on 22 August 1936 the Holy See granted priests in Spain permission 'to celebrate the Holy Sacrifice without an altar, without sacred vestments, and using, in place of a chalice, a decent drinking glass.'

It was these new dispositions that allowed Father Josemaría to say Mass in the asylum.[316] He placed the things for saying Mass inside a cabinet with the door open. If María Luisa signalled to him that someone was coming he could then close the doors and hide everything.[317]

With María Luisa's help, from then on Father Josemaría said Mass every day he was in the asylum. After Mass he would take communion to some of the fugitives hiding there. Two of these were the Marquis and Marchioness of Torres de Oran.[318]

'Being able to receive daily Communion in such circumstances was surely a gift from God,' the Marchioness said in later years.

It was about this time that Father Josemaría, alone and isolated in the asylum, found a welcomed companion. To escape the searches and mass arrests José María González joined him as another 'patient under observation'.

By the end of October the Nationalist offensive had reached the gates of Madrid and the flashes from the artillery could be seen from the asylum, much to the delight of some of the mentally ill patients. One was heard to call out, 'Now the crazy people are in Madrid and having a party. How much better it is to be here. How much more peaceful.' The Republican army was being reinforced with the newly-arrived International Brigades, volunteers from all over the world attracted by the Communist International call to save democracy in Spain. This combined force stopped the Nationalist advance at the beginning of November.

Some areas of Madrid close to the battle-front had to be evacuated. One of these districts was Ciudad Universitaria which took in Dr Cárceles Street where Father Josemaría's mother and family were still living. Hoping that the Nationalist troops would soon occupy the area Father Josemaría's family stayed on in their home until they were forced to move out towards the end of November. Then they went to a hotel in the centre of Madrid, near the Puerta del Sol where Isidoro was able to make contact with them. He took them to an apartment at 15 Caracas Street, belonging to Alvaro González whose son, José María González, had joined Father Josemaría in the asylum.

Santiago remembers the luggage the family took with them to Caracas Street: 'one suitcase with the indispensable items, and a trunk with the papers of the Work.' The contents of the trunk could have got them all arrested. They were no less than the archives of Opus Dei and they included Father Josemaría's intimate notes. The trunk attracted the attention of the porter of the Caracas Street apartments who wanted to examine the contents before allowing it on the premises. Father Josemaría's sister Carmen flatly refused to let him and told him 'on principle I do not want to open it, and would sooner leave it in the doorway.' And that was where it remained.[319]

The porter, perhaps because he was responsible for reporting all new residents to the security police and thinking that Santiago might be of military age and might get him into trouble, refused to allow him to live in the building. His mother, Doña Dolores and Isidoro decided that the best thing would be for Santiago to go and live with his brother in the asylum. Santiago was admitted as 'a companion of a patient under observation'. The trunk with the papers followed soon afterwards.[320]

The purging of fifth columnists, Fascists and traitors had filled the prisons to bursting point. Throughout the month of November the crowded prisons were systematically emptied by what was officially referred to as the 'extraction of prisoners'. At night the prisoners were loaded on to trucks and driven to the killing grounds, usually quiet places near Madrid, such as the infamous Parcuellos del Jarama district. Then they were executed en masse.[321]

Father Josemaría prayed more and more for all his sons and offered up many mortifications.

It was at this time he wrote in a letter to his spiritual sons about this. To get the letter past the censors he made out that he was loving grandfather writing to his grandchildren whose debts he had undertaken to pay. 'I want to embrace all of you,' he wrote, 'with all my soul, like the doting grandfather I am, so that whatever blows you might receive would fall on the strong back of the one writing to you. Isn't it strange that, having as many debts of my own as I do, I have been allowed to co-sign for everyone in these times of economic collapse? And I hope the payments will be asked of me. If they are, how joyfully I will give all that is needed, down to the last penny!'[322]

Strange, inexplicable things happened. 'Chiqui' (José María Hernández) and Juan Jiménez Vargas both had remarkable close shaves with death during the 'extractions' and nightly shootings.

Chiqui was on a truck with other prisoners waiting to be driven to the place of execution. His name was called out and he was ordered to get off. The truck then drove off to the designated killing area. Chiqui returned to his cell.[323] Juan was in the Porlier prison which was being emptied corridor by corridor. His turn for execution came on 26 November. The prisoners lined up and walked to the truck waiting in the street. It loaded up with prisoners and drove off. Juan and three others were left to be taken on a second trip. The truck returned just before daybreak. Half an hour passed and then it was announced the operation had ended. Those left in the corridor were spared.[324]

Father Josemaría's spiritual sons were always convinced it was his prayers that had saved them.[325]

That winter the asylum was cold and damp and Father Josemaría began to suffer very badly with rheumatism. It was decided to give him an injection of bee sting venom, a treatment that was very fashionable at the time. The effects of the bee venom were dramatic and terrifying. In fact his brother Santiago said later that Dr Suils thought they had killed him. He was left paralysed and in great pain and hardly able to move his head. He was bedridden and in agony for more than two weeks and needed help to do the least thing. At one stage he even had to be fed. His only nourishment was orange juice. He gradually recovered but was very weak and frail. But when someone brought him a heater he immediately gave it away, saying that he wasn't cold and didn't need it.[326]

His months in the asylum were taking a heavy toll of him. There was the constant tension of having to keep up the appearance of madness while he was being watched by Communist nurses. Sometimes a stranger would suddenly appear which would cause immediate unease. For any stranger could be a militia spy or a member of the security police. And all the time he was in the asylum he continually worried about his mother and family and about the members of the Work, his spiritual sons and daughters. Only through Isidoro Zorzano did he receive news of what was happening to all of them.

In January of 1937 Juan Jiménez Vargas was released from the Porlier prison as a result of Isidoro's efforts and Father Josemaría's prayers. Without any documents, and risking re-arrest, Juan hid in his parents' flat for two weeks until he also was able to get into the asylum. Then at the beginning of February Chiqui (José María Hernández) was transferred from the notorious San Antón prison in Madrid to the San Miguel de los Reyes prison in Valencia.[327]

Father Josemaría had earlier made contact again with Pedro Casciaro in Torrevieja by the simple expedient of having someone send him a postcard. A short time earlier Pedro had been called up by the Republican military authorities but because he wore glasses had been declared unfit for active service.[328]

'What joy! What relief!' Pedro remembers the postcard

brought him. So many fears and uncertainties disappeared for him the moment it arrived. All kinds of horrendous news had been filtering through about the religious persecution raging through Madrid and other parts of the country. There were stories that were later verified of mass executions and of thousands of priests being killed and of laymen and women being executed simply for being Catholics. Pedro had been worried for months about what might have happened to Father Josemaría and had been praying for him the whole time.

At the beginning of the Civil War life in Torrevieja and the Mediterranean areas of Valencia and Alicante had been much easier than in the central region of Spain. In these Mediterranean cities, surrounded by market gardens and watered by the Turia and Segura rivers, there was nothing like the hunger and the terror people were experiencing in Madrid.[329]

Though, as in all the Communist controlled areas, there was little freedom and life was very difficult and restricted. 'Without a pass you could not even go out of doors,' Pedro Casciaro remembers. 'You had to carry a pass to make any journey whatsoever. One's entire life depended on that piece of signed and sealed paper which stated who you were, why you were there and how long for, and it confirmed that you were not "an enemy of the people".'[330]

Undoubtedly the fact that Pedro's father was Provincial President of the Popular Front was a great help when it came to Pedro getting a pass to help him move about without too many restrictions. Armed with his pass Pedro even managed to go to Mass. The church in Torrevieja had been burned down but Mass was still said in the parish hall. The last Mass was said there on 25 July, the feast of Saint James, the patron saint of Spain. On this day the persecution became particularly vicious and many arrested priests were chosen to be executed throughout the Communist controlled areas. It was later found that ninety-five had been killed that day.[331] After the last Mass in the parish hall Pedro, armed with his pass, had got on his bike and found another place. He cycled to a little village called Torrelamata, using his pass to get through the numerous checkpoints on the way. The parish priest at

Torrelamata was an old man who had recently returned from Mexico after many years of priestly ministry there and was still courageously saying Mass. It was not long before the old priest was hauled up before the Village Revolutionary Committee. The priest had a great devotion to Our Lady of Guadalupe, Mexico's famous shrine. He put his trust in her and stuck to his beliefs. Amazingly his life was spared. He was allowed to go free but forbidden to say Mass. Pedro still continued to see him and he says, 'I was able to go to him for Confession and to receive Holy Communion.'[332]

Letters from Father Josemaría followed on from the first postcard. 'His letters,' says Pedro, 'were very short, often just a few hand-written lines and signed Mariano.' This was the fourth name he had been given when he was baptized. It was the name of an uncle, a widower, who later became a priest.[333] During the Civil War he, too, died because of his priesthood.

Father Josemaría was using the name Mariano to avoid putting the receiver of the letter or himself in danger. In the letters, Pedro says, 'The Father encouraged us to be very united to Our Lord during those times, not to neglect our prayer or abandon our plan of life. He urged us to plead with Our Lord constantly to cut short that terrible time of trial. He advised us always to commend ourselves to the most Blessed Virgin Mary, our safe path, asking her to protect all our lives, our faithfulness and our perseverance.'[334]

How did Father Josemaría manage to get his spiritual advice past the censors during such a virulent religious persecution which was penetrating every nook and cranny of daily existence and affecting everyone's lives?

Pedro explains, 'Little by little, without our having arranged anything (we had no opportunity to do so) a kind of private language developed among us. It contained certain key words such as when the Father mentioned "Don Manuel" he was referring to Our Lord. "Don Manuel's Mother" was the Blessed Virgin. The Father was "Grandfather" and he would make out he was an old man writing to his children and grandchildren.'[335]

One such letter reads, 'My little ones, Grandfather

would like very much to embrace you, but his plans always go up in smoke. Which means that it is better so. Nevertheless, who knows? I've not given up hope that my dreams will soon come true. In a word, Don Manuel knows what's best . . .'[336]

For quite some time Pedro Casciaro was in the dark about what had happened to his good friend Paco Botella who had left Madrid with him just before the outbreak of the Civil War. One day a letter arrived out of the blue from Paco which revealed all he had been up to. At the outbreak of the war Paco was at his home on Marquis del Turia Street in Valencia. He had got a job in the mornings in the Municipal Institute of Public Health and was taking part in vaccination campaigns with his cousin, Enrique Espinos and a friend, Amadeo de Fuenmayor. This way they had managed to acquire special passes allowing them to move around freely.

But after receiving the letter Pedro again lost touch. This was because Paco had written his address as 'M del Turia'. Giving the full name of the street would have meant writing Marquis, a term which did not go down well in those highly politicized times and could have brought him to the attention of the authorities. Pedro read the 'M' as an 'H' and thought Paco was writing from the Hotel del Turia, and sent the letter there. Which is where their correspondence ended for a time.[337] Then letters began to arrive for Pedro from Isidoro. In what Pedro describes as 'tiny copperplate handwriting', Isidoro would transmit in their coded language ideas from the Father's preaching.[338]

Pedro decided it was time he started looking for a job. But he had no experience to offer. 'I was 21 and still at university. Fortunately I got a job in a laboratory at Las Salinas de Torrevieja. The head of Department, Chuno Chorower, a Russian Jew who had done a doctorate in Germany, discovered I was reading Maths/Physics and employed me as a maths assistant.'[339]

This enabled Pedro to join the UGT (the General Workers' Union) with the other employees. He also found an old FUE (Federation of Spanish University Students) membership card, which he had joined at sixteen, and managed to swop it for a Socialist Party card. His documentation now allowed him to travel to Valencia, Alicante and other nearby towns.

'My comparative freedom,' he says, 'also meant I was able to send some food and other necessary supplies to those left behind in Madrid.'

These parcels were sent to Isidoro and contained dried cod, coffee, sugar, soap and other items belonging to Pedro's grandparents who had built up a stock of provisions before the war.[340]

Around the same time that Juan had joined Father Josemaría in the asylum, two other new comers arrived – an Air Force officer and a Falangist from Logroño called Alejandro Láscaris. The three new arrivals greatly worried the 'patients under observation' who were afraid they could be militia spies or members of the security police. Those who had been going to Father Josemaría for confession no longer left their rooms. No one walked in the garden and there was a strange, uneasy silence everywhere. Suspecting there might be a imminent raid, Dr Suils asked Láscaris to leave and then told Juan and José María González that they, too, would have to go. This made Father Josemaría suffer a great deal and after they had departed he went to see Dr Suils and told him, 'I can't stay in a place my sons have been thrown out of.'[341]

It was now March 1937 and Father Josemaría, who had been in the asylum for about five months, ever since the previous October, was determined to move to another hiding place.

The new refuge he found was the Honduran consulate, which he moved into on 14 March 1937. Before he departed from the asylum he left some of the fugitives with a supply of Holy Communions. 'He gave us small individual particles of the Mass host,' the Marchioness of Torres de Orán would recall years later, 'each wrapped carefully in cigarette papers so we could consume the particles of host without touching them.[342] I recall that incident very well because I was impressed by the profound respect he had for the Blessed Sacrament.'[343]

Father Josemaría took with him from the asylum a doctor's certificate he thought might be very useful to him if ever he was stopped and asked for his papers. Dated 14

March 1937 it read: 'As of today, Don José María Escriba [deliberate misspelling] Albás is discharged from this sanatorium. At present he is not completely cured, which means he is restricted from doing any kind of work, bearing any responsibilities, doing any travelling, or engaging in other types of activities. In the sanatorium he was accompanied by his 15-year-old brother Santiago, who should remain close to him.
The Director, Dr A Suils.'[344]

CHAPTER 40

Life in the Consulate

Father Josemaría's new refuge, the Honduran consulate, despite its grand sounding name, was not a recognized diplomatic building. It was in fact the home of Salvadorian diplomat Pedro Jaime de Matheu who also acted as the Honduran Consul in Madrid. Taking advantage of his diplomatic position he had requested and had received diplomatic immunity for his home on the Paseo de la Castellana. Countless people whose lives were in danger because they were known Christians found refuge in his consulate during the Civil War.[345] Many other embassies and consulates, all of which were closely watched by the security police, had also opened their doors to offer refuge to the victims of the communist terror.

Once inside the Honduran consulate Father Josemaría felt a sense of elation. He was still a hunted priest, but now he was free once again openly to be a priest of God and to say Mass and carry out all his priestly duties. Thanks to the generosity of the de Matheu family the Honduran consulate also became a home and refuge for Father Josemaría's brother Santiago, José María Gonzáles, Alvaro del Portillo, Juan Jiménez Vargas and Eduardo Alastrué, a student who used to be a regular visitor at one of the residences.[346]

It was José María Gonzáles who, after being thrown out of the asylum, had discivered that the consulate was taking in people trying to escape the Communist terror. This was because he was a friend of a friend of the consul's son in law, Rodriguez-Candela. And, after being given refuge José María Gonzáles told the de Matheu family about the plight of Father Josemaría and they agreed to take also Father Josemaría into their home together with his brother and some of his members.[347]

Father Josemaría was particularly happy to be reunited with Alvaro who had suffered a great deal since their last meeting. Alvaro had been hiding in the Finnish embassy until early in December 1936 when it had been raided by the militia. He and the other refugees were arrested and imprisoned in the notorious San Antón jail where he had nearly had his brains blown out when a pistol was put to his temple and he was accused of looking like a priest.[348]

Alvaro had been put on trial on 28 January 1937. The next day, 29 January, he was set free. And again he went on the run.[349]

Eduardo Alastrué was another person who had narrowly escaped execution. He had been imprisoned in a checa on Fomento Street in November. His captors had been about to kill him when they suddenly changed their minds and let him go.[350]

Father Josemaría was always very grateful to the de Matheu family for sheltering him and his sons for more than five months. Without that refuge it was odds on that he would have been caught in what had become a relentlessly efficient persecution. Many years later he would joke that, in Spanish, Honduras meant deep waters. 'There is a saying,' he said, 'stay clear of deep waters. I took refuge in the Legation of Honduras in Madrid and I've never regretted it. There were many refugees there, all of us under the threat of death. We suffered terrible hunger...'[351]

Three days after arriving he wrote to his sons in Valencia: 'I saw poor Josemaría and he assured me that he is no longer in the insane asylum (this is his current obsession) but has got into deep waters [honduras]. He is very happy. The doctor lets me see him every day.' [Meaning he was able to say Mass every day].[352]

Father Josemaría's mother arrived at the consulate to see him in the last week in March. But because he was so thin and wasted and wearing laymen's clothes, she didn't recognize him. It was not until after he had spoken to her and said, 'How wonderful to see you, mother,' that she realized it was her son standing before her.

It was also at this time that Juan Jiménez Vargas received an order from the medical association to join a battalion of the anarchist Spartacus Brigade as a medical lieutenant on the Jarama front. Juan, with the agreement of the Father, left to take this posting. The plan was that he would try to cross over to the Nationalists' lines as soon as possible after joining the battalion. But every time he had the opportunity something seemed to hold him back. 'I found myself unable to cross over with the Father remaining in Madrid,' he said. On his next leave Juan returned to Madrid and entered the consulate using the name Ricardo Escrivá.[353]

Overcrowding and hunger were all part of daily life in the legation. The consul's house had two floors and there were thirty refugees on each floor, making sixty in all. Father Josemaría and his companions had to make do with whatever space they could find for themselves in the rooms or corridors. At night they slept in the dining room under a massive circular table. In the middle of May they were allocated a tiny room on the lower floor. The room measured about nine square metres and its only furnishings were four mattresses.[354] These were rolled up during the day and used as seats. The only source of light and ventilation was from a narrow window, high up and overlooking a courtyard. A naked light bulb dangled on a wire from the ceiling and had to be left on for most of the day.[355]

In a humorous letter to those in Valencia, Father Josemaría gives us a vivid description of their cramped quarters: 'There isn't room to spread out all five of our mattresses. Four are enough to completely carpet the floor ... One window, which looks out on a dark patio – very dark. Beneath the window a small packing crate with some books and a bottle for banquets [wine for saying Mass]. On top of the crate, two small suitcases. (I'm writing this letter with one of them on my lap – after writing in a hundred thousand positions, awfully painful for the muscles ...) Next to the crate, two other small suitcases in a corner of the room, on top of which are a valise and a tin box where we keep everyone's toiletries. Right next to that the door ... (You can enter whenever you like – the door doesn't shut; there's something wrong with it.) The only thing left for you to admire is the rope that cuts across a corner of the room and serves to hold five towels. And also the beautiful lampshade, of genuine newspaper, which in a light-hearted moment this grandfather placed on the bare bulb hanging from a dirty wire. Don't even think of touching the light switch because if you do it will be a lot of trouble to get the light back on; the switch is broken ...'[356]

The room was also infested with beetles and bed bugs.

In another letter he wrote: 'This is a paradise of cockroaches. Some are quite big, as solemn and lustrous as a sacred Egyptian beetle; others are the size of a pinhead. And what a harmony of colours! White, red, silver, gold, brown and black – it makes one want to praise one's Maker.' And in another letter: 'Today, when Eduardo opened a book, a magnificent bedbug emerged ... At least the cockroaches will see they are well accompanied.'[357]

In this tiny, dingy room with all its beetles and bugs and squalor they lived, prayed, worked, studied and slept.

From the day he arrived, to the day he left the consulate, Father Josemaría said Mass daily.[358] This Mass was the centre and focal point of the little group's spiritual lives. The consul and his family also attended this Mass and an open invitation was extended to all the other refugees. But most of them were too afraid. They feared that the militia might make a surprise raid and catch them hearing Mass which would be certain death for them.

Suitcases placed on top of the empty crate served as the Mass altar.[359] Sometimes a small table was available and this would be used instead. A crystal glass served as a chalice, except when the consul's family lent Father Josemaría a gold cup.[360] The family donated this gold cup to the Work shortly after the Father's death.

Father Josemaría said Mass wearing a dark business suit, which was all he possessed. He read the prayers of the liturgy from a small missal. The atmosphere reminded

Life in the Consulate 271

those attending of the early Christians in the catacombs. Eduardo Alastrué who had taken it upon himself to record as faithfully as possible what was happening at the time wrote:

> He could not have celebrated with greater fervour and dignity had he been clothed in the richest vestments in the most noble cathedral. As there were no time constraints, we responded slowly, savouring each word, speaking not only with our lips but also our minds and hearts. The dialogue between the celebrant and the people took on great meaning as we gathered round the makeshift altar, a very small but authentic representation of God's people. We truly were a tiny portion of the Church supplicant, alive and ever praying amid widespread disaster. We came forth from that prayer renewed and strengthened, refreshed in mind and body.[361]

And each day Father Josemaría preached a meditation. Eduardo records, 'Seated on the mattresses, in semi-darkness ... we listened ... His words now serene, now energetic and charged with emotion, but always bearing light, poured over us and seemed to nestle within our soul.'

'They were all,' Eduardo tells us, 'centred in one way or another on Christ: his person, life, words and passion. Here he found inexhaustive material: contemplating Christ slowly and lovingly following step by step his miracles, his teaching, his suffering. It was as if were hearing the Gospel anew ...'

After Mass the Blessed Sacrament was put into two round silver boxes which were kept in a writing desk in one of the consul's private rooms. 'Night and day a small oil lamp burned before it,' the consul's daughter remembers. 'Father Josemaría and his group spent long intervals there keeping Our Lord company ...[362] and we tried to make sure they were not disturbed.'

For the other refugees life in the consulate was harsh, tense and monotonous. Most were professional men and some had their wives with them. They were of all ages, lawyers, doctors, engineers, teachers and soldiers; there was also an artist and a small child.

The day began with them all having to await their turn to use the bathroom. Then the rest of the day seemed to stretch endlessly ahead and they spent the time talking, dreaming of the future, playing cards or going back to bed and trying to sleep. 'Some,' Eduardo Alastrué later notes, 'spent the time silently mourning their misfortunes. Others poured out their troubles, bitterly lamenting family reverses, career or business losses, the uncertain future. Ever present was the fear awakened by past sufferings and persecutions, a fear that painted the world outside our refuge in brutal colours. In some cases fear spilled over into hatred for the enemy, a hatred powerless for the moment but buoyed up by the prospect of future revenge.'[363]

Often, at the slightest provocation, fierce quarrels would break out.

The consul's son-in-law, Rodriguez-Candela, noticed how different Father Josemaría's behaviour was from the other refugees. 'I was amazed,' he said, 'at his serene assessment of events ... His words never betrayed hatred or anger ... When the rest of us celebrated victories, Father Josemaría kept quiet.

'The civil war had everyone's nerves on edge but we never saw the slightest sign of irritation in Father Josemaría. He was always serene, at peace and in complete control of himself.[364] He was a person who made living together easy and enjoyable. He never caused problems or made negative comments about either the Communists or the Nationalists, not even about the bombings and the hardships ...[365] Without fuss he spread serenity and joy, transmitting his peaceful confidence to those around him.'[366]

At midday a meagre lunch was served in the consulate. This usually consisted of stale carob beans, which in normal times are used as animal feed.[367] Alvaro always remembered the beans. They were partly rotten and, he said, 'they also contained what we jokingly termed "protein" – tiny bugs of various colours, yellow, brown and red.'[368]

And there was an equally frugal supper quite late at

night. The subject of food became an obsession with many of the refugees and their imagination became tormented by memories of pre-war abundance. Then they would lament even more over the privations they were then suffering. This would in turn make them more miserable and depressed. And the ever present fear was that any day the fragile diplomatic immunity could be broken and the militia would raid the consulate. And if that happened, they knew all too well that it would mean the death sentence for most of them. Father Josemaría, by contrast, taught his companions to turn all their difficulties and wants into offerings to God and into opportunities to show their love for Him. From the first moment he entered the consulate he had been determined to make his companions' forced inactivity bear fruit. As he later wrote in *The Way*: 'The plants lay hidden under the snow. And the farmer, the owner of the land, remarked with satisfaction: "Now they are growing on the inside." I thought of you and your forced inactivity. Tell me, are you too growing "on the inside"?'[369]

To help them grow on the inside he worked out a timetable. As well as the Mass and meditations, there were also cheerful get-togethers, praying the Rosary, reading, writing and studying.[370] Father Josemaría somehow managed to turn their tiny room into 'a university of the mind and spirit.'

Several hours a day they spent studying foreign languages so that when the war was over they would be able to take Opus Dei to all parts of world. Father Josemaría asked Alvaro to learn Japanese.[371]

'What if I told you that in the heart of the Marxist tyranny in Madrid, a friend of yours was studying Japanese, intent on introducing our way to university students in Tokyo,'[372] Father Josemaría would write a few months later. This was in a newsletter he launched, which was written on an ancient typewriter and sent to members and friends on the various war fronts.

Another point he was to write in *The Way* also referred to these months spent in the legation:

Outside events have placed you in voluntary confinement, worse perhaps, because of its circumstances, than the confinement of a prison. You have suffered an eclipse of your personality.

On all sides you feel yourself hemmed in: selfishness, curiosity, misunderstanding, people talking behind your back. All right. So what? Have you forgotten your free-will and that power of yours as a 'child'? The absence of flowers and leaves (external actions) does not exclude the growth and activity of the roots (interior life). Work. Things will change, and you will yield more fruit than before, and sweeter too.[373]

Father Josemaría himself set all of them an example of how to make good use of their confinement. He wrote a great deal, read the classics and re-read his theological text books. The little room every day seemed to become brighter and happier, a place fill with prayer, cheerfulness and study.

Eduardo Alastrué writes of this time,

The Father by his word and example helped us to abandon ourselves completely in God's hands, which brought us such joy and peace.[374] It was as if our poor needs, the bleak hardships of seclusion and the danger hovering over us engendered a hidden delight. We travelled the path of God's will with hearts brimming with joy. I recall José María González's simple and sincere comment one day, 'This can't go on. There's too much happiness.'[375]

They tried to spread this happiness, cheerfulness and optimism to the other refugees.

Several members of religious orders had also taken refuge in the consulate and Father Josemaría had a special concern for them. Father Recaredo Ventosa, who lived on the upper floor with other members of the Congregation of the Sacred Heart, said, 'I got to know Father Josemaría very quickly. We became good friends. After speaking to me for the first time he asked me to hear his confession. He went to confession with me many times during his stay in the legation.[376] I would like to emphasise his love for the Sacrament of Confession. He confessed at least weekly.'

It was while Father Josemaría was in the consulate that the atrocities in the Republican controlled areas of Spain were made known to the world by Pope Pius XI. In his encyclical *Divini Redemptoris* of 19 March 1937, he condemned the errors and evils arising from Marxism. 'The Communist scourge has been unleashed in Spain,' he said, 'with a more than frenzied violence. It is not this or that church, this or that convent which has been destroyed, but wherever possible, they are destroying all of the churches, all of the convents, and every trace of the Christian religion, even where this is linked to the great monuments of art and science. The Communist frenzy has not been limited to the murder of bishops and thousands of priests and members of the religious orders of men and women ... but they have found a much greater number of victims among all classes of laymen who, still today, are being murdered en masse for the mere fact of being good Christians, or, at least opposed to Communist atheism.'[377]

Isidoro Zorzano, with his Argentine citizenship, was still able to move freely about Madrid and keep Father Josemaría in touch with the others. Eduardo Alastrué gave his written summaries of Father Josemaría's meditations to Isidoro who then learned them off by heart. Afterwards he went out and repeated them to the others scattered all over Madrid. In this way he was even able to give the meditations to people who were in prison.[378]

And Father Josemaría, well before the days of ministers of the Eucharist, also used Isidoro to distribute Holy Communion.[379] The sacred hosts were wrapped in small corporals which Father Josemaría's sister Carmen, with a special joy and dedication, had made specially for that purpose. Isidoro would then take the sacred hosts wrapped in the corporals to people in all parts of the city.[380]

Alvaro's younger brother Carlos, aged eleven, and his sister Teresa, aged nine, also helped. They were able to go in and out of the consulate without attracting the attention of the guards on duty outside the building and sometimes they carried messages out to Isidoro in their shoes.[381]

During his days in the consulate Father Josemaría ate virtually nothing. As a result he lost almost fifty kilograms in weight, or around 110lbs.[382]

What at this time really made Father Josemaría suffer, Alvaro remembers, was knowing all that Christians were undergoing in Madrid and not being able to go out and help them.[383] He felt he himself needed to do more, to atone, to make reparation for all that was happening.

Alvaro also gave this frightening and graphic account of how he tried to atone:

> Once he (Father Josemaría) asked the others to leave the room. Since I was sick and feverish, I couldn't do so. I was wrapped in a blanket on one of the mattresses ... The Father told me, 'Cover your head with the blanket.' I obeyed and shortly afterwards heard him using the formidable discipline he himself had made. I was curious, so I counted. I'll never forget it. One thousand powerful blows. The floor was covered with blood, but he thoroughly cleaned it before the others returned.[384]

Pedro Casciario, still on his own in his small Mediterranean enclave, was busy working out ways to escape from Spain and the Communist tyranny.

'I knew,' he says, 'that my mission in life was to carry out Opus Dei; so I thought that if I escaped abroad I could continue the Work in total freedom.'

The country he would have like to have gone to was England. His grandfather Julio then recalled that he had never renounced his British citizenship. So he and Pedro both went off to the British consulate in Alicante and after several applications both obtained British passports.

The next step, Pedro decided, was to get to the United Kingdom with his grandfather. 'I persuaded him,' Pedro says 'that as a British subject he could do that. It seemed feasible. We even obtained an invitation to attend King George VI's coronation ceremony. We asked permission to travel, arguing that because of my grandfather's age and state of health I had to accompany him. Everything seemed to go smoothly until I applied to the Civil Government in Albacete for permission.'

Then things went badly wrong and he nearly ended up in jail. Another escape plan he had was to borrow a boat and sail to an English cruiser anchored in the port of Cartagena. But his family and friends strongly advised him to drop the idea. During all this time he was trying as best he could to follow his Christian plan of life as a member of Opus Dei.[385]

> Among other things, I tried to make the most of my time, as the Father had taught me. This surprised my family quite a lot. 'Why are you studying if you don't know what is going to happen?' they inquired.
>
> My logic went the other way round. It was precisely because I did not know what was going to happen that I thought the best thing to do was to make the most of my time and continue being apostolic. As the Father had taught me to do, I began with my own family. I spoke to my brother Pepe who was finding his feet as a growing man in the midst of all the convulsion.

His brother Pepe remembers it well:

> One day my brother Pedro suggested a plan of life to me. He gave me a copy of *The Imitation of Christ* by Thomas á Kempis to help me pray for a while every day. He gave me a Bible in French, by l'Abbé Crampon, for me to use for spiritual reading and practise my French at the same time, and he lent me a book by Chateaubriand called *Le genie du Christianisme*. He recommended I take up French and told me always to keep busy. I put all this into practice in a rather unusual fashion. As all the young men on the estate had been called up, we had to stand in for them as best we could. It fell to me to look after the sheep and cattle. So during those months I spent many hours reading Chateaubriand, among the sheep in the shade of the almond trees.[386]

It was about this time, when Pedro's escape plans were coming to nothing, that he received another letter from

Father Josemaría. Pedro would always remember these letters he received from the Father, especially the little details. 'He would always begin with an affectionate touch,' Pedro says. 'For instance he would draw the initial "P" of my name in an artistic manner, with long curling stokes.'

This particular letter, dated 7 April 1937 was one of the many he wrote from the Honduran consulate. In it Father Josemaría asked Pedro to do all he could to help Chiqui (José María Hernández) who had been transferred to a prison in Valencia. The transfer had been a mistake. Chiqui had been sentenced to death by a People's Tribunal and should have been shot.

'Writing in code, the Father asked me,' Pedro explains, 'to take him if possible to the Alicante countryside to recuperate after he came out of the sanatorium (that is, the prison).[387]

Chiqui, however, would not be released from prison for another three months and by that time Pedro, even though he had earlier been classed unfit for active service, would have been called up and be a solider-clerk in a Red army cavalry unit.

On 6 June 1937 Pedro received another letter from the Father who, he says, 'evoked our visits to the Countess of Humanes'. (She was the blind lady who had handed over her jewels to Father Josemaría and liked to show Pedro her pictures and antiques.) The letter went on to say, 'Did I tell you that hardly had the good lady died when an armed group invaded the house and looted everything right down to the floorboards?' 'Then,' Pedro says, 'he told me about a possible trip to Valencia, which cheered me up no end. "Though nothing is definite, it looks as though Josemaría will probably leave quite soon. If he goes to Valencia, Ignacio (This is, Isidoro) will write and ask you if you could go and see him."'[388]

Then came the second military call up. Pedro explains:

As things got worse, the auxiliary services were mobilised too, and I had to go to the Army Recruitment Centre in Albacete ... and from Albacete we were taken by lorry to a military camp at Torre Guil, a farm five kilometres from Murcia. The house was large, like Los Hoyos, but it was absolutely inadequate for the 4,000 recruits concentrated there. Chaos reigned. For instance, we were supposed to be grouped into three companies: people with tuberculosis, people who had trachoma, and the 'glass brigade' – those of us who wore spectacles. In actual fact we were all mixed together. We slept on the floor and, needless to say, there were not enough mattresses for everyone. One night it happened that I was sleeping beside a man with tuberculosis who began to vomit blood. Thank God, he survived. The food was very wholesome given the circumstances: rice, oranges and wine, plenty of wine. Outside the military camp there was an inn where you could drink as much as you could pay for. Discipline was very lax (in Guil there were practically no latrines and no way at all to wash). I met some acquaintances from Albacete there. One of them was permanently semi-drunk. One day he confessed to me, perfectly openly, that he tried to be sozzled as much time as he could in order to more or less bear the appalling situation in which we found ourselves. It was the only way he had found of not sinking into deep depression.

A medical committee came to give everyone cooped up there a very superficial check over. Some were freed and allowed to go home because of their ill health. Some from the 'glass brigade' were declared fit for any military service and a third set, in which I was included, were destined to go to the medical corps or military offices.[389]

Pedro was posted to the Headquarters of the Remounting Unit, a cavalry section which had been transferred from Madrid to Valencia. Pedro could hardly believe his luck. He was convinced that this posting must have come about through the intercession of his Guardian Angel. Not only would he be united with his good friend Paco Botella in Valencia but this was the very city where Father Josemaría in his letter said he could soon be visiting.[390]

CHAPTER 41

In Workmen's Overalls

Father Josemaría, while in hiding in the Honduran Consulate in Madrid, constantly worried about the plight of Catholics throughout the city. By this time thousands of priests had been executed and about half the bishops of Spain had been killed. Those priests who had survived had either escaped from the Republican zone or, like himself, were in hiding.[391] As a result it was almost impossible for Catholics to find a priest in Madrid and many were dying without being able to receive the Sacrament of Penance or Holy Communion. Father Josemaría was plagued by a feeling of helplessness. He was a priest but he felt he wasn't being of much help to them. What could he do? This line of thinking led him to making a decision that would again put him in danger. He would, he decided, have to leave the safety of the Honduran Consulate and return to moving about the streets of Madrid. This way, he would be able to care for many of those people who were in such desperate need of a priest.

Among the list of priests killed about this time was Father Josemaría's godfather, his Uncle Mariano, who had been ordained priest at a late age and was then an old man.[392] He had never harmed anyone. His only crime was to be a priest and for this he was executed. Another victim connected with Father Josemaría's family was a gentle, elderly nun who had been like a sister to Father

Josemaría's mother.[393] She had devoted herself to teaching little children to read. But the Communists had made it a crime to be a nun and for this she too had been executed.

The areas under the Republicans were now tightly controlled police states and anyone found without identity papers was immediately arrested and interrogated. Father Josemaría knew it would be suicide to go back out on the streets without some form of identity papers. But how could a hunted priest who would be shot on sight obtain identity papers? No doubt this problem would be the constant subject of his conversations with God at this time as he asked for help and light.

In the month of July 1937, Pedro Casciaro moved to Valencia to become a soldier at the Headquarters of the Cavalry Remounting Unit, and at the same time to be reunited with Paco Botella.

The Remounting Unit headquarters was in a large house near the Turia and as a soldier clerk Pedro found himself directly subordinate to a cavalry major. The major had worked his way up through the ranks, from corporal to sergeant to officer rank. He was about fifty and Pedro describes him as 'a big rough fellow with a kind heart.' Above the major was the colonel-in-chief, 'a good man who had taken voluntary retirement when Azaña came to power but had then been forced to rejoin the Republican army. He was very distinguished looking; a tall, slender man of fifty plus,' Pedro says. And Pedro thought the colonel looked on him 'with a certain benevolence.' Some months later Pedro's life would be in his hands and his benevolence would be tested to the full.[394]

Pedro had to find his own accommodation in Valencia. As the city was very crowded because of the war and he was very hard up he ended up a 'in a run-down lodging house in a seedy area of the city.'[395]

Every evening after finishing work at the Remounting Unit headquarters Pedro would go to Paco's home. During this period he was able to receive Holy Communion every day in the Botella home because Paco kept some consecrated hosts locked in a desk. Pedro also spent a good deal of time with Paco's parents, Don Francisco and Doña Enriqueta while waiting for Paco to return home.

The two friends, Pedro and Paco, helped each other all they could and drew even closer.[396]

Pedro discovered that Paco also had also been receiving letters from the Father from the Honduran consulate. One, dated 28 March 1937, reads:

> Here you have this poor old man evacuated to Widow Honduras' house, sleeping on the floor in the dining room (great fun) with four members of my family. Now I'm really feeling my age. I have lost nearly 30 kilos and actually I feel better, though I was ill in bed (what a luxury) for more than a month. I am awaiting Ricardo with great anxiety because I need him. When he comes I will write and tell you. I am on tenterhooks not having news of my children who are away, but I'm always hopeful that I'll be able to embrace them all again when the war ends.
>
> As for Josemaría, I must tell you that he assures me that it is precisely in these disunited times that he manages to be most closely united with his friend whose little donkey he is, as he carries a lot on top.[397]

The Ricardo referred to in the letter was Ricardo Fernández who, the day before the outbreak of the Civil War, had left Madrid with Paco. Ricardo had been conscripted into the Republican army and sent to Teruel, the capital of the southern most province of Aragon. As an architect he had been assigned to building the Teruel fortifications. A few months later this battlefront would be the scene of some of the most bitter fighting of the Civil War. Ricardo knew he was being closely watched but on 17 May 1937 managed to escape across the frontline to the Nationalist zone.[398] He had crossed over just in time. A few days later an order for his arrest as a suspected Fascist arrived from Madrid.[399] It was not until early June that the news of Ricardo's escape reached Father Josemaría in the Honduran consulate.

And in July news also filtered through that Chiqui had

been released from prison.[400]

Despite the great clampdown on religion and the massacre of priests, Pedro and Paco still managed to get to regular confession:

> Paco informed me that there were two old priests (dressed as country folk) in Parterre, who dedicated themselves to administering the Sacraments in spite of the risk it involved. If anyone informed on them they would be arrested and most probably shot. Outwardly they looked like two old men who, in common with many others, were sitting in the sun and looking after their grandchildren for there were lots of children playing round about.
> The system for going to Confession was very simple. You approached one of them, gave the established greeting and walked round making your confession and afterwards received absolution. And off you went...[401]

Father Josemaría was still struggling to find a way to obtain some form of official documentation that would allow him to leave the Honduran consulate. More than anything else now he wanted to be able to move about Madrid so that he could offer his priestly ministry to people in a city now gripped by famine. One day he had a talk with the Honduran consul, Pedro Jaime de Matheu, and the consul agreed to provide him with something that might help. This was a typewritten letter on Honduras consulate headed notepaper bearing Father Josemaría's passport photograph and fingerprints. It stated that: 'José ESCRIBA ALBAS [again a deliberate misspelling of Escrivá], 35 years of age, single, is in the service of this Ministry of Foreign Affairs as Chief Supply Officer.'[402]

He was delighted with the document and to get the passport photo it required, he risked leaving the consulate and going to a photographer. Juan Jiménez Vargas went with him and had his picture taken at the same time.

The consul not only provided Father Josemaría with his identity document but as well, gave him one of his good suits and a tie to go with it.[403] Father Josemaría also had a card that someone had obtained for him from an anarchist syndicate at the outbreak of the Civil War that identified him as an anarchist lawyer.[404] He was all too aware, however, that his new consulate 'papers' and anarchist identity card would pass only casual checks. They would be useless if he were arrested or came to the attention of the secret police.

On the last day of August 1937, after six months in the consulate, he made his farewells and went off to begin an intense priestly apostolate. He went first to Isidoro Zorzano's apartment where he was reunited with Chiqui, Manuel Sainz and Rafael Calvo. After his release from prison Chiqui had been conscripted into the Communist-controlled army of Andalusia and was spending a few days in Madrid before rejoining them. Manuel Sainz was the owner of the flat in Sagasta Street which had provided Father Josemaría with his first hiding place. And it was Manuel who had been arrested when he returned home during the militia search. He too had recently been released from prison. Rafael Calvo, who was also trapped in Valencia at the beginning of the war, had been assigned to the International Brigades and had got two days' leave just to see the Father before joining them.[405]

Afterwards, Father Josemaría went to his new hideout, a rented room that Eduardo Alastrué's father had found for him on fourth floor of No 67, Ayala Street. The room, which looked out on the street, had no bed, only mattresses on the floor.[406]

Once free to move about again, one of Father Josemaría's first tasks was to go to the Panamanian consulate. And from the Panamanians 'on the recommendation' of the Honduran consul, he obtained an identity document for Juan Jiménez Vargas similar to the one the Hondurans had given him.

The Panamanian 'document' with Juan's passport photo on it – the photo he had had taken with Father Josemaría – bore the name Ricardo Escrivá, which was the name Juan was using at the time to escape the attention of the security police. Juan was now able to leave the Honduras consulate and join Father Josemaría in his new hideout.[407]

As he continued moving around, caring for one person

after another and saying many Rosaries as he walked along, Father Josemaría began to feel there was something missing, something which he knew would help him a great deal: it was a picture of Our Lady. He decided he would somehow have to get one. He could then keep it in his new home. But where could he find a picture of Our Lady in Republican controlled Madrid? Selling holy pictures was proscribed. But he also knew that foreigners were not bound by the anti-religious laws so he decided to make use of his Honduran 'papers' to try to obtain the picture of Our Lady that he felt he so badly needed. He found a shop that before the war had sold religious pictures and specialized in picture frames and prints. On entering the shop he asked straight out if they had a picture of Our Lady.

'They were alarmed when I asked for a picture of Our Lady,' he said. 'I showed them my diplomatic "papers", and they furtively brought one from a back room.'[408] It was a small elegantly-framed picture of Our Lady of Sorrows which many years later would stand on the desk in the room where he and Alvaro worked in the Villa Tevere, Rome.[409]

During those dangerous days in Madrid, this picture brought great joy to his heart. A glance at Our Lady every time he entered or left his room was enough to keep him going.[410]

'We kept it in the cramped quarters I shared with Juan. The day after we left, the house was bombed.'[411]

Each day from then on, Father Josemaría, wearing either the suit given him by the consul or workman's overalls, would leave his room and carry out his priestly apostolate throughout the city, convinced his Guardian Angel would lead him to where he was most needed. He said Mass, took people Holy Communion, preached, gave meditations and offered comfort and hope to countless numbers of people. He heard innumerable confessions, often walking along the streets under the noses of the secret police and the Communist militias.

Father Josemaría in later years rarely spoke of those days in Madrid but on one occasion said,

I walked about Madrid ... sometimes wearing overalls,

other times in a fashionable suit and tie with the Honduran flag on my lapel.[412]

He would celebrate Mass as best he could, in any nook or cranny, without vestments or sacred vessels. He used a glass for the chalice and a plate for the patten. He didn't have a missal. He knew the canon by heart. He went from house to house to give communion to anyone who asked for it. He carried the Blessed Sacrament wrapped in tiny corporals made by his sister Carmen. He kept them in a lady's cigarette case, which he covered with a small Honduran flag as added protection.

Many times he slept with his clothes on, with the Blessed Sacrament wrapped in his arms.[413]

'I heard many confessions in the street,' he said. 'I would take someone by the arm and hear his confession as we walked along.'

Throughout his life Father Josemaría always whole-heartedly forgave anyone seeking to harm him. 'Even during the persecution we tried to love everyone. We never considered anyone an enemy,' he said.[414]

'If someone was dying, I would go and attend to him.' One of them was Alvaro del Portillo's father, Don Ramón. He had been arrested in August 1936 but it was not until the beginning of 1937 that his family was informed of his whereabouts. He was in fact being held in the same jail as his son Alvaro, the San Antón. The two never saw each other and Alvaro had no idea his father was a fellow prisoner.

When Don Ramón was released he was a very sick man and was later diagnosed to have tuberculosis of the larnyx. Despite medical treatment his condition quickly deteriorated and word was sent to Alvaro in the Honduran consulate who in turn got a message out to Father Josemaría. He immediately went to see him.

'I went to his home,' Father Josemaría said, 'and Alvaro's sister announced, "The doctor is here." I heard his confession and gave him the Last Rites, and no one was the wiser.'

Alvaro's sister, Pilar, recalled that Father Josemaría arrived dressed in something like a lab coat such as a doctor or a shopkeeper wore. The holy oils were in a syringe and the Blessed Sacrament in the lady's cigarette case kept in a small bag decorated with the flag of Honduras.

Don Ramón, who died a few weeks later, was greatly comforted by Father Josemaría's visit.[415]

If anyone at any time came to Father Josemaría and said there was someone who needed a priest he would immediately go with them, even though he realized that any such request could be a trap. And he was always conscious of the fact that wherever he went and whatever he did, there was always the danger of being recognized and betrayed.

It was amazing what he accomplished. At the very centre of one of modern Europe's cruellest religious persecutions he was able to go about offering hope and happiness to so many people. He was especially dedicated to caring for the sick and people on their deathbeds, afraid they would die without the Sacraments.

He had many narrow escapes. One day he was going to say Mass at the home of Alejandro Guzman, a man who had been generous in helping him set up the first residence. Father Josemaría was just about to enter the house when a woman grabbed him by the arm and loudly exclaimed as if they were old friends, 'How good to see you!'

She then led him from the house and, when she thought they were far enough away, said in a low voice, 'Forgive me, Father Josemaría. Were you going to say Mass there?'

'Yes,' Father Josemaría answered.

'Well,' the woman said, 'they're searching the house from top to bottom at this very moment. If you go in they'll take you and kill you.'

Father Josemaría moved on.[416]

It was about this time that he heard of a community of Third Order Capuchin nuns who had run the city's Villa Luz hospital and were in hiding. He offered them his assistance.

One of them, Sister Ascension Quiroga, later explained, 'We had taken refuge in a small hotel a friend had rented for us. We were afraid, almost in a state of terror. We had switched to wearing ordinary clothes and had even begun to use makeup to hide the fact that we were nuns.'[417]

Another nun of a different Order who was also hiding in the hotel told them about 'a priest who could do us a lot of spiritual good in such trying times.'

The priest was Father Josemaría.

Sister Ascension said, 'He gave us a talk and what he said impressed us so much that we renewed our desires to give ourselves totally to Jesus Christ, as on the day of our religious profession. I distinctly remember Father Josemaría speaking to us of our cowardice. He said: "We are cowards. We are afraid to stand up for God."

'The way he spoke impressed me. He wasn't preaching. We were listening to a saint voicing his personal prayer. I think all of us (at least I did) left that meditation confirmed in our vocation, with a hunger to give ourselves.[418]

'From that day on, we never used make-up again. We continued to live in the Communist zone but with a deep desire to imitate Jesus ... inspired by Father Josemaría's words to seek a more loving union with Our Lord.'

Father Josemaría helped many other nuns in hiding and said Mass for them whenever he could.

Then, through Professor José María Albareda, who used to receive spiritual direction from him, he heard about a married couple who were looking for a priest to baptize their newborn baby.

(The professor was a well-known research scientist and academic and about the same age as Father Josemaría. He had made several breakthroughs in agricultural chemistry and had worked as a scientist and university lecturer in England, France and Germany.[419] He was a friend of Domingo Díaz-Ambrona and his wife who had taken refuge in the Cuban Embassy.)

When the time came for Domingo's wife to have her baby she had been transferred to the Riesgo Hospital; which at the time was under the protection of the English flag. There she had given birth to a daughter, Guadalupe. Father Josemaría agreed to go to the Riego clinic at seven o'clock on a certain day to baptize the baby. But the baby's father, Domingo, putting perhaps too much trust in the security offered by the English flag and not realizing the danger Father Josemaría was in, began talking about the baptism and inviting godparents and friends to the ceremony. This had only to get to the ears of the security police and they would lie in wait for the priest. But Father Josemaría decided to go ahead and baptize the baby.

Domingo explains what happened next, 'The priest arrived at five in the afternoon, two hours early, stayed just long enough for the baptism and left. Everything happened so quickly that we didn't even ask him his name. It was only afterwards that I found out it was Father Josemaría. His behaviour was a lesson in courage and prudence for all of us in those difficult times.'

Domingo adds, 'I tried to get him to stay, but he replied, "Many souls have need of me".'[420]

Early one evening, this time dressed in overalls, Father Josemaría met a young man called Tomás Alvira. Tomás was very impressed by the young priest's strong personality and by the joy and optimism that radiated from him in such hazardous times.[421]

'I continued to see him,' says Tomás. 'I witnessed how, in very dangerous circumstances, he risked his own life to renew his apostolic work, administering the sacraments and consoling everyone he could.

'I was amazed when one day he invited me to make a retreat with four others. My surprise was understandable, given the situation in Madrid. Not a single church or chapel was open. Many had been burned and sacked. I myself had seen a person arrested for wearing a medal of Our Lady.'

Anything connected with religion was proscribed and there were spies and informers everywhere. Tomás, however, happily accepted the invitation.

'The retreat,' he says, 'had to be carefully organised because any gathering might arouse suspicion. In Madrid each apartment block was watched by a person called "a control". So we each went separately to the apartment where we were meeting. Father Josemaría would arrive and give a meditation and afterwards we'd all leave one by one. And walking along in the street we would continue to pray and say the Rosary etc.

'Then we would go to another flat where one of us lived and have the next meditation. The retreat lasted three days and entailed great risk,' he says.

On the last day of the retreat Father Josemaría celebrated Mass in Tomás Alvira's house. He said it on a table, without wearing vestments and using a glass as a chalice.[422] One man who was very impressed by the retreat was Professor José María Albareda. On 8 September he asked to join the Work.[423]

Not content with desecrating and closing the churches, the Communists had also gone around destroying every religious image they came across, in the streets or in the squares of the city or on any public buildings or monuments. But they had missed one image of Our Lady. This was carved in the stone base of the monument to Christopher Columbus at the end of La Castellana. Every time Father Josemaría passed that way, he would give Our Lady a discreet but very fervent greeting and pray for the Church that was undergoing such fierce, inhuman and unrelenting persecution.[424]

CHAPTER 42

The Plan of Escape

To all those close to Father Josemaría it became abundantly clear that if he continued to stay in the city it would only be a matter of time before he was captured. They came to the conclusion that they would have to find a way of getting him out of Madrid as quickly as possible. The first plan they came up with was quite simple and would not put Father Josemaría at any great risk. Or so they thought.

They would obtain a genuine birth certificate belonging to someone who had been born in a foreign country and replace the original name, age and details with Father Josemaría's name, age and details. Then they would take the doctored birth certificate to the embassy of the country concerned and get a genuine passport. And with such a passport Father Josemaría would be free to travel to wherever he chose.[425]

Tomás Alvira soon managed to get hold of an Argentinian birth certificate from a teacher friend of his and began work on it. 'I erased the name, age etc., using chemicals,' Tomás says. 'But, as this involved quite a few number of lines, the paper wrinkled. So I ironed it and it turned out quite well. We filled in Father Josemaría's personal data using a typewriter with matching type.'

When finished he carefully examined the birth certificate and was quite satisfied that changes made stood a very good chance of passing unnoticed. Tomás then took the birth certificate to the Argentinian embassy and applied for a passport. The officials there looked at the birth certificate, didn't notice anything amiss and told Tomás the passport would take three or four days.

It was Father Josemaría who went to pick up the passport. But in the intervening days the chemicals used for the erasions had discoloured the paper where the alterations had been made. It was obvious that the birth certificate had been tampered with.

Father Josemaría was confronted by an embassy official who demanded to know why the birth certificate had been changed. 'I am a lawyer and a priest,' Father Josemaría replied. 'Under the circumstances, as a lawyer I defend and justify it. As a priest, I give it my blessing.' He then left the embassy.[426]

Another way of escaping had to be found. It was about this time that Professor José María Albareda received word that his brother Ginésa and his sister-in-law had managed to escape through the Republican controlled zone and cross the border into France. Barcelona, they learned, was the place to make for. From that city it was possible to escape over the Pyrenees out of the red zone and into Andorra and from there into France.[427] Father Josemaría, after much prayer and thought, decided they should try it. It was the Republican government's policy at this time to evacuate the city and people were being encouraged to leave. In fact it had been decreed that only those with work papers justifying their stay in the capital had the right to remain. Checks by the police and militia on those still in the city became more rigorous as a result. This in turn made life more precarious than ever for those on the run.

To travel anywhere in the Republican controlled zones safe-conduct passes were needed. As it was government policy to move people out of Madrid these now appeared not too difficult to obtain. Father Josemaría acquired his safe-conduct pass using his anarchist lawyer's membership card. From the CNT's Regional Union for Public Services 'Comrade Escriba' received this testimonial:

Madrid, 5 October, 1937
To the Passport Division of the Police Headquarters:
Greetings, comrades. We hope you will authorize and

grant safe conduct for travel to Barcelona and return within a period of 30 days, for taking care of family matters, to the comrade of this 'Lawyers' Group' José Escriba Albas, ID number 522.

Yours and for the cause,
on behalf of the Committee.
Guillermo Zendón, Secretary[428]

And, by various other methods, passes were also obtained by Juan Jiménez Vargas, Professor José María Albareda, Tomás Alvira and Manuel Sainz.

They could now make their plans for getting to Barcelona. This too presented a problem. No trains were running because the railway line out of the city had been cut by the advancing Nationalist army. The only way out of Madrid was by road. But finding a car or some other vehicle in the besieged city they knew would be very difficult. As the final preparations were being made for leaving Madrid, Father Josemaría began to be assailed by terrible doubts. Juan Jiménez Vargas saw him one Saturday and was delighted to hear that he had finally made up his mind to leave Madrid. But the next day, Sunday, Father Josemaría told him he had changed his mind.

'He saw very clearly the need to cross to the other zone,' Juan recalled, 'but he couldn't bear the thought of leaving behind those unable to go.' Among these were his mother Dolores and his brother and sister, Santiago and Carmen, Alvaro del Portillo and Eduardo Alastrué, who were still in hiding in the Honduras consulate and Vincente Rodríguez, who was in the Norwegian embassy.

Father Josemaría, Juan says, 'grew more and more upset, thinking he was getting out while they remained behind.'

But the others kept insisting he must try to escape and his mother Dolores agreed and added her arguments to theirs.[429] His mother would not only remain in Madrid with her two children but she would continue to risk her life taking care of the archives and all the documents of the Work.

'She hid them inside a mattress, and whenever the

militia men came to make a search, she took to her bed as if she did not feel very well – which certainly was the truth!' Alvaro would later say. 'And in this way she succeeded in keeping safe the records and personal papers of her son. Among these were real treasures, such as some notes the Father had written about his interior experiences and other graces he had received from God, some early thoughts and plans regarding the development of the Work, and many other very precious texts.'[430]

Finally, after much agonizing, Father Josemaría decided he would attempt to escape.[431] Isidoro Zorzano with his Argentine citizenship and freedom to move about Madrid would become the Director and take over the responsibility of looking after those left behind.

The escape party would go first to Valencia. There Father Josemaría would be able to see his two sons, Pedro Casciaro who was now in the Red army and Paco Botella who was about to be conscripted at any time. For Father Josemaría seeing them both again was of paramount importance.

From Valencia they could then travel by train to Barcelona. And once in Barcelona, the next step would be to try to make contact with certain groups of smugglers. These were men who were now making a living leading parties of refugees to freedom over the Pyrenees and into Andorra.

Juan Jiménez Vargas was the first to depart. He managed to get a lift out of Madrid on a truck transporting barrels of wine which took him as far as Tembleque. From there he was able to get a train to Valencia, arriving on 6 October, 1937.[432] That day Pedro Casciaro and Paco Botella had the surprise of their lives when Juan Jiménez Vargas suddenly appeared. 'He was very thin,' Pedro remembers. 'His hair was very short and his features were more pronounced than usual because of the privations of the war. Dark glasses did not help.'[433]

Juan, who was a man of few words although always very precise and clear, told them that that the Father would be coming in two days' time with several others on their way to the Pyrenees. From there they would try to cross to Andorra.[434]

And one day later, on 8 October, Father Josemaría left

Madrid in a hired car together with Professor José María Albareda, Tomás Alvira and Manuel Sainz.[435]

When they reached a place called Puerto de Contreras the car came to a sudden halt and they found themselves staring at kneeling militiamen with rifles trained on the car. But all the militia wanted was to see was their papers and after inspecting them they let the car through. Father Josemaría and his companions arrived in Valencia without further incident at about eight o'clock that night and made straight for the Botella home.[436]

When Pedro Casciaro called that night he found Paco's father looking very frightened. Given the constant tension and near panic prevailing at that time in the Republican zone this was not surprising.

'He told me,' Pedro recalled, 'that some friends of ours had just arrived from Madrid and that they were in the parlour.

'I walked into the room. Paco was with them. In the fading evening light coming in from the balcony. I could make out Juan (Jiménez Vargas) and someone else I did not recognize. He was a very thin man, well-dressed in a dark grey suit. As soon as he saw me this person clasped me in his arms and said, "Perico, I am so happy to see you again!" I was astounded. It was the Father. The voice was the Father's, but he had changed so much! When I was sure it really was him I became all excited and began to weep with joy and he had to calm me down.[437]

'While he was talking to me I was noticing the striking changes in the man I had last seen fifteen months ago when he had given me his blessing before I left for Albacete. I had always known him wearing a cassock and looking energetic and healthy. Now he was so astonishingly thin. He must have lost more than 30 kilograms. His cheeks were sunken, accentuating his broad forehead. His eyes seemed more penetrating. He had new glasses with thicker lenses. His hair was longer and parted on one side. Finally, I noticed a small, but to me very significant detail. He was wearing a tie with a very neat knot. The only thing that hadn't changed was his voice.[438]

'And while I was looking at him so attentively, the Father was talking about fulfilling God's will. He was saying that it was not easy to understand God's way of doing things, nor was it easy to see all the good we were going to draw out of the tragic circumstances. But he conveyed to us his conviction that God was determined that the Work would be accomplished and that He would not fail to help us. We on our part had to try to regain the freedom we needed in order to be able to talk about God anywhere and everywhere. But we also had to make a big effort and do everything humanly possible "to escape this hell where God cannot even be mentioned."' Pedro says that the Father then told them that it seemed to be possible from Barcelona to cross to the Nationalist zone. Other people had managed it. And he said he had only made the decision to attempt it after a lot of prayer.

'They explained then the plan to us,' Pedro recalls. 'They hoped to leave the very next day by train for Barcelona. From there they would send news to Paco and me and would perhaps be able to arrange things so that we could go with them.[439]

'After such a long separation that first meeting with the Father seemed very short. We left early because we did not want to worry Paco's parents. Any group of people holding unauthorised meetings could arouse suspicion and was dangerous ... We arranged to meet the next day for lunch if possible, but it would have to be somewhere that a relatively large group could gather without attracting much attention.'[440]

Juan Jiménez Vargas, after taking Father Josemaría and José María Albareda to the house where Professor Sellés was living and where they would stay the night, returned to speak to Pedro and Paco once again. 'We strolled along the Marquis de Turia for some time,' Pedro says. 'He talked about what the Father had just been saying, stressing the transcendence of those moments in the history of the Work. He spoke about maturity on the human level, the importance of looking for the divine meaning in things. He also explained to us how the Lord's call had to be placed before everything else. We could not use our youth as an excuse. Despite our age we had to be aware that we had to carry out the Work, which over-rode any other plans and commitments, however pressing they might seem. While Juan was talking to us, Paco and I realised that he was passing on to us the ideas he had heard from the Father and was perhaps obeying a specific request from the Father to prepare us for what would happen afterwards. When Juan left us we asked each other what the main idea was that he had been trying to convey. One of us humorously remarked, "Get it into your head that, as from today, we have stopped being a couple of carefree young guys and have no choice but to start being responsible men."'[441]

Meanwhile, in Professor Sellés' house, Father Josemaría had been informed about the doorman of the building. He also was a priest who had miraculously escaped execution. As he was being driven off to be shot, a Communist, who had only recently joined the party and disapproved of his bloodthirsty comrades, talked his fellow revolutionaries into leaving him in his hands. Then he not only spared the priest's life but found him the job as a doorman. Every morning this priest said Mass in Professor Sellés' apartment where they kept the Blessed Sacrament. After some hesitation the Father let it be known to the doorman who he was. The two priests made their confessions to each other and served each other's Mass with the others coming over to attend.[442]

Father Josemaría's was rather a special Mass that morning. He was able to wear vestments. A pair of candles were put out and lit on the makeshift altar. The vestments had been hidden away at the beginning of the persecution and the Sellés family had brought them out for this occasion.[443]

Father Josemaría was very grateful for the family's help and hospitality and wanted to show his thanks in some way. So he asked Pedro and Paco to get the children some sweets. It was a difficult request to fulfil in wartime Valencia. But in the end they managed to find some enormous caramels that were traditionally distributed during Holy Week processions before the war.

At midday they all met up as discreetly as possible in a very modest restaurant in the old town, near the market and the warehouses. It was a restaurant patronized by soldiers and militiamen.

Pedro says, 'I used to go there sometimes, so I knew the place well. Then something happened there which was common enough in wartime. We were having lunch when some militiamen came in asking people for their documents. They didn't ask everyone, just a few at each table. There was a moment of great tension. I went pale. Little by little the militia drew nearer to our table and I started shaking.'

At that moment Pedro also became aware that he was the only one whose documents were in order. If they asked anyone else at the table they would all be arrested. 'The Father also realised this,' Pedro says 'and he whispered to me, "Stay calm! Pray to the Guardian Angels". The militia then came to our table. And the only papers they asked to see were mine. They looked at them and left.'[445]

Once again they were all convinced they had been saved by their Guardian Angels who it soon became clear would have to look after them even more in the days ahead. Making contact with the smugglers who could be trusted to lead them to freedom over the Pyrenees and through forests and ravines infested with militia and border guards would proved much more difficult than they had been led to believe. Some smugglers took their groups into the mountains and then demanded more money than had originally been agreed upon. This left the refugees with no other choice than to pay up or be stranded. On their own, abandoned in the mountains, the odds were against them surviving. Even if they did manage to keep themselves alive, they would inevitably be caught by either militia patrols or border guards and shot.

Worse still, they were to learn that some smugglers were in the pay of the border guards and led refugees into prearranged ambushes where they were massacred.

To underline the dangers involved in trying to escape over the mountains a sensational story appeared in the newspapers. It told how border guards had caught up with an escape party in the mountains. The escape party had been completely wiped out. The story was being published by the authorities as a warning to any would-be escapers.[446] The message was clear: 'If you try to escape you will die. Border guards do not take prisoners!'

Undeterred, and placing their trust in God and the continued assistance of their Guardian Angels, they decided to face all the dangers and hazards that escaping involved.

They moved to Barcelona and after numerous delays and difficulties found smugglers who could be trusted. After being on the run for more than a month Father Josemaría and his seven fellow fugitives – Juan Jiménez Vargas, José María Albareda, Pedro Casciaro, Paco Botella, Miguel Fisac, Tomás Alvira and Manuel Sainz – joined an escape party led by the smugglers and began their dangerous trek across the Pyrenees. It was soon clear to them all that with every step they took they were receiving abundant help from heaven. They avoided the militia patrols, they overcame extreme exhaustion and survived the bitter winter weather of the mountains. On 2 December 1937 every one of them reached the safety of Andorra. They had escaped from 'this hell on earth where God cannot even be mentioned' to freedom. To the freedom of being able to seek God and holiness in their everyday lives and daily work. And to spread this message of hope throughout a troubled world.

Epilogue

José María Albareda became a distinguished scientist after the war. He was appointed Professor of Pharmacy at the University of Madrid, and later President of the Superior Council of Scientific Research, responsible for the fostering and coordination of scientific research in Spain. He was the first Rector of the University of Navarre, Pamplona. In 1959 he was ordained priest. He died in 1966.

Juan Jiménez Vargas resumed his career in medicine, specializing in physiology and biochemistry, and later became Professor at the University of Navarre. He was the first Director of its hospital and medical school. He died in 1992.

Pedro Casciaro and **Paco Botella** both became priests. Fr Francisco Botella (as he was known after his ordination) worked in Spain until his death in 1987, while Fr Pedro Casciaro helped to start the work of Opus Dei in Mexico. He died in 1995.

Miguel Fisac resumed his career as an architect and became internationally renowned, winning several prestigious awards for his work.

Tomás Alvira was among the first of the many thousands of married people to join Opus Dei after Pope Pius XII granted the Church's definitive approval on 16 June 1950. He became an expert in the field of education and the family, researching and writing several standard works. He founded a well-known chain of schools ('Fomento de Centros de Enseñanza'). He died in 1995.

Manuel Sainz resumed his career as a Civil Engineer. He died in 1995.

Isidoro Zorzano stayed in Madrid until the end of the war, and afterwards worked as an engineer in the regeneration of the Spanish railway network. He died in 1943 and his cause of canonization opened in 1948.

Alvaro del Portillo escaped from Madrid by enlisting in the Republican army and at the battlefront crossing no man's land to the Nationalist zone. He became a priest after the war and succeeded Father Josemaría at the head of Opus Dei. Bishop Alvaro Portillo died in 1994, and his cause of canonization opened in 2003.

Father Josemaría's teaching about the universal call to sanctity and the role of laymen and women became a keynote of Vatican II and is now the official teaching of the Catholic Church. He was canonized by Pope John Paul II and became Saint Josemaría, the pioneer of lay sanctity, on 6 October 2002.

Sources

General Archive of the Prelature of Opus Dei, *Archivo General de la Prelatura* (abbreviated to AGP), Viale Bruno Buozzi 75, Rome, Italy.

Historical Register of the Founder, *Registro Histórico del Fundador* (RHF) [section within AGP].

Intimate notes, *Apuntes íntimos*. Personal and confidential notes made by St Josemaría from March 1930 onwards and which was not to be read until after his death.

Assorted writings of the Founder, *Autógrafos Varios del Fundador* (AVF).

Personal letters of the Founder, *Espistolario del Fundador* (EF), cited by number.

Document (D).

Collections of printed documents including notes taken in get-togethers with St Josemaría (P01, P02, P03 etc.) [sections with AGP].

Letters written to all members (Letter) cited by date and section number.

Newsletters giving information about him and his teachings after his death.

Bibliography

Azevedo, Hugo de, *Uma Luz no mundo*, Lisbon, Prumo, 1988.
Beatification Booklet, *Blessed Josemaría Escrivá Founder of Opus Dei,* Rome, Opus Dei Central Postulation Office, 1992.
Berglar, Peter, *Opus Dei: Life and Work of its Founder*, Princeton, Scepter, 1994.
——, *Opus Dei: Vida y Obra del Fundador*, Madrid, Rialp, 1987.
Bernal, Salvador, *Alvaro del Portillo*, Sydney, Little Hills Press, 1999.
——, *Profile of the Founder of Opus Dei*, London/New York, Scepter, 1977.
Casciaro, Pedro, *Dream and Your Dreams Will fall short*, London, Scepter, 1997.
Cavalleri, Cesare, *Immersed in God*, Princeton, Scepter and Manila, Sinag-Tala, 1966.
Cejas, José Miguel, *Vidal del Beato Josemaría*, Madrid, Rialp, 1992.
Coverdale, John F., *Uncommon Faith*, Princeton, Scepter, 2002.
Crozier, Brian, *Franco. A Biographical History*, London Eyre & Spottiswoode, 1967.
Escrivá, St Josemaría, *The Way*, London, Scepter, 1965.
——, *Christ is Passing By*, Dublin, Veritas, 1974.
——, *The Forge*, London/New York, Scepter, 1988.

―――, *Friends of God*, London, Scepter, 1981.
―――, *Furrow*, London/New York, Scepter, 1987.
―――, *Holy Rosary*, Dublin, Four Courts Press, 1979.
―――, *In Love with the Church*, London, Scepter, 1989.
―――, *The Way of the Cross*, London, Scepter, 1983.
―――, *Conversations with Josemaría Escrivá*, Dublin, Scepter, 1968.
Gondrand, François, *At God's Pace*, London/New York, Scepter, 1989.
Helming, Dennis, *Footprints in the Snow*, London/New York, Scepter, 1986.
Preston, Paul, *Franco. A Biography*, London, Fontana, 1993.
Sastre, Ana, *Tiempo de Caminar*, Madrid, Rialp, 1989.
Vázquez de Prada, Andrés, *El Fundador del Opus Dei*, Madrid, Rialp, 1983.
―――, *The Founder of Opus Dei, Vol. I*, Princeton, Scepter, 2001.
―――, *The Founder of Opus Dei, Vol. II*, Princeton, Scepter, 2003.

Notes

PART I Prelude to Civil War

Chapter 2

1. Cavalleri, *Immersed in God*, p. 43.
2. Ibid.
3. Ibid., p. 44.
4. Bernal, *Profile of the Founder of Opus Dei*, p. 20.
5. Escrivá, *The Way*, no. 310.
6. Newsletter no. 5, p. 3.
7. Ibid., p. 5.

Chapter 3

8. Escrivá, *Holy Rosary*, 4th Glorious Mystery.
9. Cavalleri, *Immersed in God*, p. 44.
10. Bernal, *Profile of the Founder of Opus Dei*, p. 18.
11. Ibid., p. 19.
12. Ibid., p. 32.
13. Ibid.
14. Ibid.
15. Vázquez de Prada, *The Founder of Opus Dei*, vol. I, p. 37.

Chapter 4

16. Ibid., p. 491.
17. Escrivá, St Josemaría [AGP, P06, I, p. 206].
18. Bernal, *Profile of the Founder of Opus Dei*, p. 33.

Chapter 5

19. Vázquez de Prada, *The Founder of Opus Dei*, vol. I, p. 511.
20. Ibid., p. 64.

306 Notes

[21] Escrivá, *The Way*, no. 82.
[22] Bernal, *Profile of the Founder of Opus Dei*, p. 220.
[23] Ibid., p. 61.
[24] Cavalleri, *Immersed in God*, p. 48.
[25] Bernal, *Profile of the Founder of Opus Dei*, p. 59.
[26] Cavalleri, *Immersed in God*, p. 46.
[27] Cited by Alvaro del Portillo, in Sum.76, Vázquez de Prada, *The Founder of Opus Dei*, vol. I, p. 75.

Chapter 6

[28] Blessed Josemaría Escrivá, Beatification booklet, p. 17.
[29] Vázquez de Prada, *The Founder of Opus Dei*, vol. I, p. 70.
[30] Blessed Josemaría Escrivá, Beatification Booklet, p. 19.
[31] Vázquez de Prada, *The Founder of Opus Dei*, vol. I, p. 75.
[32] Helming, *Footprints in the Snow*, p. 13.
[33] Vázquez de Prada, *The Founder of Opus Dei*, vol. I, p. 78.

Chapter 7

[34] Cavalleri, *Immersed in God*, p. 48.
[35] Vázquez de Prada, *The Founder of Opus Dei*, vol. I, p. 96.
[36] Cavalleri, *Immersed in God*, p. 49.
[37] Ibid.
[38] Vázquez de Prada, *The Founder of Opus Dei*, vol. I, p. 99.
[39] Ibid., p. 101.
[40] Ibid.
[41] Ibid., p. 98.
[42] Escrivá, *The Way*, no. 131.
[43] Cavalleri, *Immersed in God*, p. 159.

Chapter 8

[44] Escrivá, *The Way*, no. 340.
[45] Bernal, *Profile of the Founder of Opus Dei*, p. 69.
[46] Vázquez de Prada, *The Founder of Opus Dei*, vol. I, p. 132.
[47] Bernal, *Profile of the Founder of Opus Dei*, p. 71.
[48] Gondrand, François, *At God's Pace*, p. 39.
[49] Bernal, *Profile of the Founder of Opus Dei*, p. 64.

Chapter 9

[50] Ibid., p. 30.
[51] Cavalleri, *Immersed in God*, pp. 65, 66.
[52] Vázquez de Prada, *The Founder of Opus Dei*, vol. I, p. 141.
[53] Ibid., p. 544.
[54] Escrivá, St Josemariá [AGP, P04, 1972, II, p. 758].
[55] Bernal, *Profile of the Founder of Opus Dei*, p. 75.
[56] Blessed Josemaría Escrivá, Beatification Booklet, p. 25.

Chapter 10

[57] Vázquez de Prada, *The Founder of Opus Dei*, vol. I, p. 43.
[58] Ibid., p. 155.
[59] Ibid., p. 140.
[60] Ibid.
[61] Ibid., p. 168.
[62] Ibid., p. 160.
[63] Ibid., p. 171.
[64] Ibid., p. 170.
[65] Gondrand, François, *At God's Pace*, p. 45.

Chapter 11

[66] Vázquez de Prada, *The Founder of Opus Dei*, vol. I, p. 192.
[67] Ibid., p. 206.
[68] Ibid., p. 211.
[69] Ibid.
[70] Bernal, *Profile of the Founder of Opus Dei*, p. 116.

Chapter 12

[71] Cavalleri, *Immersed in God*, p. 54.
[72] Escrivá, *Christ Is Passing By*, nos. 110–111.
[73] Blessed Josemaría Escrivá, Beatification Booklet, p. 29.
[74] Bernal, *Profile of the Founder of Opus Dei*, p. 110.
[75] Blessed Josemaría Escrivá, Beatification Booklet, p. 32.
[76] Cavalleri, *Immersed in God*, p. 166.
[77] Ibid., p. 100.
[78] Escrivá, *The Way*, nos. 81, 82.
[79] Vázquez de Prada, *The Founder of Opus Dei*, vol. I, p. 242.
[80] Bernal, *Profile of the Founder of Opus Dei*, p. 136.
[81] Blessed Josemaría Escrivá, Beatification Booklet, p. 32.
[82] Vázquez de Prada, *The Founder of Opus Dei*, vol. I, p. 243.
[83] Cavalleri, *Immersed in God*, p. 54.
[84] Vázquez de Prada, *The Founder of Opus Dei*, vol. I, p. 250.
[85] Cavalleri, *Immersed in God*, p. 56.
[86] Vázquez de Prada, *The Founder of Opus Dei*, vol. I, p. 252.

Chapter 13

[87] Cavalleri, *Immersed in God*, p. 93.
[88] Ibid.
[89] Bernal, *Profile of the Founder of Opus Dei*, p. 109.
[90] Escrivá, *Conversations*, p. 65.
[91] Bernal, *Profile of the Founder of Opus Dei*, p. 110.
[92] Cavalleri, *Immersed in God*, p. 88.
[93] Bernal, *Profile of the Founder of Opus Dei*, p. 188.
[94] Ibid., pp. 187, 188.
[95] Blessed Josemaría Escrivá, Beatification Booklet, p. 38.
[96] Cavalleri, *Immersed in God*, p. 166.

[97] Vázquez de Prada, *the Founder of Opus Dei*, vol. I, p. 218.
[98] Ibid., p. 255.
[99] Ibid.
[100] Ibid.
[101] Ibid., p. 414.
[102] Ibid., pp. 626, 627.
[103] Cavalleri, *Immersed in God*, p. 33.
[104] Escrivá, *The Way*, no. 8.
[105] Vázquez de Prada, *The Founder of Opus Dei*, vol. I, p. 342.
[106] Gondrand, François, *At God's Pace*, p. 78.
[107] Vázquez de Prada, *The Founder of Opus Dei*, vol. I, p. 342.

Chapter 14

[108] Ibid., p. 561.
[109] Ibid., p. 269.
[110] Ibid., p. 270.
[111] Ibid.
[112] Ibid.
[113] Ibid., p. 271.
[114] Ibid., p. 584.
[115] Ibid., pp. 236, 271.
[116] Ibid., p. 273.
[117] Ibid., p. 272.
[118] Ibid., p. 275.

Chapter 15

[119] Ibid., p. 281.
[120] Ibid., p. 284.
[121] Ibid., p. 285.
[122] Ibid., p. 286.
[123] Escrivá, *Holy Rosary*, 1st Joyful Mystery.
[124] Escrivá, *Holy Rosary*, Introduction.
[125] Escrivá, *The Way*, Prologue.

Chapter 16

[126] Vázquez de Prada, *The Founder of Opus Dei*, vol. I, p. 287.
[127] Bernal, *Profile of the Founder of Opus Dei*, p. 129.
[128] Vázquez de Prada, *The Founder of Opus Dei*, vol. I, p. 289.
[129] Ibid., p. 291.
[130] Ibid., p. 294.
[131] Ibid., p. 295.
[132] Blessed Josemaría Escrivá, Beatification Booklet, p. 34.
[133] Escrivá, *The Way*, no. 267.
[134] Blessed Josemaría Escrivá, Beatification Booklet, p. 34.
[135] Cavalleri, *Immersed in God*, p. 181.
[136] Ibid.
[137] Ibid.

Chapter 17

[138] Vázquez de Prada, *The Founder of Opus Dei*, vol. I, p. 324.
[139] Ibid.
[140] Ibid.
[141] Bernal, *Profile of the Founder of Opus Dei*, p. 152.
[142] Escrivá, *The Way*, no. 626.
[143] Bernal, *Profile of the Founder of Opus Dei*, p. 179.
[144] Escrivá, *The Way*, nos. 340, 335.
[145] Vázquez de Prada, *The Founder of Opus Dei*, vol. I, p. 301.
[146] Ibid., p. 302.
[147] Ibid., p. 307.

Chapter 18

[148] Ibid., p. 330.
[149] Cavalleri, *Immersed in God*, p. 89.
[150] Vázquez de Prada, *The Founder of Opus Dei*, vol. I, p. 332.
[151] Ibid., p. 336.
[152] Ibid., Appendix 15, p. 487.

Chapter 19

[153] Cavalleri, *Immersed in God*, p. 87.
[154] Vázquez de Prada, *The Founder of Opus Dei*, vol. I, note 105, p. 586.
[155] Ibid., p. 278.
[156] Ibid., p. 321.
[157] Bernal, *Profile of the Founder of Opus Dei*, pp. 178–179.
[158] Blessed Josemaría Escrivá, Beatification Booklet, p. 38.

Chapter 20

[159] Vázquez de Prada, *The Founder of Opus Dei*, vol. I, p. 294.
[160] Escrivá, *The Way*, no. 91.
[161] Vázquez de Prada, *The Founder of Opus Dei*, vol. I, p. 262.
[162] Escrivá, *Christ Is Passing By*, no. 181.
[163] Vázquez de Prada, *The Founder of Opus Dei*, vol. I, p. 257.
[164] Ibid., p. 313.
[165] Escrivá, *The Way*, no. 565.
[166] Ibid., no. 562.
[167] Ibid., no. 570.
[168] Ibid., no. 916.
[169] Helming, *Footprints in the Snow*, p. 25.
[170] Vázquez de Prada, *The Founder of Opus Dei*, vol. I, p. 309.
[171] Ibid., p. 310.
[172] Ibid.
[173] Escrivá, *The Way*, no. 854.
[174] Ibid., no. 855.
[175] Ibid., no. 860.
[176] Vázquez de Prada, *The Founder of Opus Dei*, vol. I, p. 308.
[177] Ibid., p. 109.

Chapter 21

[178] Gondrand, *At God's Pace*, Letter, January 9, 1932, p. 89.
[179] Bernalm *Profile of the Founder of Opus Dei*, p. 289.
[180] Escrivá, *The Way*, no. 208.
[181] Vázquez de Prada, *The Founder of Opus Dei*, vol. I, p. 339.
[182] Ibid., p. 327.
[183] Ibid.
[184] Escrivá, *The Way*, no. 817.
[185] Cavalleri, *Immersed in God*, p. 100.
[186] Ibid., p. 187.

Chapter 22

[187] Vázquez de Prada, *The Founder of Opus Dei*, vol. I, p. 354.
[188] Bernal, *Profile of the Founder of Opus Dei*, p. 286.
[189] Vázquez de Prada, *The Founder of Opus Dei*, vol. I, p. 353.
[190] Ibid., p. 356.
[191] Ibid., p. 363.
[192] Ibid., pp. 346, 486.
[193] Ibid., p. 369.
[194] Escrivá, *The Way*, no. 301.
[195] Vázquez de Prada, *The Founder of Opus Dei*, vol. I, p. 378.
[196] Escrivá, *The Way*, no. 808.

Chapter 23

[197] Newsletter no. 5, p. 9.
[198] Vázquez de Prada, *The Founder of Opus Dei*, vol. I, p. 371.
[199] Cavalleri, *Immersed in God*, p. 170.
[200] Vázquez de Prada, *The Founder of Opus Dei*, vol. I, p. 389.
[201] Ibid.
[202] Escrivá, *The Way*, no. 382.
[203] Bernal, *Profile of the Founder of Opus Dei*, p. 214.
[204] Ibid., p. 215.

Chapter 24

[205] Cavalleri, *Immersed in God*, p. 157.
[206] Vázquez de Prada, *The Founder of Opus Dei*, vol. I, p. 390.
[207] Ibid.
[208] Ibid., p. 391.
[209] Bernal, *Profile of the Founder of Opus Dei*, p. 186.
[210] Vázeuez de Prada, *The Founder of Opus Dei*, vol. I, p. 393.
[211] Cavalleri, *Immersed in God*, p. 151 and Escrivá, *The Way*, no. 638.

Chapter 25

[212] Vázquez de Prada, *The Founder of Opus Dei*, vol. I, p. 396.
[213] Cavalleri, *Immersed in God*, p. 137.
[214] Ibid., p. 127.
[215] Bernal, *Profile of the Founder of Opus Dei*, p. 190.

[216] Escrivá, *Christ Is Passing By*, no. 24.
[217] Bernal, *Profile of the Founer of Opus Dei*, p. 50.
[218] Cavalleri, *Immersed in God*, p. 107.
[219] Vázquez de Prada, *The Founder of Opus Dei*, vol. I, p. 399.

Chapter 26

[220] Escrivá, *The Way*, nos. 76–80.
[221] Bernal, *Profile of the Founder of Opus Dei*, p. 124.
[222] Ibid., p. 121.
[223] Vázquez de Prada, *The Founder of Opus Dei*, vol. I, p. 409.
[224] Ibid., p. 623.
[225] Vázquez de Prada, *The Founder of Opus Dei*, vol. I, p. 403.
[226] Ibid.
[227] Ibid., p. 404.
[228] Ibid., p. 405.
[229] Ibid.
[230] Cavalleri, *Immersed in God*, p. 55.
[231] Bernal, *Profile of the Founder of Opus Dei*, p. 310.
[232] Ibid., p. 311.
[233] Escrivá, *The Way*, no. 12.

Chapter 27

[234] Bernal, *Alvaro del Portillo*, p. 17.
[235] Ibid., p. 19.

Chapter 28

[236] Casciaro, *Dream and Your Dreams Will fall short*, p. 23.
[237] Helming, *Footprints in the Snow*, p. 28.
[238] Casciaro, *Dream and Your Dreams Will fall short*, p. 28.
[239] Escrivá, *The Way*, no. 537.
[240] Vázquez de Prada, *The Founder of Opus Dei*, vol. I, p. 421.
[241] Ibid., p. 418.
[242] Casciaro, *Dream and Your Dreams Will fall short*, p. 29.

Chapter 29

[243] Ibid., p. 47.
[244] Bernal, *Alvaro del Portillo*, p. 19.
[245] Cavalleri, *Immersed in God*, p. 132.
[246] Ibid., p. 106.
[247] Ibid., p. 148.

Chapter 30

[248] Bernal, *Profile of the Founder of Opus Dei*, p. 228.

Chapter 31

[249] Escrivá, *The Way*, no. 982.
[250] Escrivá, *The Way*, no. 848.
[251] Vázquez de Prada, *The Founder of Opus Dei*, vol. I, p. 445.

Chapter 32

[252] Ibid., p. 446.
[253] Ibid.
[254] Cavalleri, *Immersed in God*, p. 116.
[255] Casciaro, *Dream and You Dreams Will fall short*, p. 70.

Chapter 33

[256] Cavalleri, *Immersed in God*, p. 145.
[257] Casciaro, *Dream and Your Dreams Will fall short*, p. 78.

Chapter 34

[258] Ibid., p. 88.
[259] Vázquez de Prada, *The Founder of Opus Dei*, vol. I, p. 453.
[260] Ibid.
[261] Ibid.
[262] Ibid., p. 454.
[263] Ibid.
[264] Berglar, *Opus Dei: Life and Work of its Founder*, p. 120.
[265] Escrivá, *Friends of God*, p. 223.
[266] Gondrand, François, *At God's Pace*, p. 131.
[267] De Azevedo, *Uma Luz no mundo*, p. 103.

PART II The Hunted Priest

Chapter 35

[268] Casciaro, *Dream and Your Dreams Will fall short*, p. 93.
[269] Escrivá, St Josemaría, *Notes taken in a get-together, 24-XII-1959* [AGP, P03, 1981, p. 127].
[270] Berglar, *Opus Dei: Life and Work of its Founder*, p. 126.
[271] Vázquez de Prada, *The Founder of Opus Dei*, vol. II, p. 489.
[272] Ibid., pp. 489–490.

Chapter 36

[273] Ibid., p. 20.
[274] Bernal, *Alvaro del Portillo*, p. 58.
[275] Vázquez de Prada, *The Founder of Opus Dei*, p. 167.

Chapter 37

[276] De Azevedo, *Uma Luz no mundo*, p. 110.
[277] Gondrand, François, *At God's Pace*, p. 138.
[278] Ibid.
[279] Vázquez de Prada, *The Founder of Opus Dei*, vol. II, p. 24.
[280] Ibid.
[281] Cejas, *Vida del Beato Josemaría*, p. 93.
[282] Vázquez de Prada, *The Founder of Opus Dei*, vol. II, p. 27.
[283] Cejas, *Vida del Beato Josemaría*, p. 93.

[284] Sastre, *Tiempo de Caminar*, p. 197.
[285] Coverdale, *Uncommon Faith*, p. 201.
[286] Vázquez de Prada, *The Founder of Opus Dei*, vol. II, p. 28.
[287] Sastre, *Tiempo de Caminar*, p. 197.

Chapter 38

[288] Gondrand, François, *At God's Pace*, p. 137.
[289] Vázquez de Prada, *The Founder of Opus Dei*, vol. II, p. 28.
[290] Escrivá, St Josemaría, *Notes taken in a get-together, 26-XII-1968* [AGP, P03, 1981, pp. 132–133].
[291] Bernal, *Alvaro del Portillo*, p. 57.
[292] De Azevedo, *Uma Luz no mundo*, p. 112.
[293] Cavalleri, *Immersed in God*, p. 91.
[294] Ibid., p. 92.
[295] De Azevedo, *Uma Luz no mundo*, p. 113.
[296] Cavalleri, *Immersed in God*, p. 92.
[297] Vázquez de Prada, *The Founder of Opus Dei*, p. 170.
[298] Sastre, *Tiempo de Caminar*, p. 198.
[299] Cavalleri, *Immersed in God*, p. 144.
[300] Gondrand, François, *At God's Pace*, p. 139.
[301] Vázquez de Prada, *The Founder of Opus Dei*, vol. II, p. 32.
[302] Ibid., p. 33.

Chapter 39

[303] Ibid.
[304] Ibid.
[305] Ibid., p. 34.
[306] Ibid., p. 37.
[307] Ibid., p. 39.
[308] Ibid., pp. 40, 41.
[309] Ibid., p. 495.
[310] Ibid., p. 36.
[311] Ibid., p. 37.
[312] Ibid., p. 41.
[313] Ibid., p. 172.
[314] Berglar, *Opus Dei: Vida y obra del Fundador*, p. 407 (omitted in English language edition).
[315] Vázquez de Prada, *The Founder of Opus Dei*, vol. II, p. 42.
[316] Gondrand, François, *At God's Pace*, p. 141 and Vázquez de Prada, *The Founder of Opus Dei*, vol. II, p. 36.
[317] Coverdale, *Uncommon Faith*, p. 205.
[318] Vázquez de Prada, *The Founder of Opus Dei*, vol. II, p. 42.
[319] Ibid., p. 40.
[320] Ibid., p. 41.
[321] Ibid., p. 39.
[322] Ibid., p. 76.
[323] Ibid., p. 45.
[324] Ibid., p. 46.

[325] Ibid., p. 45.
[326] Ibid., p. 43.
[327] Gondrand, François, *At God's Pace*, p. 141 and Vázquez de Prada, *The Founder of Opus Dei*, vol. II, pp. 46–47.
[328] Casciaro, *Dream and Your Dreams Will fall short*, p. 100.
[329] Ibid., p. 102.
[330] Ibid., p. 101.
[331] Ibid., p. 100.
[332] Ibid., p. 101.
[333] Ibid., p. 103.
[334] Ibid.
[335] Ibid., p. 104.
[336] Vázquez de Prada, *The Founder of Opus Dei*, vol. II, p. 115.
[337] Casciaro, *Dream and Your Dreams Will fall short*, p. 104.
[338] Ibid., p. 103.
[339] Ibid., p. 106.
[340] Ibid., p. 107.
[341] Vázquez de Prada, *The Founder of Opus Dei*, vol. II, p. 46.
[342] Ibid., p. 50.
[343] Coverdale, *Uncommon Faith*, p. 205.
[344] Vázquez de Prada, *The Founder of Opus Dei*, vol. II, p. 50.

Chapter 40

[345] Ibid., p. 58.
[346] Gondrand, François, *At God's Pace*, p. 142.
[347] Vázquez de Prada, *The Founder of Opus Dei*, vol. II, p. 48.
[348] Bernal, *Alvaro del Portillo*, p. 58.
[349] Ibid., p. 59.
[350] Vázquez de Prada, *The Founder of Opus Dei*, vol. II, p. 61.
[351] Escrivá, St Josemaría, *Notes taken in a get-together, 17-II-1967* [AGP, P03, 1981, p. 244].
[352] Vázquez de Prada, *The Founder of Opus Dei*, Vol. II, p. 50.
[353] Ibid., p. 55.
[354] Ibid., p. 62.
[355] Gondrand, François, *At God's Pace*, p. 142.
[356] Vázquez de Prada, *The Founder of Opus Dei*, vol. II, p. 62.
[357] Ibid., p. 63.
[358] Gondrand, François, *At God's Pace*, p. 142.
[359] De Azevedo, *Uma Luz no mundo*, p. 119.
[360] Gondrand, François, *At God's Pace*, p. 142.
[361] De Azevedo, *Uma Luz no mundo*, p. 119.
[362] Ibid.
[363] Coverdale, *Uncommon Faith*, p. 222.
[364] De Azevedo, *Uma Luz no mundo*, p. 118.
[365] Vázquez de Prada, *The Founder of Opus Dei*, vol. II, p. 77.
[366] Coverdale, *Uncommon Faith*, p. 224.
[367] Ibid., p. 221.
[368] Mgr Alvaro del Portillo, *Notes taken in a get-together, 11-III-1979* [AGP, P03, 1981, pp. 259–261].

369 Escrivá, *The Way*, no. 294.
370 Coverdale, *Uncommon Faith*, p. 223.
371 Ibid.
372 Escrivá, St Josemaría, [AGP, P03, 1981, pp. 253–256].
373 Escrivá, *The Way*, no. 697.
374 De Azevedo, *Uma Luz no mundo*, p. 119.
375 Coverdale, *Uncommon Faith*, p. 226.
376 Vázquez de Prada, *The Founder of Opus Dei*, vol. II, p. 81.
377 Ibid., p. 56.
378 Coverdale, *Uncommon Faith*, p. 228.
379 Vázquez de Prada, *The Founder of Opus Dei*, vol. II, p. 64.
380 Ibid., p. 175.
381 Pero-Sanz, José Miguel, *Isidoro Zorzano*, p. 206.
382 Gondrand, François, *At God's Pace*, p. 144.
383 Sastre, *Tiempo de Caminar*, p. 204.
384 De Azevedo, *Uma Luz no mundo*, p. 120.
385 Casciaro, *Dream and Your Dreams Will fall short*, p. 108.
386 Ibid., p. 109.
387 Ibid., p. 110.
388 Ibid.
389 Ibid., p. 112.
390 Ibid.

Chapter 41

391 Vázquez de Prada, *The Founder of Opus Dei*, p. 176.
392 Ibid., p. 493.
393 Ibid., p. 498.
394 Casciaro, *Dream and Your Dreams Will fall short*, p. 113.
395 Ibid., p. 114.
396 Ibid., p. 113.
397 Ibid., p. 117.
398 Vázquez de Prada, *The Founder of Opus Dei*, vol. II, p. 55.
399 Ibid., p. 106.
400 Casciaro, *Dream and Your Dreams Will fall short*, p. 114.
401 Ibid.
402 Vázquez de Prada, *The Founder of Opus Dei*, vol. II, p. 97.
403 Ibid., p. 98.
404 Ibid., p. 44, 117.
405 Ibid., p. 98.
406 Ibid., p. 99.
407 Ibid.
408 Sastre, *Tiempo de Caminar*, p. 204.
409 Vázquez de Prada, *The Founder of Opus Dei*, vol. II, p. 126.
410 Gondrand, François, *At God's Pace*, p. 146.
411 Sastre, *Tiempo de Caminar*, p. 204.
412 Escrivá, St Josemaría, *Notes taken in a get-together, 10-XI-1969* [AGP, P03, 1981, p. 367].
413 Ibid., p. 307.

316 *Notes*

414 Escrivá, St Josemaría, *Notes taken in a get-together, 10-XI-1969* [AGP, P03, 1981, pp. 368–369].
415 Bernal, *Alvaro del Portillo*, p. 60.
416 Coverdale, *Uncommon Faith*, p. 232.
417 Vázquez de Prada, *The Founder of Opus Dei*, vol. II, p. 112.
418 Coverdale, *Uncommon Faith*, p. 232.
419 Rios, Enrique Gutierrez, *José María Albareda*, pp. 33–68.
420 Cavalleri, *Immersed in God*, p. 23.
421 Bernal, *Profile of the Founder of Opus Dei*, p. 233.
422 Coverdale, *Uncommon Faith*, p. 233.
423 Vázquez de Prada, *The Founder of Opus Dei*, vol. II, p. 103.
424 Gondrand, François, *At God's Pace*, p. 146.

Chapter 42

425 Vázquez de Prada, *The Founder of Opus Dei*, vol. II, p. 94.
426 Ibid.
427 Rios, Enrique Gutierrez, *José María Albareda*, p. 112.
428 Vázquez de Prada, *The Founder of Opus Dei*, vol. II, p. 123.
429 Bernal, *Profile of the Founder of Opus Dei*, p. 233.
430 Cavalleri, *Immersed in God*, p. 67.
431 De Azevedo, *Uma Luz no mundo*, p. 123.
432 Vázquez de Prada, *The Founder of Opus Dei*, vol. II, p. 124.
433 Casciaro, *Dream and Your Dreams Will fall short*, p. 115.
434 Ibid., p. 118.
435 Coverdale, *Uncommon Faith*, p. 236.
436 Vázquez de Prada, *The Founder of Opus Dei*, vol. II, p. 126.
437 Casciaro, *Dream and Your Dreams Will fall short*, p. 118.
438 Ibid., p. 119.
439 Ibid., p. 120.
440 Ibid., p.120.
441 Ibid., p. 121.
442 Vázquez de Prada, *The Founder of Opus Dei*, vol. II, p. 125.
443 Casciaro, *Dream and Your Dreams Will fall short*, p. 121.
444 Ibid., p. 122.
445 Ibid., p. 123.
446 Sastre, *Tiempo de Caminar*, p. 209.

Printed in the United Kingdom
by Lightning Source UK Ltd.
102421UKS00002B/49-309